The Amish Ways

Eddie Swartzentruber

© 2024 Global Brother SRL
All rights reserved

This book is protected by copyright.
Subject to statutory exception and to the provision of relevant collective licensing agreements, no reproduction of any part may take place without the written permission of the publisher.

Legal Disclaimer

The contents of the book titled *The Amish Ways* are intended solely for informational and educational purposes. The authors and publishers of this book expressly disclaim any and all liability arising from the use, application, or interpretation of the information contained herein. No warranties, express or implied, are made with respect to the accuracy, completeness, or reliability of the information presented, and the authors and publishers assume no responsibility for any errors or omissions.

This book is not a substitute for professional advice, guidance, or services, whether medical, agricultural, or otherwise. Any reliance upon the information provided is at the sole discretion and risk of the reader. The techniques, practices, and remedies discussed in this publication may not be appropriate or effective in all situations, and the authors and publishers do not warrant or guarantee any specific outcomes or results.

The reader is strongly advised to seek professional consultation where necessary, including but not limited to matters of health, safety, food preservation, legal compliance, and environmental conditions. The application of any information from this book must be undertaken with careful consideration of local laws, regulations, and individual circumstances. Furthermore, readers are advised to consult with licensed professionals prior to implementing any techniques related to health, medical remedies, agriculture, or construction.

By using this book, the reader agrees that neither the authors nor the publishers shall be held liable for any direct, indirect, incidental, or consequential damages or losses resulting from the use or misuse of the information contained within. The reader assumes full responsibility for any actions taken based on the material presented in this book, and all legal claims arising from such use shall be expressly waived.

This disclaimer serves as a binding legal agreement between the reader and the authors and publishers of *The Amish Ways*.

About Eddie Swartzentruber

Eddie was born and raised in the Swartzentruber community, one of the most conservative Amish groups. His family, originally from Ohio, relocated to Minnesota, where they initially engaged in dairy farming. However, they later switched to construction because businesses wouldn't accept non-refrigerated milk.

Like his nine older brothers, Eddie was born on the family farm. He recalls that neither he nor his brothers ever visited a hospital during their upbringing. Instead, they relied on natural, homemade remedies passed down through generations.

Eddie also remembers never visiting a regular store for food. Everything his family consumed was grown and prepared by them. He recalls a large pantry at home, filled with jars of food that could sustain them for months.

In their community, riding in cars was prohibited except for medical emergencies. They avoided the use of electricity and indoor plumbing altogether.

Despite these restrictions, they found ingenious ways to remain self-sufficient. Eddie had the unique opportunity to witness these methods firsthand. From his family, he learned the projects and skills that make the Amish self-reliant and prepared for any crisis that might imminently affect America.

His father taught him a lot about mechanics. Eddie could take the engine out of a combine, completely disassemble it, and then put it all back together. Eddie believes that the Amish can remain calm in the middle of absolute chaos as their skills will not let them down.

He never forgot what he experienced during his "Amish Years." Seeing how soft and dependent the rest of the world has become, he has decided to share these Amish secrets for the first time ever in this book.

Dedication

To my father, who taught me everything I know about homesteading, living off the grid, and leading a self-sufficient and sustainable lifestyle.

To my mother, who loved me and was always there to nurture me back to health in times of sickness. Mom taught me everything I know about home remedies, avoiding pharmacies, and treating illness in a natural, healthy way.

TABLE OF CONTENTS

- Legal Disclaimer 2
- About Eddie Swartzentruber 3

THE AMISH WAY OF GARDENING — 8

- **General Information on Amish Gardening** . 9
- **Guide to Amish Companion Planting** 16
  - *Advantages of Companion Planting* 16
  - *Types of Effective Amish Companion Crops* 17
  - *Companion Planting in Amish Medicinal Flower Gardens* 22
  - *Crop Rotation Amish Style* 23
  - *How to Transform Your Garden for Crop Rotation* .. 24
  - *Herbal Pest Control Spray* 25
  - *Amish Seeds: What Are "Heirloom" Seeds?* 26
  - *How Can I Use Companion Planting and Natural Preventionin an Emergency?* 26
- **Raised Beds with Hoop House** 28
  - *The Benefits of Using Raised Beds* 28
  - *How to Select Your Site* 28
  - *How to Make Your Raised Bed* 29
  - *How to Fill Your Raised Bed* 30
  - *Which Plants Can I Grow in the Raised Bed?* 31
  - *Making a Hoop House over Your Raised Bed* 32
  - *Maintenance of Your Raised Bed and a Crop Rotation Plan* 33
- **How the Amish Grow Potatoes in Thin Air** 35
- **How to Build a Year-Round Underground Food Garden** 40

USING PLANTS THE AMISH WAY — 48

- **How to Forage the Amish Way** 49
  - *General Foraging Guidelines* 49
  - *Mistakes to Avoid When Foraging* 49
  - *Plants You Can Forage* 50
- **Medicinal Plants You Can Forage** 63
- **Amish Medicinal Garden You Should Have in Your Backyard** 80
- **Amish Cough Syrup and Throat Drops** . 89
  - *Amish Cough Syrup Recipe:"Snake Juice"* 89
  - *Amish Cough DropsRecipe* 90
- **Amish Plasters** 91
  - *Amish Mustard Plaster* 92
  - *Amish Onion & Garlic Plaster* 93
  - *Warming Plaster for Pain: Ginger, Cinnamon, and Cayenne Pain Relief Plaster* 94
- **Amish Antibiotics** 96
  - *Amish "Super Tonic" - A Potent, All-Purpose Herbal Remedy* 96
  - *Amish "Amoxicillin"* 97
- **Amish Painkillers** 99
  - *Amish Multi-Purpose Pain Relief Elixir* 99
  - *Amish Major Pain Relief Tincture* 101
  - *Snake Juice* 102
- **Amish Black Drawing Salve** 103
  - *Amish Black Drawing Salve* 106
- **Burns and Wounds Ointment** 107
  - *Burn and Wound Ointment* 110
- **Deep, Penetrating Ointment for Aching Joints and Sore Muscles.** 111
  - *Aching Joints & Sore Muscles Ointment* 111
- **Amish Parasite Flush** 112
  - *Amish Parasite Flush Tincture* 112
  - *The Ingredients and Their Anti-Parasitic Properties* 114
- **How to Treat a Cavity the Amish Way** . 116

- **Homemade Dental Care Products** 118
  - DIY Amish Toothpaste 118
  - Herbal Mouth Rinses........................118

- **Amish Strength Juice**...................119
  - Amish Strength Tincture 119
  - Amish Strength Tonic 120

PRESERVING FOOD THE AMISH WAY — 121

- **Food Preservation Methods** 122
  - How Natural Preservatives and Techniques Work. 123
  - Amish Preservation Techniques 123
  - Cold Pickling 123
  - Old-Fashioned Amish Ice-Box Pickles.... 124
  - Sun Drying and Solar Dehydration 125
  - Water Glassing Eggs 127
  - Water-Glassed Eggs 127
  - Water Bath Canning the Garden Harvest........... 128
  - Canned Tomatoes 128
  - Pressure Canning 130
  - Pressure Canned Chicken 130
  - Preparing Lard Like the Amish 132
  - Lard Recipe.. 132

- **Drying Beef** 134
  - Dried Beef General Principles.............. 134
  - Amish Style Dried Beef 134
  - Storage... 136
  - Shelf Life 136
  - Amish Dried Beef Gravy 136

- **How to make Forever Butter** 137
  - The Importance and Uses of Ghee for the Amish Community 137
  - Traditional Preparation of Ghee 137
  - Making Forever Butter 138

- **Long-Lasting Amish Recipes** 140
  - Beef Stew with Vegetables.................. 143
  - Chicken Soup 144
  - Beef Chili... 146
  - Amish Poor Man's Steak..................... 147
  - Vegetable Soup................................... 149
  - Pork Sausage...................................... 150
  - Hot Packing 151

- Broth for Canning Meat......................151
- Canning Reminders 151
- The Canning Process 152

- **Amish Root Cellar**......................153
  - Building a Root Cellar....................... 154
  - What Foods Do the Amish Store in a Wood Barrel Root Cellar?............................. 156
  - Store Meat Like the Amish 157
  - Practical Tips and Recommendations for Storing Cured Meat in a Barrel Root Cellar 157
  - Wood Barrel Root Cellar Food Storage and Shelf-Life Tips................................... 158
  - Potential Challenges and Safety Precautions........ 158

- **Amish Pantries 101** 159
  - The Perfect Location for Building a Pantry........... 159
  - How to Build a Pantry 160
  - What to Store Inside Your Amish-Style Pantry 161
  - 1. Dried Meat 161
  - 2. Cheese 162
    - Jack Cheese...................................... 162
  - 3. Canned Goods................................ 163
    - Eggs Covered in Salt 163
    - Amish Friendship Bread Starter (for Canning)................................... 163
    - Amish Friendship Bread (Using the Starter) ... 164
  - 4. Herbs... 164
    - Painkiller in a Jar............................ 165
  - How to Organize the Pantry 165

- **Building an Amish Buried Fridge**.......166
  - Where to Build Your Amish Buried Fridge............166
  - Building Your Amish Buried Fridge: A Step-by-Step Guide 167
  - Additional Tips 168

- **Amish Smokehouse** 169
  - Building an Amish Smokehouse 169
  - Tips and Tricks 173
  - Maintenance Advice for Your Wooden Smokehouse 173

- Be Aware of This When You Smoke Your Meat!.... 174
- The Process 174
- What Could Go Wrong 174
- Remember 175

Self-Sufficiency The Amish Way — 176

- **Amish Traditional Lighting Sources**..... 177
  - Kerosene Lamps 177
  - Propane and Naphtha Fuel Lamps 177
  - Hurricane Lamps 178
  - Candles 178
  - Solar Powered Lamps 178
  - Hand-Dipped Amish Candles 179
  - Molded Candles in Portable Containers 180
  - Homemade Lamp Oil for Emergency Lighting 181
    - Recipe 1: Crisco and Vegetable Oil Blend 181
    - Recipe 2: Olive Oil and Vegetable Oil Blend..... 182

- **Amish Techniques Used for House and Water Heating** 183
  - House Heating 184
  - Water Heating 185

- **Amish Air-Powered Tools that Make You Self-Sufficient** 186
  - Amish Alternatives to Electricity 186
  - Wind and Air Power 186
  - Collecting and Compressing Air 187
  - Pneumatic Tools that Use Air in Place of Electricity 188
  - Ceiling Fans as an Alternative to AC 189

- **How to Preserve Water the Amish Way** ..190
  - Underground Cisterns 190

- Above-Ground Storage Tanks 191
- Rooftop Rainwater Harvesting 191
- Recycling Greywater 192
- Secondary Water Sources 192
- Methods and Techniques to Test Water Quality 193

- **Amish Wells** 194
  - How to Dig a Hand Dug Well 195
  - How to Install a Driven Well 197
  - How to Install a Spring Fed Well 198

- **DIY Amish Water Filter** 200

- **Amish Livestock** 202
  - Animals You May Find in Amish Farms 202
  - What Do the Amish Feed Their Livestock? 204
  - How the Amish Keep Livestock Healthy 205

- **DIY Amish Chicken Coop** 206

- **Essential Items the Amish Always Keep on Hand** 211

- **DIY Off-Grid Washing Machine** 214
  - How Does the Off-Grid Washing Machine Work? . 214
  - What Detergent to Use? 214
  - Building the DIY Off-Grid Washing Machine 215
  - Operation of the DIY Washing Machine 217
  - Modifications You Might Consider 217

- **Why The Amish Paint Their Barns Red** .. 218

Using Money The Amish Way — 220

- **Handling Money Like the Amish** 221

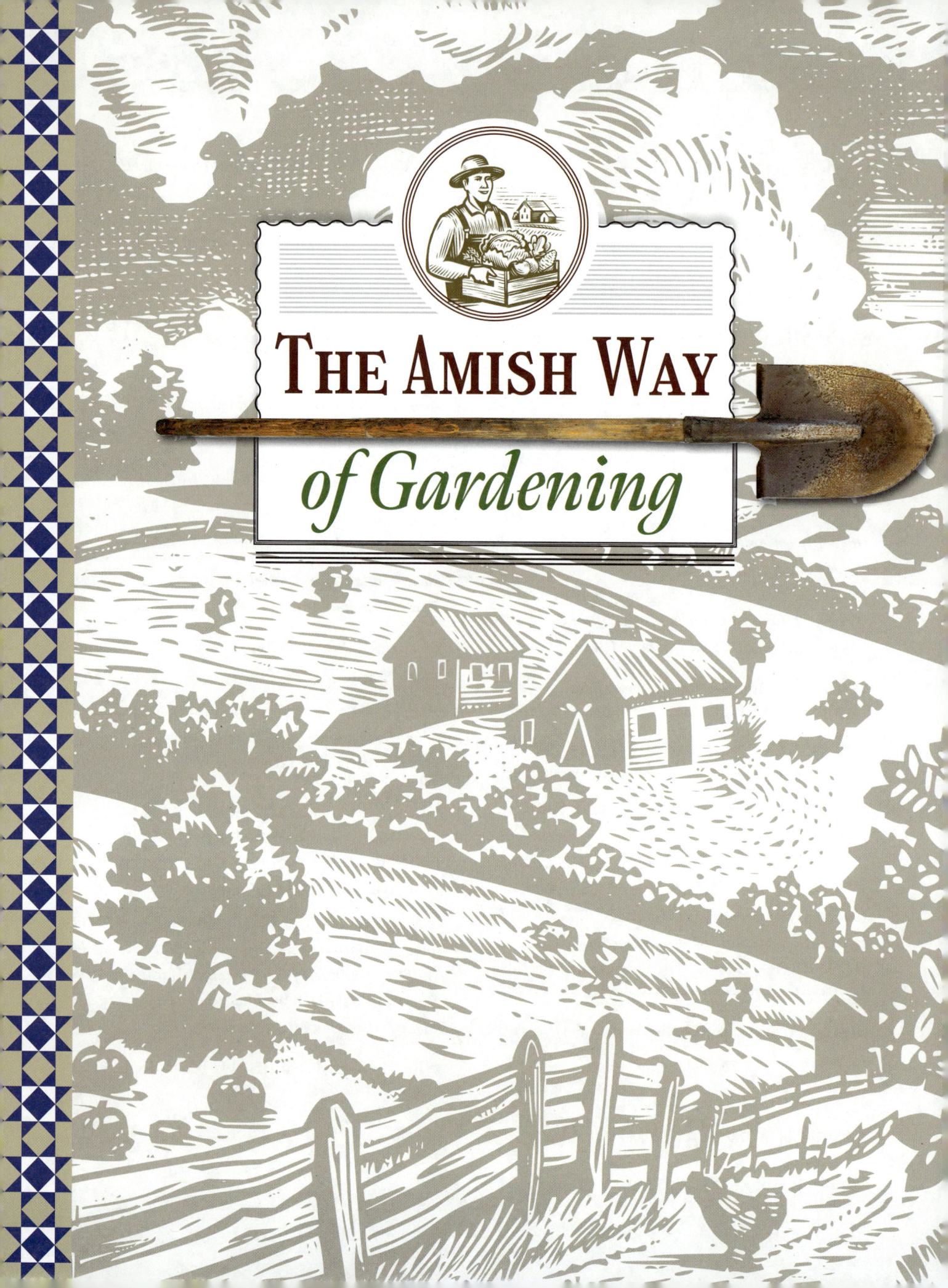

The Amish Way
of Gardening

General Information on Amish Gardening

Amish have always been known as excellent farmers dating back hundreds of years. In this chapter, you will learn the secrets and methods of growing a lot of food to feed a big family throughout the year.

1. PLANNING AND LAYOUT

Not being allowed to use any electricity, the Amish are almost completely dependent on rain, so we will only live in areas that receive enough annual rainfall to support the crops. When choosing a place to garden, especially for a SHTF scenario, you'll need to keep this in mind. The Amish typically locate a few large gardens close to the house, while livestock pastures and crops are usually kept farther away. It is best to choose garden locations in sunny areas with good topsoil and free of rocks, preferably close to the house or where you will be preparing the harvest for canning, like an outside kitchen.

Mark the area where you want the garden by pounding 4 sticks in the ground, keeping it in the shape of a square or rectangle, as it is easier to plow or till this way. Growing up with my Amish family, I was always the one who'd go outside to find those sticks and bury them in the ground. Remember to leave room between fences and buildings for garden tools to be used whether it be a tiller or a plow.

2. PREPARING THE SOIL (FERTILIZER)

Every fall and winter, Amish will take manure left behind by the livestock in the barn and put it on the garden. They will cover the garden first then the fields where their crops are raised. They will use whatever they have on hand including horse, cow, rabbit, sheep, duck, pig, and chicken manure. Included in the manure is the bedding used whether it be straw or wood shavings.

This will also help to aerate the soil a little for less soil compaction. You will want to put this on in the fall and winter so that as the snow melts or it gets rained on, it will leach the nutrients from the manure into the soil providing healthier soil for your plants come spring. When adding manure to your garden, put on a liberal amount covering the ground nicely. Raw manure is fine to put on in thicker amounts, if it sits for a few months leaching into the soil. However, if you purchase composted manure, you will want to use it according to the sellers' instructions, as it can burn the plants when spread too thick. Amish typically don't use composted manure, but rather raw manure from the barn, simply because it is readily available to them. A horse drawn manure spreader (like the one in the bottom left image) is used in the fields, spreading the

THE AMISH WAY *of Gardening*

3. SPRING PREPPING

In the early spring, as soon as the ground is dry enough and not too muddy, the Amish will plow their gardens and fields. Typically, this is done with a team of 3-4 horses hitched to a plow. They will plow in rows flipping the dirt over neatly, and nicely burying the manure that was put on top over the winter. You can achieve this by hand, using a shovel and turning over the soil (one full shovel at a time). Although doable for small gardens, it is not recommended for larger areas, as it is time-consuming and even dangerous for your health.

The plow leaves the ground a little uneven and lumpy, so the Amish usually follow the plowing with a harrow, making multiple passes, smoothing the soil out, and making it easier for planting. This is also done with a couple of horses, pulling the harrow behind them. A garden rake or better yet, a landscape rake can be used to do this by hand.

The Amish will typically prepare the garden when they have the horses hitched up to prepare the fields. However, if you don't use horses, a gas-powered tiller can be used to do these two steps leaving your soil even smoother and fluffier than the plow and harrow method. The gas tiller is allowed in some Amish communities, but not in the more

manure evenly, as it is flung into the air by paddles that are driven by the wheels.

Sometimes, the spreaders are used in bigger gardens but a wheelbarrow and pitchfork will be used to spread it by hand in the smaller gardens. A chore left to the young boys in the family. Manure is mostly what Amish use, although some might add store bought natural fertilizers, lime or nitrogen to supplement to the soil as needed.

The Amish Way of Gardening

conservative ones (like the Swartzentruber), who still do not allow modern tools. A small tractor with implements could also take the place of a team of horses. As it is harder to own and take care of horses, it might seem more logical to get a tractor, however you must keep in mind that in a grid down situation, fuel for your tractor will most likely not be available.

On the other hand, if you choose not to have horses, a plow or a tiller, you can try the *Back-to-Eden gardening method*, **which does not require either tool**. This method has been adopted by a few Amish communities, but this technique will take a few years to get the garden fully established, although it is a great no-till, weed-free alternative. The Back-to-Eden gardening method is therefore a more natural way of gardening, which will take you back to the old ways.

The Back to Eden gardening method is known as a weed-free way of gardening. Weeds will still come up, but very little compared to the till method, and the weeds that do grow are easier to pull. The cover, in this case wood chips, will hold and release moisture as needed, and will protect the garden from washouts during heavy rain. The wood chips will also keep the sun from baking the soil, allowing the worms to work the soil underneath making it healthier day by day. This method is great in hot dry climates as it conserves water. You will want to keep adding wood chips every year as the originals start to break down. It will take a few years to have a garden with soft fluffy dirt but is worth the wait. My wife and I switched to this method in the Idaho high desert and are now using it in a wetter climate in Michigan.

Here is how it's done:

1. To start this type of garden, you'll have to choose your garden spot and cover it all with 2-3 layers of cardboard or newspapers. You will have to do this in the fall, so it is ready for the growing season in the spring. You should only have to do this once. The cardboard can come from used shipping boxes that don't have any shiny surfaces or stickers. You will want to remove the packaging tape as well.

2. Once the ground is covered with cardboard, you will cover it with a 6–8-inch layer of compost and wood chips or wood shavings. As it sits over winter, the cardboard will kill any grass or vegetation underneath and the wood chips will gather and hold moisture and allow healthy worms to work the soil underneath.

3. By spring, the cardboard will have mostly deteriorated and all that's needed for planting is to push the wood chips aside a bit and plant the produce according to the instructions.

4. Once the plants start getting bigger, you can push the wood chips back around the plant to help prevent weeds.

- MANURE
- WOOD CHIPS
- COMPOST
- NEWSPAPER

4. PLANTING

The planting period is of course the beginning of spring; however, this also depends on the vegetables you want to plant. Root plants, such as potatoes are planted in late April and more fragile plants like corn, beans, peas and tomatoes are planted after the last frost is expected, which is typically in early to mid-May. Amish will plant almost everything that grows in their region and can be preserved over the winter, potatoes usually being the most abundant crop found in their gardens, as they provide a lot of delicious calories for the physically hard-working families. They are easy to grow, harvest, preserve and cook, making them the ideal survival food. Almost every Amish dinner will have potatoes in their meal plan. Other garden produce grown in Amish gardens are sweet corn, green beans, peas, radishes, onions, red beets, cucumbers, pickles, squash, pumpkin, cantaloupe, watermelons, strawberries, carrots, tomatoes, peppermint, garlic, flowers, peppers, rhubarb and some herbs. Sweet corn is often planted in stages, about 2 weeks apart, to allow for a longer corn on the cob season.

Amish will plant everything in straight rows, to make it easier for weed control. Sticks and string is used to get the rows straight. This is important as you will want to use a cultivator or tiller between the rows throughout the summer for weed control.

Here is how it's done:

1. Start on one side of your garden and put 1 wooden stake on each end of the garden making sure, you are a tiller or cultivator width from the edge.

2. Run a string from one stake to the other approximately 6-10 inches from the ground.

3. Then take a garden hoe (a V-shaped one works best for this) and make a furrow the length of the garden under the string leaving room for your tiller or cultivator at each end. The depth of the furrow will depend on the seed requirements you are planting.

4. Drop the seeds in the furrow following the spacing recommendations on the package.

5. After this, take a garden rake and carefully cover the seeds. If so desired, mark each end of the row so you know where the row is at until the plants start growing.

6. Then, measure from the existing row to the new row and put the stakes and string in, repeating the steps for each row. When coming up with the measurement for spacing between the rows, you will need the width of your tiller or cultivator PLUS the width of the fully grown plant you are planting. This way, when tilling the pathway between the rows you are not cutting into the plant roots. Strawberries, peppermint and similar plants are usually planted in 2-3-foot-wide rows the length of the garden. This is desirable as they are plants that spread through the roots and the width is perfect for being able to reach the center from each side for weeding and harvest. A great way to keep these plants from spreading too much is to build garden boxes with 6-inch sides in whatever lengths and widths you desire.

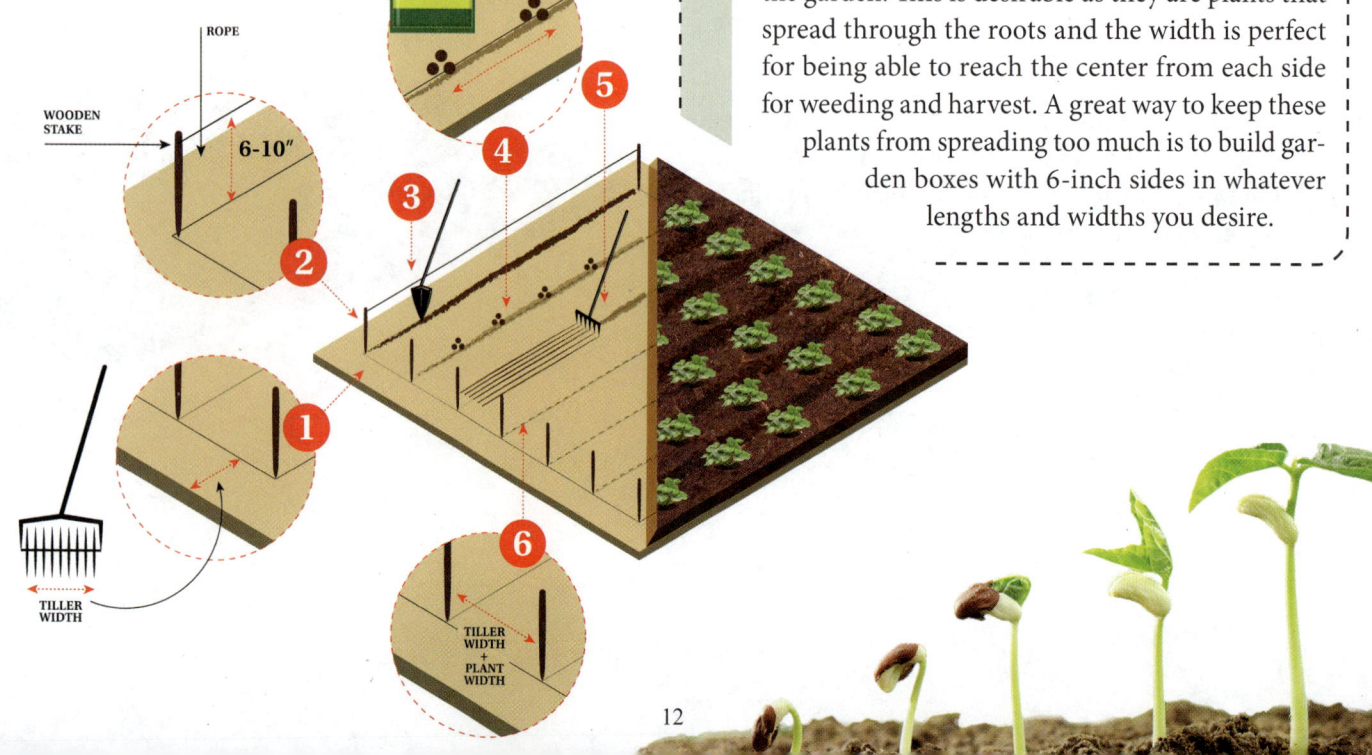

5. WEED CONTROL

Once the plants in the garden start to grow, so will the weeds. And they need to be kept under control. If you planted your produce in proper rows, you will start with taking the cultivator or tiller between the rows and along the edges, uprooting the weeds in the pathways. These weeds are then picked up to keep the garden looking clean. The Amish do this with a tiller, a team of horses and cultivator, a hand pushed cultivator, or simply with a hoe. Then it's time to get down on your hands and knees starting down each row, pulling the weeds by hand from between the plants. This has to be done multiple times a summer.

Amish gardens are typically kept weed-free and clean-looking, and this is almost always done without chemicals. It is a time-consuming but very healthy process. Many days and evenings are spent with families in the garden pulling weeds. This job typically falls to the women and young children, but when men aren't doing field work, they will join in.

Although this was a dreaded job as a kid, in my opinion, it was great opportunity for quality time together as a family. It is also a great opportunity to spend some time alone away from the busy world, to reflect and ground yourself to the simple things in life.

Driving through the Amish country, you may find families working in the garden together. Picture the father driving the horse drawn cultivator while a younger child is sitting on top riding the horse and the mother and the other siblings are tending to the rest of the garden in the cool of the evening as the sun goes down. This is a beautiful picture of family, creation, and God working in harmony.

6. FRUIT

Fruit is also a popular food source among the Amish. Most live in northern climates, so they will mostly grow apples, pears, grapes, raspberries, and some peaches. Orchards are typically kept close to the gardens and fertilized in the same way. Depending on the family, fruit trees are left to grow or trimmed back for easier picking. If pruning is done, the job usually falls on the father or older sons of the family. Pruning is done with a hand saw or pruning shears. Unlike the garden, pesticides are often used on fruit trees to keep the insects from completely destroying the crops. It is not easy growing nice fruit organically with something to keep the bugs away.

Although Amish grow table grapes, the majority of grapes grown are concord grapes grown for the purpose of juices and wine. Grape juice makes a cool delicious drink in the hot summers and the wine is made for communion church and other special occasions. Amish do not typically drink to get intoxicated but will enjoy an alcoholic beverage occasionally. Apples are canned or stored in root cellars. Peaches and pears are canned for later use.

7. GROWING TIPS

Amish will mostly grow bean and pea varieties that are self-supporting plants so no trellis or support is needed. Tomato cages are used to support the tomato plants as they get larger.

One Amish community I know, adds milk crates over their tomatoes until they get tall, then switch to cages. They claim the young tomato plants grow faster and are stronger when they do this. When asked for the reason, they couldn't say but claimed it definitely seems to make a difference.

8. HARVEST TIME

As the produce starts to ripen, the women will start to harvest, preserve, and store the food to be used throughout the year until the next harvest season. Amish are a close-knit community and share much information with each other. The size of the garden and amount of food planted is determined from the experience of many generations of families and handed down to the children who are just starting their own families and gardens. The amount of food you want to grow will most likely take you a few seasons to figure out. Seeds are cheap, so you can always grow extra and give to neighbors and friends, but on the other hand, don't overwhelm yourself as it can be discouraging. Starting small is usually a better way of learning what your family's needs are when it comes to gardening.

Strawberries are picked, washed and used right away for deserts or strawberry shortcake, or turned into jams to spread onto toast for breakfasts throughout the rest of the year. Amish who are allowed to have refrigeration will mostly make freezer jam with the strawberries and it is absolutely delicious.

Corn on the cob becomes part of dinner most evenings as it starts to ripen. Whatever does not get eaten right away is cut off the cob and canned. Lots of corn is canned or frozen depending on if refrigeration is allowed. Freezing corn is the preferred method as it tastes nice and fresh when thawed out and heated up. Corn on the cob was always something we looked forward to as children.

Green beans and peas are picked and canned. The wife will pick the green beans in a bucket, find the nearest shade tree, and sit down with the children helping to break them into the right lengths for preserving. It's the same way with the peas. Gather the children, and grandma, if she lives next door and remove the peas from the pod. These are time consuming jobs and although I would groan and whine when we had to do it, I look back now and cherish the time spent with my then young mother.

Watermelons are picked and dropped into the livestock's water trough to cool off in the water until it can be enjoyed the next evening. Muskmelons are also not preserved but eaten as they ripen.

Tomatoes are harvested and canned as salsa, tomato paste, tomato juice or soup. Root vegetables like potatoes, onions, and carrots are left in the ground as long as possible then pulled and stored in the root cellar.

9. CLEAN UP

As the produce gets harvested, the leftover plants, like corn stalks, are tossed into the pasture where the livestock graze so they pick through and eat what they please. Chickens love this. Some smaller softer plants may be left in the garden to be tilled in the following spring. You do not want to leave corn stalks, tomato plants, and other tough vine plants in the garden as they won't break down over one winter and will get tangled in your plow, tiller or cultivator the following year. If you don't have chickens or livestock a great alternative is to start a compost pile, letting it breakdown and then reintroducing it to your garden. Raking it in a pile in the middle of the garden and burning it could also be done if the plants aren't too wet. The ashes are good for gardens.

Some Amish might plant a cover crop for the winter. Personally, I think it is good to keep the soil covered one way or another as it encourages worms to work the soil underneath making it healthy.

Using the Amish way of gardening is productive and efficient for large amounts of food but we (my wife and I) have chosen the "Back to Eden" method for our gardens, continually adding organic matter to the top of our garden to control weeds and continually provide nutrients to the soil. This keeps moisture in and keeps the soil from getting baked by the sun. We do not till or plow our soil. It seems like a more natural, going with nature, way of gardening.

Guide to Amish Companion Planting

Companion Planting is a natural method of growing particular plants side by side for pest prevention, because one offers the other a growing advantage, or because both plants enjoy similar conditions. The Amish have used this method for years and choose typical plants to boost the harvest of their typical crops: tomatoes, potatoes, beans, sweetcorn, maize for cattle feed, barley, strawberries, and tobacco. The Amish community prefers not to use chemicals and always opts for traditional gardening tools and methods, to keep their soil healthy working alongside "Mother Nature". Also, as underlined before, the Amish keep their own animals, meaning they have a good supply of animal manure, a valuable natural fertilizer, that helps them achieve good harvests throughout the year. In this chapter, we will focus on how the Amish farmers use Companion Planting to grow crops without chemicals, and encourage pollinators to visit crops. Read on to see how to apply this to your own survival garden.

Advantages of Companion Planting

The main advantage of companion planting is that it reduces the pests visiting your chosen plant while also increasing biodiversity. If you visit an Amish farm, you will notice brightly coloured marigold flowers in rows next to carrots, onions, corn and cabbages, that provide insects and pollinators with a feast. The strong smell will also distract the carrot rust flies away from your carrots.

Aphids, which are dangerous for crops, choose marigolds or nasturtiums instead of plants from the cabbage family so you can watch pests like thrips, greenflies, and whiteflies whizz over your vegetables, to get to these flowers. Strong smells and bright colours are a lure for pests and deter them from your plants.

Another advantage to planting two plants together is that they like the same conditions and this will benefit your soil. Peas and beans leave nitrogen in their roots, for the next crop to enjoy. Cabbages, kale, or broccoli can be planted after peas, along with oats, especially if, like the Amish, you have animals to feed. Cabbage family plants grow right through the winter and the winter oats thrive alongside them. Both benefit from the nitrogen left by the peas. In this picture, you can see oats already dried in the background, with broccoli in front of them. This way, the oats become fodder for cattle afterward, or process it yourself for cooking and preparing long-lasting recipes.

One other important advantage of companion planting is the prevention of soil erosion. If you do not grow this combination, then plant cover crops like clover or green ma-

The Amish Way of Gardening

nures in the fall, to prevent soil blowing away. You can dig these back into the soil in spring and some crops are edible (e.g., mustard or corn salad). If you have plants growing over winter, the fertile topsoil stays in place even in strong winds. Soil gets blown away easily if fields are left bare.

Types of Effective Amish Companion Crops

If you drive past any Amish farm, these 10 crops can usually be seen growing in the fields or for sale in the farm shop. Here is a small guide to adopting Amish companions for your chosen vegetables and fruit:

1. Tomatoes with Herbs

"Amish Paste" tomatoes are Heirloom seeds saved from original tomato seeds from the Pennsylvania Amish communities, and these tomatoes can be eaten fresh in summer salads but traditionally they were made into "Amish Paste", which is a natural way to save tomatoes for winter use out of season.

Herbs like basil and cilantro love the same soil, watering conditions, and sunlight hours as tomatoes, so these are excellent companions. The strong scent of Basil also repels tomato and tobacco hornworm (*Manduca quinquemaculata*), which provides added protection in northern states, where this pest is a major problem.

Companion planting in your garden:

Planting outdoor tomatoes in a group with cucumber, herbs, squash, or sweet peas, is another alternative for smaller gardens. All these plants need the same soil, watering conditions, and staking for support as they climb, so anywhere you have a gap, plant tomatoes with similar crops. Make sure you stake the tomatoes before planting though to avoid root damage.

Indoors, inside a glasshouse, you can plant tomatoes with the same crops but try to change the position of the plants each year and nourish the soil well, with manure nd homemade compost.

2. Potatoes with Salads/Spinach

These are staple crops for Amish communities and they grow over several months underground, so you can plant faster-growing crops like lettuce at the surface level, in between rows of potatoes. "Early Ohio" is an Heirloom potato that you can try. To grow alongside these, try any plant with shallow roots (like spinach), which doesn't dig deep for nutrients.

In a small garden where space is tight, you can companion plant potatoes, squashes, and kale together. The potatoes (dark green leaves in the center) and squash (bright green larger leaves far right) both like deep, rich soil, and they are planted side by side. In the picture (top left), small kale plants are situated at a distance and these will grow much slower than the other two crops. When the potatoes and squash are harvested, the kale can overwinter in the same spot.

<u>*Do not*</u> plant potatoes near tomatoes, because both crops are vulnerable to blight. Avoid carrots and root crops, whose deep taproots will impact the size of the potato crop growing underneath.

3. Strawberries with Borage

I know summer has arrived when I notice pots of small, sweet strawberries for sale near Amish farms and in Amish craft and food shops. Amish strawberries come early, but you can extend the season by buying plants that fruit at different times.

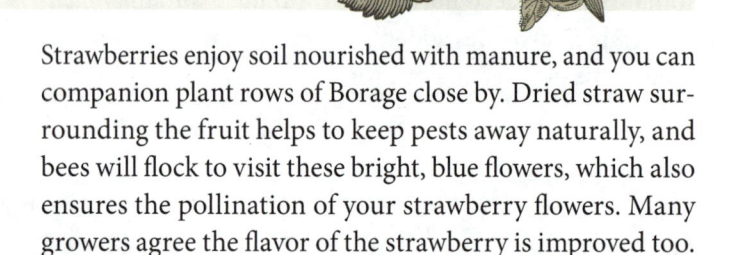

Strawberries enjoy soil nourished with manure, and you can companion plant rows of Borage close by. Dried straw surrounding the fruit helps to keep pests away naturally, and bees will flock to visit these bright, blue flowers, which also ensures the pollination of your strawberry flowers. Many growers agree the flavor of the strawberry is improved too.

The Amish Way *of Gardening*

4. Sweetcorn with Cantaloupe Melon

Sweetcorn takes a long season to grow and you need space. Amish farmers plant the seed earlier than most farms in March and harvest the corn early in June, but you may prefer to start it later after the last frost and cut cobs in the fall. Amish farmers plant a second crop of sweetcorn to use as animal feed during the winter. In your garden, plant sweetcorn in rows in a square shape with at least 6 x 6 seeds about 9 inches apart, to aid pollination. The crop is usually wind-pollinated.

This crop takes up a lot of space before the cobs form, so anything you can plant at its feet keeps the roots of the sweetcorn cool, even on hot days. Amish methods advise cantaloupe melon for this, as it spreads with large leaves and gorgeous yellow flowers which bring in bees to pollinate.

Amaranth, spinach, and borage (seen in the picture) are alternative companions for sweetcorn in your vegetable garden because they grow well early on when the corn stalks are small, providing leaf cover to block out weeds, and also shade for the roots of the corn as the weather warms up.

Borage brings in pollinators too, which is another advantage and you can eat the flowers and foliage. Amaranth leaves are great in salads with edible seeds and their pretty flowers add charm to any summer garden.

5. Onions (or Garlic or Leeks) with Marigold Flowers

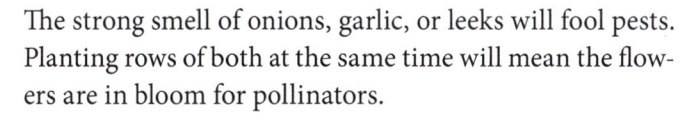

The strong smell of onions, garlic, or leeks will fool pests. Planting rows of both at the same time will mean the flowers are in bloom for pollinators.

Companion plant in your garden:

Other Amish companion plantings with onions include lettuce, or try planting rows of onions with carrots and beets.

See beans and leeks below too.

6. Beets or Carrots with Lettuce or Onions

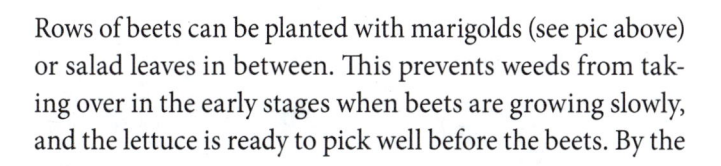

Rows of beets can be planted with marigolds (see pic above) or salad leaves in between. This prevents weeds from taking over in the early stages when beets are growing slowly, and the lettuce is ready to pick well before the beets. By the time you harvest lettuce, the beets will have top foliage and go on to develop into thick roots without the usual trouble of weeds. Many Amish farms also plant onions next to rows of roots like these to avoid pests.

THE AMISH WAY *of Gardening*

7. Cabbages (or Kale) with Marigolds, Nasturtiums, or Leeks

Cabbage, Brussels sprouts, kale, and any plant in the cabbage family (known as Brassicas) are susceptible to aphids, thrips, greenflies, and being nibbled by the caterpillars of the Cabbage White butterfly. However, some flowers will attract these insects away from your crop because pests prefer the flowers and leaves of the companion plant.

Kale and leeks inter-planted. Pests do not like the smell of the leeks so they avoid the area and this benefits the kale.

You can also add another layer of protection such as netting (or fleece), which will not allow Cabbage root flies to penetrate or allow the cabbage moth to lay eggs on your cabbages.

Nasturtiums are an excellent example. Plant rows of them beside the cabbages, and watch the pests aim directly for them rather than your crop. The leaves and flowers are edible and they have a sweet, peppery taste so you can nibble on them as well. These flowers fit into a flower garden as easily as your vegetable garden.

Marigolds do the same trick as nasturtiums - see a picture of them in the onions section above.

8. Leeks with Beans or Peas

Leeks take a long time to grow and they start as tiny seedlings. Sow the seeds in a pot at home in May and then you need to make holes for them in the soil, like in the picture from June onwards. Then drop one individual leek into each hole and water it in. Do not fill in this hole with soil. Water these young leeks every day until the roots settle into the hole. Gradually, the leek swells and grows in size over the fall and into the colder winter weather, when you can pick them from November to March.

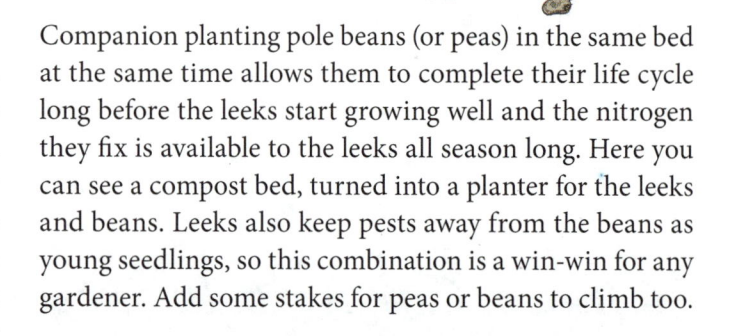

Companion planting pole beans (or peas) in the same bed at the same time allows them to complete their life cycle long before the leeks start growing well and the nitrogen they fix is available to the leeks all season long. Here you can see a compost bed, turned into a planter for the leeks and beans. Leeks also keep pests away from the beans as young seedlings, so this combination is a win-win for any gardener. Add some stakes for peas or beans to climb too.

9. Asparagus and Herbs

Asparagus is a delicious spear-shaped vegetable only available for about 3 months in early spring. It can be frozen or canned but it is best fresh! It stays in the same bed for over 20 years and needs care when planting. The soil must be weed-free and then plant 2-year-old seedlings (called crowns) into the soil and water them in well. Their roots are shallow, so be careful weeding. Every year you need to add a layer of manure or leaf mold over the winter to retain fertility. Planting basil alongside asparagus will deter pests like the Asparagus beetle because basil has such a powerful scent.

Plant basil seeds next to the asparagus bed, or plant in a whole herb grown at home, without damaging the fragile roots of the asparagus. Cilantro and parsley work well too. The advantage is fewer pests and lots of fresh herbs to pick too.

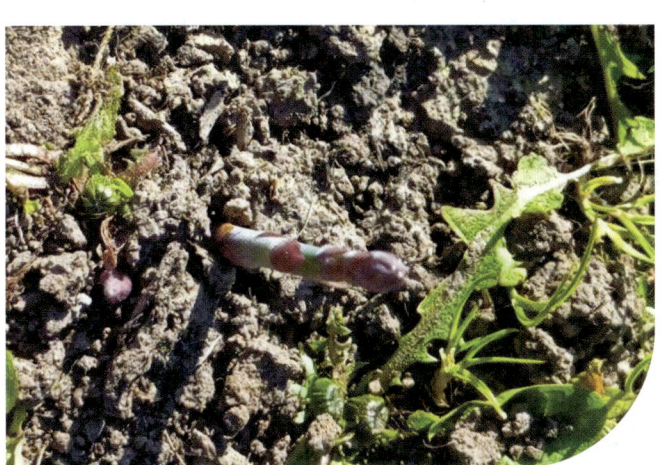

10. Barley and Beans or Peas

Barley is an Amish staple crop and you can companion plant barley with rows of peas on the edges of the crop, because these fix nitrogen into the soil which benefits the barley, and will cause the seed heads to grow to a better size. You get a second crop of tasty peas and healthier soil too.

THE AMISH WAY *of Gardening*

Companion Planting in Amish Medicinal Flower Gardens

All Amish homes have a vegetable plot and while the stricter Amish communities (e.g. the Swartzentruber community in Homes County, Ohio) do not have flower gardens, many Amish communities encourage flower growing as a creative hobby that can provide flowers for vases, nectar for pollinators, as well as herbs and medicinal plants too. In Amish flower gardens, medicinal herbs are often inter-planted among the other blooms, offering bees and pollinators a welcome place to collect their nectar.

Choose flowers you love for your Amish-style flower garden. Sunflowers give endless joy as they bloom, and seeds can be dried and eaten. Gourds are a traditional Amish companion plant for sunflowers. Plant lavender to attract bees, and other herbs with medicinal qualities, like Feverfew are common in Amish flower gardens.

Comfrey (*Symphytum oficinale*) attracts bees in droves and the leaves can be used to make a liquid feed for plants. Just add some green leaves to a bucket of water to soak for 4-5 days and then water your tomatoes or hungry plants with this. You can also add leaves directly to the soil to increase nutrients or add them direct to the composting system.

You may regard Stinging nettles as a weed but Amish gardeners know that butterflies use their leaves for egg laying, and here is a tip. You can also use these leaves to make dried nettle tea, or nettle soup as a spring tonic. By carefully picking leaves (wearing gloves), then soaking them in water for a week, you can make homemade nettle feed for tomatoes and other hungry crops.

Now you know all the advantages of Companion Planting, let's look at the secrets of Amish Crop Rotation which will help your soil retain its nutrients by changing the crop each year.

Feverfew (Tanacetum parthenium)

The Amish Way *of Gardening*

Crop Rotation Amish Style

Visiting an Amish craft and food store is a wonderful way to find out more about this farming community. You probably visit to buy the delicious farm fruit and vegetables but you can also find handmade wooden toys and items, and basket-weaving gifts. The first thing you will notice driving there is that Amish farms do not use machinery to till the land, but horse-drawn carriages so that their precious soil does not get compacted. Another method of keeping Amish soils healthy is by not growing the same crop in the same soil every year. Certain crops extract nutrients from the soil so if you do not alternate your crops, the soil may become depleted.

This is known as Crop Rotation and this is a basic tenet of Amish cultivation. Manure from animals is used as a natural fertilizer because Amish communities do not use herbicides, chemicals, or manmade fertilizers. Crop Rotation helps to avoid diseases that remain in the soil by changing the crop annually. Pests are also confused by the change so this helps to keep them under control too. The idea is to have a 4-year cycle of plants and then rotate these from one location to another every year so that by year 5 you return to the original plot to start over again. Planting different crops every year allows their precious soil to recover, as potatoes will take some nutrients but planting peas straight afterward allows the soil to have free access to nitrogen. In your garden, this is a wonderful method to adopt which will increase soil health, reduce disease, and allow wildlife to thrive. Here is a guide for a 4-year crop rotation cycle.

Year	Plant	Spread manure or not?	Alternative fertilizer
1	*HUNGRY CROPS* Annual vegetables - Eggplant, tomatoes, squash, zucchini, etc; Herbs	Yes	Can also mulch to retain moisture.
2	*LEGUMES AND ONION FAMILY* Peas, Beans, Onions, Garlic, Leeks	Yes	Can also mulch to retain moisture.
3	*BRASSICAS – THE CABBAGE FAMILY* Cabbage, Kale, Sprouts etc.	No	Lime the patch to make the soil pH suitable.
4	*ROOTS* Carrots, Parsnips, Swedes, Beets	No	General compost or mulch.
Perennial beds	*PLANTS THAT STAY FOR AT LEAST 3 YEARS* Asparagus; Strawberries; Fruit trees; Herbs.	Yes Yes Yes Yes	Yes Also wood ash; Compost; Hay, straw; Leaf mold; Comfrey leaves.

THE AMISH WAY *of Gardening*

How to Transform Your Garden for Crop Rotation

1. If you have never dug the ground before, prepare the soil by placing a layer of mulch or cardboard to reduce light and moisture for a week or two before planting. You can then remove the weeds easily by pulling, and the soil is easier to dig. Do not use weed killers, herbicides, or pesticides as these are frowned upon in Amish agriculture. Garden split into sections for crop rotation

2. Divide the growing area into 4 different sections and you can use paths to avoid standing on the soil and to make it easier to harvest crops.

3. Prepare the soil. Apply a layer of well-rotted manure, for areas where you plant hungry crops but not for cabbage plants, or root crops. For plants that do not like manure, apply a mulch of dried leaves instead, use fresh comfrey leaves, or use general homemade compost to boost fertility.

4. Set aside pots or another area for perennial crops such as asparagus and fruit bushes.

5. Think about crops your family enjoys eating, and then check the Crop Rotation plan above for ideas about which ones can be planted together. If possible, use Heirloom seeds (see more information about the seeds below) that you can save year on year. Then find suitable companions from the list above to complement them. Make notes in the chart with your companion plants.

6. Plan to harvest and preserve your crops for winter months as the Amish community does.

7. If you do not have one already, then make a composting area to use waste material and transform it into a free, viable soil improver.

The Amish Way *of Gardening*

FAQs

Do Amish communities compost waste?

Yes, and so should you, because this produces perfect soil enrichers in a system that uses everything. Add mown grass cuttings, fallen leaves in the fall, green waste from the kitchen, stems of plants, pruned twigs, potato peelings, and eggshells unless you are using them to keep slugs away…

How do you protect your plants from slugs, snails and other pests?

Here is an Amish tip on pest control and deterrents for slugs. On one visit to an Amish farm shop, I was buying a wicker laundry basket as the craftsmanship of Amish basket-weaving is famous. I asked the staff about something unusual I saw in the fields on my journey there. Some new small crops were surrounded with brownish pieces around the stem and I couldn't make out at a distance what this was. The shop assistant told me! "We use everything available and egg shells are great to keep slugs at bay. They hate crossing them and not only that, eggshells are free, and they also add a valuable nutrient to the soil; calcium. "A great gardening tip straight from the horse's mouth, so to speak".

A new kale plant with used tea leaves, stones, and comfrey leaves

A new kale seedling with eggshell deterrent and comfrey leaves

In your own garden, save your used eggshells and dry them out for a few days. Then crush them and lay them around the stem of any vulnerable seedlings. For extra protection, if you have dandelion or comfrey leaves available, use these as decoys spread around the plant as food for the slugs. Slugs can feast on those leaves before they reach your plants and then they meet eggshells, so they decide to move on. You can also add used tea or coffee grounds because slugs and snails avoid these too.

Herbal Pest Control Spray

Medicinal plants can create a natural pest control spray for use in the garden and inside the house. Garlic contains a compound called allicin and is famed for its antioxidant, anti-bacterial, and anti-inflammatory properties. As a companion plant in the garden, the powerful fragrance helps repel slugs, aphids, and carrot flies, but you can also use garlic to make a natural pest control spray. Here's a quick and simple recipe.

Instructions

Puree two garlic bulbs with one tablespoon of vegetable oil.

Leave overnight, strain in the morning, and then add one teaspoon of mild liquid soap and four cups of water to create enough to fill a spray container. Store in the fridge until needed.

Use the spray in the evening on plants suffering from insect infestation, spraying on both sides of the leaves and applying every few days until the insects are gone.

This spray can also be used as an insect deterrent every week or fortnight on healthy plants.

Plants with a strong fragrance, like lavender, can repel garden pests while attracting pollinators and offer the perfect home fragrance when dried or used to create an essential oil for healing and calming. Rosemary is also used for its essential oils and in food preparation and is known to repel slugs and snails in the garden.

Also, if you try to grow the same crop on a plot year after year, you'll quickly notice yields starting to fall, and you're more likely to lose crops to parasites or disease.

To avoid this, use each plot for a different crop every year, so you don't strip all the nutrients out of the soil – and, every fifth year, leave the plot fallow; give it a year off. That, combined with growing peas or beans one of the other years, will preserve the soil. Fallow plots can be planted with grass or a grazing crop, like clover.

Amish Seeds: What Are "Heirloom" Seeds?

Heirloom seeds are food and flower seeds that have been saved by families for over 50 years, and they are passed down from one generation to the next. The Amish prefer to buy seeds from local companies than from big multinationals and some strict Amish communities ban the use of GMO (or transgenic) corn.

Amish Heirloom seeds include the famous "Amish paste" tomato seeds that originally grew in the Pennsylvania Amish communities. Heirloom Potato tubers such as the "Early Ohio are very popular on Amish farms and there are many varieties of potatoes to suit each region available. Heirloom potatoes such as "Amish White Bunch" potatoes" are actually sweet potatoes.

To be self-sufficient, saving your own seed is important. The benefit of using heirloom seeds is that you know they are trusted by generations of growers, and it saves you cash by being able to plant them every year if you dry them and store them carefully. These seeds have been shown to improve biodiversity by retaining seeds that are not one standard type, and they come in as many varieties as there are growers. The Amish prefer to buy seeds from local community sellers rather than rely on large multinational companies.

Many heirloom seeds are organic and this fits in with the Amish lifestyle, where all farming work is done with protection of the natural world and respecting soil, plants, and wildlife as part of a lifestyle that does no damage to the planet.

How Can I Use Companion Planting and Natural Prevention in an Emergency?

An emergency can take many shapes and forms from a simple power cut to extreme temperatures, a pandemic, flooding, fires out of control, terrorism, or even war, as we have seen in recent years. After the last few years, you probably keep a supply of candles at home and matches, a lighter, or a way of lighting them too. Here are a few more ideas to help.

Electrical Blackout

Remember that the Amish community does not use electricity or electrical tools, so a blackout for them is the same as any other day. Where we might struggle, they can turn to their food storage cupboard for preserved food, or just go to the farm to pick food in daylight hours. This is a good incentive to follow their example and have some preserved food and winter crops growing on your property that you can go out and pick. You also need to make sure your storage area is protected from either floods or fire if possible, by keeping food supplies elevated or wrapped in waterproofed or fireproofed materials and areas.

Flooding

If you follow the crop rotation plan outlined in this chapter, you will already have some food growing over winter to stop soil erosion. This alone helps to mitigate the worst effects of flooding because your soil will absorb a lot of the excess water. You can buffer your land for this even more by planting nature-friendly hedgerows or fruit bushes and trees around your growing garden.

Although plants in the ground will be drenched, soil that has been composted absorbs water better than an asphalt driveway for example, and will be a lot easier to clean up afterward. Flood water may be contaminated though, so the soil should be carefully checked after floods recede and tested.

In any emergency, it is essential to have drinking water available. If you do not have cupboards full of bottled water, then fill a bath and any suitable containers with spare water from the taps for safe drinking, in case water is completely cut off and it is a good idea to store some water treatments tablets too, because flood water is not necessarily hygienic either. Remind the family that water is rationed too to avoid drinking it all on the first day. Saved fruit juice is useful here and ice cubes can be melted too.

Fire Prevention

Protection from fire is hard but it very much depends on your preparation. Take the advice offered by your local authority and do not put yourself, your family, or your livestock in danger.

- A good preventative measure is to water your land thoroughly when you know a fire is coming your way. Wet soil will not burn as easily as land in drought, and this one action may save your crops, your home, your animals, and your homestead. You will have saved water for irrigation and may have gray water stored as well. In an emergency, it needs to be spread on a strip wide enough strip to prevent fire from crossing. As wide as possible but at least 10 feet. Keep freezers closed to avoid the contents being destroyed in a blackout but in a fire situation, you can open them once, and strip ice from any freezers to melt, and use them as safe drinking water or use frozen food bags to soothe burned flesh.

- A useful natural tip is to grow cacti and succulents close to your house, food storage areas, and animal houses. Succulents retain water in their fleshy leaves and when approached by fire, the water begins to evaporate. The plants wilt and rarely catch fire but their whole structure disintegrates and what is left is a moist, mush of watery plant flesh. This will help to stop fire from crossing that area by lowering the temperature, raising the humidity, and hopefully stop the fire from passing.

- Some plants are known to resist fire whereas others are extremely flammable. One way to check the plants close to your house, garden, or animal sheds is to cut some foliage or a small branch from shrubs and trees close to the farmland. Try to burn these and see if they ignite quickly. If this is the case and fire is a real risk in your region, rethink plants close to buildings and try adding some plants known to be fire retardants.

- Fires are very unpredictable and depend on wind to move in one direction. If there is a stream, a lake, or a reservoir on your property, get close to it.

- Soak old blankets in the bath and use these as protection around doorways.

- Have transport ready in case you need it! Wind direction can change a fire quickly so even canoes on a river, or any method to get away fast is essential. Wrap wet blankets or towels around vulnerable animals or children if the fire is really close. Get the kids in waterproofs and soak towels to place around them if the fire gets dangerously close.

Economic Downturn

Most of us have faced this recently with the pandemic closely followed by the war in Ukraine which has affected food supplies worldwide. Being able to grow your own food is healthy and saves cash, and how to preserve it is a skill this chapter has taught you. Maybe some of these preserved foods can be sold to make an income. Learn more about the climate in your region, ways to improve the soil, how to source seeds from a local community or save your own and make a plan for how much food you can produce. The Amish way of life shows that we can work alongside nature to produce more food, and perhaps think about living a simpler life.

The secrets of Amish companion planting and crop rotation should be very clear now. Use what you have learned to choose excellent seeds and plant them using the annual crop rotation plan along with companion planting. Knowing a little about natural fire and disaster planning could save you in any emergency so get planting fire-resistant and water-blocking hedges and plants. By using natural methods, you can have great-tasting food like the Amish, without damaging the planet or your soil.

Raised Beds with Hoop House

The Benefits of Using Raised Beds

It is not just the Amish who use raised beds. Gardeners all over the world adore them for providing growing space in a small space, creating a protected site for particular plants, where soil conditions can be carefully amended and controlled, and pests can be excluded using the barriers. The depth of the bed provides a thick layer of soil, and weeds can be removed from the start by careful preparation. In areas where the soil retains a lot of water for example in areas with a high amount of clay in the soil, raised beds can solve the problem by using a layer of sand, small stones, vermiculite, or gravel to improve drainage.

Raised beds are also fantastic for anybody with mobility issues as you do not have to work at ground level and even if using a wheelchair, you can access the garden area at waist height. These beds can have a topsoil layer of manure or compost applied annually to boost fertility, to ensure that the plants growing in the beds have rich soil with good water retention. Remember that the Amish prefer to work with nature so they do not use manmade chemicals to kill either weeds or pests, so if you want to grow the Amish way, try to understand this principle. Learn to distract pests by companion planting, or physical removal to the compost heap, and you can remove weeds at the construction stage of your raised beds to keep them in check.

How to Select Your Site

If you can, observe the area during the previous winter or for at least a few days before construction to check how the sun reaches the site for your proposed raised bed(s). Notice how long the sunlight shines directly on there and if the raised bed will be in the shade for much of the day. You can also check whether the rain drains away easily or tends to become waterlogged, whether there is a tap close by or other water supplies, and if frost or the likelihood of getting some may affect your choice of plants.

Raised beds need direct sunlight for about 6-8 hours per day in the summer season for plants to grow well so try to choose an area where there are no overhanging bushes, trees, high hedges, walls, or sheds that could cast shadows over the area. You may be able to prune tall hedges or remove large branches but you cannot move a wall or building so observe the area well and see where the direct sun settles throughout the day before deciding where your raised bed will finally be located.

The Amish Way *of Gardening*

In soil that becomes easily waterlogged by rain during the winter, you may need to add some sand, pebbles, or gravel into the raised bed to improve the drainage. Sandy soil may need some other components added so that all the goodness is retained, and not allowed to soak away at the first sign of rain.

Is there a water supply close by? If not, can you add a water-collecting barrel? Vegetables and fruit are thirsty for water in hot summer weather and another alternative is to use a drip watering system to water plants regularly without out the hard work.

How to Make Your Raised Bed

An easy method is to buy a ready made Amish raised bed kit with fitted wood sections and instructions, but you can also just use some wood or planks you have available. There are some beautiful Amish designs with interlocking woodwork for sturdy construction and if you want your raised bed to last for a long time, this may be a good option.

If making a DIY version, you need 4 planks, to make a basic rectangular shape and some nails to secure the corners.

Warning

If using pallets, check the stamps to make sure that none of them have been sprayed with toxic chemicals.

Stamp	Meaning
MB	It indicates methyl bromide. This is **toxic** and unsafe for growing food, so you should never use wood with an MB stamp.
BM	Debarked and is safe to use.
HT	Heat treated with no dangerous chemicals.
KD	Kiln dried, which is fine for DIY work too.

Step 1

First, lay the boards in situ and mark the corners using 4 poles or sticks for each raised bed. Try to make sure they have a 90-degree angle when you raise the boards at the corners.

You can tie a layer of string from one corner to the next, then remove the boards so you can work on the soil easily.

Step 2

Dig out the top layer of grass (or whatever is growing there), and set it aside upside down to replace (upside down) as valuable topsoil at the end.

Remove any perennial weeds, shred them, and compost them separately to avoid the seeds spreading.

Step 3

Next, rake the earth and add a layer of cardboard (or some agricultural mesh) to exclude weeds, which will keep the area weed-free.

Now you can start to assemble the beds.

Step 4

For rectangular beds, place the longer boards in situ and the shorter ones at right angles and then slot them together if using a preassembled kit. You can just use a drill and nails to fix the corners. Some Amish craftsmen will construct interlocking corners for a perfect fit but don't worry if your carpentry skills are not this perfect. What you need is a solid shape with a base that will suppress weeds, and form a surface to lay your soil on.

For square beds, lay the 4 boards flat on the ground around the card and begin to secure the corners. Add bolts or nails to secure them in place, or if Amish-made beds, you can just fit one section into the other. Use bricks to hold them in place while you ensure they are at right angles to each other. Drill nails into the corners to secure them, and then once all 4 corners are in place, you can remove the bricks and move on to the next bed if there will be several beds.

Some gardeners enjoy making raised beds to fit a particular shape or area in their garden. I have seen very creative triangular raised beds for example. However, this may require some expert carpentry skills. You know your garden and you know where the sun shines, where the water supply is and what best suits the plants you want to grow so make a bed that suits your garden well.

Step 5

Finally, if you are planning more than one raised bed, try to design the path between them before construction. This could be grass but this will need cutting regularly, or you could lay permanent paving stones or even wood chips. Both are excellent weed deterrents but remember that for gardeners with mobility issues, you need to make it easy to move on the surrounding path. Having permanent wood chips on the area will stop weeds from developing but these can also leach the soil underneath of nutrients. Flat paving stones are useful, gravel is an alternative but not if you need to push wheels around the bed.

How to Fill Your Raised Bed

This can be the most expensive part of making raised beds because the soil needs to be deep, rich, and able to support the plants you choose over a long period. Usually, a raised bed is anywhere between 18 inches to 2-3 feet deep although some gardeners use even deeper ones for fruit bush or tree planting.

If you measure the longest side of your bed, multiplied by the width and then by the height, you get an idea of the volume of soil you will need. So if your bed measures 6 feet long by 2 feet wide, and is 1 foot tall, then you are going to need a lot of soil to fill it. If cost is no issue, you can order a large delivery of premium topsoil to fill your new raised beds but most people prefer to use available materials. The Amish will fill a deep raised bed with whatever material they have available from the garden. There may be twigs and branches pruned from trees and fruit bushes, larger branches, stones, wood chips, straw or hay and fresh grass cuttings, coffee grounds and plant kitchen waste, eggshells, nettles and comfrey leaves, small pebbles, a compost heap and a supply of well composted, animal manure. All of these can be utilized to fill your new raised beds.

Be careful when adding manure if it has not been fully composted. Leaving manure to season for 6 months to a year is the norm to avoid any pathogens contained in it. These will dissolve over time into the heap and the high volume and the heat of composting kill off any nasties. You need to keep fresh manure away from delicate new plant roots so for example if you have both animal and chicken manure, place the chicken manure on top of the wood pieces, and then add a layer of straw followed by the composted animal manure and another layer of leaf mold or eggshells, nettles etc to keep the raised bed as layers through which nature will continue to add and break down and contribute to the overall health of the soil. For the Amish, the soil is a gift from the Creator, a living material full of live creatures like worms and insects burrowing in the soil and burrowing through it eating leaves, depositing waste, and adding valuable air tunnels, if they are worms.

At ground level, your raised bed needs to have a layer that can restrict weeds and many gardeners often spread a layer of recycled cardboard (or plastic) to do this. The Amish will not favor using plastic though, as it is an unnatural material but cardboard comes from tree pulp so this would be fine. Try not to use printed or colored cardboard though, because those chemicals could seep into the soil so just use plain recycled boxes or cardboard. Another alternative the Amish use is dried grass, or straw or hay, because they use no chemicals anywhere and these will simply rot down over time, adding nutrients to the soil in your raised bed.

The Amish Way *of Gardening*

Onto this layer, you can add pruned twigs and small branches, preferably cut into small pieces and raked to make a thin layer of wood on top of the card. Allow some air pockets too so that roots will have plenty of oxygen. Bigger branches of wood will fill up the bed well and they rot down over time, adding moisture and goodness to the soil but make sure they are not thicker than a few inches in width because these will take a long time to rot down. Rotting branches will eventually add a level of moisture to the bed but if they are very large, energy goes into the decomposition that would otherwise feed your plants so keep the logs thin and cut them into pieces as small as possible.

If drainage is an issue, depending on your soil type, now is the time to add sand, pebbles, or gravel for good drainage. If you prefer, you can use vermiculite here too, as a useful mineral that retains moisture in the bed. The Amish like to add a layer to cover the wood using organic leaf molds from their gardens, such as nettle, comfrey, or dandelion leaves, which will decompose over time, adding valuable nutrients to the mix. At this stage, I like to water the bed to settle it into a flat growing area.

The base is now settled and you need to start adding layers of available materials such as the topsoil you removed at the beginning, compost, and manure that has been composted. The Amish will use layers of materials that are readily available but their best-known natural ingredient is animal manure because this provides a really rich soil conditioner, fantastic for a variety of plants. If you have access to fresh animal or poultry manure, remember not to apply it fresh. You need to allow it to break down for about 6 months to 1 year to ensure it is free of any leftover pests, pathogens, or weeds. It is also important to only use it for certain plants in your raised bed so be cautious about using manure for every crop because it is too rich for the roots of some. Crop Rotation (see more below) is a system for incorporating manure for 2 years and compost in the years following this to suit the crops that will grow there so keep a record of what you apply, and the plants you grow, and never apply manure for cabbage family or root crops.

Which Plants Can I Grow in the Raised Bed?

Plan crops in your raised bed in a cycle of changing plants called Crop Rotation, which is a basic tenet of Amish agriculture that sows seed in cycles so that the soil never becomes depleted. The Amish keep their soil fertile by changing the crop in any area every year over a 3-4 year cycle because growing the same plant on the same soil year after year will cause deterioration and also allow pests to stay in the soil, so rotating the crop encourages healthier soil. Remember that in kitchen gardens the Amish love to plant flowers to attract pollinators and that these can also help to attract pests away from your crop. See the chapter on companion planting for more details.

Having 4 raised beds will allow you to plan a Crop Rotation system that allows you to plant and amend the soil in each bed to suit the plant you intend to grow there. For example, hungry crops like squash, cucumbers, and tomatoes need manure to grow well in year 1 so a layer is applied in the first year. This raised bed can have peas or beans planted in year 2 as they fix nitrogen in the roots and will love the manure you apply. In year 3 you can try cauliflower, cabbage, or any plant from that family, but do not add manure. Year 4 will be a no-manure year but you can spread a layer of homemade compost for a crop of carrots, radishes, and beets. Plant some marigolds, and calendulas close to your carrots, nasturtiums, and wildflowers in any available space to bring in the bees and you are certainly adhering to Amish planting principles. The following year, move everything to the next bed along so that year becomes year 2 and so on. In this way, you are ensuring that the soil has time to recover and that the same minerals and nutrients are being replaced by swapping the plants.

Raised beds tend to be from 18 inches to 2 feet deep so choose plants whose roots do not dive too far underground.

Raised beds are perfect for annual plants, such as tomatoes, chili peppers, bell peppers, annual herbs like basil or coriander, eggplants, zucchini, etc. They grow for one season, you harvest them, and then you can cut the stem, and leave the roots to compost in the bed over the winter. Root crops are suitable too because your careful soil preparation means there are no small stones to make shapes in your carrots or beets and a quick crop of radishes can be planted for an early crop. Perennial plants like strawberries enjoy 3-4 years in the same bed and you can easily pot up any runners into new pots running from the raised bed.

You can ensure a fresh layer of topsoil is added to each raised bed in the fall and before planting, they have excellent drainage, and the deep soil offers plants a great growing site. Maybe set up an automatic drip watering system too if you have a lot of other gardening to do.

Making a Hoop House over Your Raised Bed

A hoop house is a covered area held in place over your raised bed using hoops or wire covered with plastic, mesh, cotton, or fleece which protects your crops from pests and/or extends the growing season by keeping plants warmer and frost and snow-free. The Amish are well-known for their beautifully constructed wooden cold frames, which can be opened in hot weather or closed if frost is forecast. Hoop houses work in the same way but they tend to stay in place for the summer season. The Amish method will usually allow them to be used for extending the growing season in cooler months by using hinged covers that can be opened or closed depending on the weather.

How to Make a Simple Hoop House

You need to make a structure that will cover the entire raised bed from one side of the raised bed to the other, for example, using a series of hoops covered with a material that allows light to penetrate but keeps weather (or pests) out. Allow at least 3 hoops per bed, or 4 if it is very long. You can buy these from your gardening store or make your own using strong wire threaded through piping or simply use bamboo shaped into hoops. You place these on either side of the raised bed and secure them with screws. A good tip is to use recycled tops from plastic bottles, make a hole in them, and use that to screw the cap onto the base of the wooden raised bed. Then the end of your wire hoop can fit easily into the cap and the tension should keep it upright. You could also add a few extra layers of plastic or wire running along the longest side of the raised bed, one at each side of the base and one at the top of the hoop.

Over the hoops and supports, you will drape the cover and then secure this at the edges. The cover can then be slotted over these supports.

Using two hinges will make the whole process very easy so you can lift the cover when picking or weeding. The Amish make bespoke covers hinged like this to suit the size of the space available and you may be able to find one readymade in your local Amish store. You need to be able to easily access the raised bed to weed and pick plants so just make sure the cover is loose to allow you to do this.

Cheaper options could be using wire from unwanted hangers to make the hoops and draping an old net curtain as a cover, that allows light through but not caterpillars, moths, or insects for crops that do not need insect pollination such as carrots or cabbage family. Another idea is to use an old window frame (or door) as the cover and fit hinges to it to secure it to the raised bed. The Amish will try to avoid plastic materials, so they will use wooden frames and glass, or natural materials such as fine woven cotton but for ease of use in your garden, a roll of polyethylene plastic used as the cover will be viable for 3-4 years use. These are readily available from most hardware stores too. Having a Hoop House that has hinges means it will fit the exact size of your raised bed, and it can lifted in hot weather and replaced if bad weather is forecast.

Maintenance of Your Raised Bed and a Crop Rotation Plan

Your raised bed is a container filled with soil, so you can understand why you need to keep adding material to ensure the fertility is maintained. Adding composted animal manure is a well-known Amish method of ensuring the fertility and health of their soil and remember they do not use pesticides or weedkillers either, instead relying on companion planting and techniques to keep pests off their crops. Adding leaf mold is another free natural method of boosting fertility and leaves can be picked from comfrey, nettles and dandelions for this usage. Some crops fix nitrogen into the soil as they grow (legumes, peas, and beans) and this provides valuable soil for the crop that follows afterward.

Although manure is a fabulous fertilizer, not all plants like it so when using manure, it is important to check each year where you added it the previous year. Then, you can decide which crops will follow in the next planting season. This chart below gives you a handy reference for whether you need to add manure or compost in which year of the Crop Rotation cycle.

Year	Sow	Manure?	Irrigation notes
1	**HUNGRY CROPS** Cucumber, Eggplant, Herbs, Chili pepper, Squash, Tomatoes	Yes	Water frequently, particularly in hot weather. Apply liquid feeds at fruiting time. Water if stems droop!
2	**LEGUMES (Nitrogen Fixers) and the ONION FAMILY** Peas, Beans, Garlic, Onions, Leeks	Yes	Water at least twice weekly and in hot weather.
3	**CABBAGE FAMILY** Cabbage, Kale, Brussel Sprouts	No Apply Compost	Water at sowing time, and at least weekly after that.
4	**ROOTS** Beets, Carrots, Radishes, Parsnips, Swede	No Apply Compost	Water at sowing time, then weekly or in hot weather.
5	**RETURN** As above	Yes	Plant a new crop.
6	**PERENNIAL CROPS** (for at least 3 years in the same place) Asparagus (20+ yrs), Red currants (5+ yrs), Blackcurrants (5+ yrs), Raspberries (5+ yrs), Strawberries (3 yrs)	Yes	Water at least weekly during summer and at fruiting time.

The Amish Way *of Gardening*

FAQs

How deep does the raised bed need to be?

For growing fruit or vegetables, it is best to allow at least 18 inches and up to 2 feet. For vegetables, check the root size carefully from your seed packets and make sure they are suitable for raised bed growing. Choosing seeds carefully will mean that you are not disappointed with the harvest.

If you want to try fruiting shrubs or dwarf fruit and nut trees in raised beds, remember that the harvest will not be as bountiful as growing them in soil as nature intended. You will need to allow taller beds to accommodate deeper root growth. Simply construct a raised bed with two or three layers of wood and fill them up with more soil.

How often should I water my raised bed?

For any growing plant, you need to provide soil, sunshine, and water and you will need to water more when it is first made, or when the sunshine is bright. If you see your tomatoes are drooping over, time to water! I prefer to water at least 2-3 times per week in summer and a lot less or no watering in winter. Setting up an automatic watering system is useful if you have many beds, to save you time. You can target the roots this way and not waste water hosing the leaves. Feel the soil if in doubt. If it is very dry then water well. Try to water early in the morning.

Tips

- Your soil in a raised bed warms up quicker than soil at ground level in spring so you can extend your growing season by planting seeds earlier than at ground level. There is more pest protection too as the soil is at a height.

- In the fall, you can transform your raised bed into a cold frame by adding a protective layer over the top to keep out colder air, storms or frost. A wooden frame draped with protective material will keep the plants growing in it protected and warmer for longer. This extends your growing season, and you can also grow some lettuces and greens in the fall to keep eating well later in the year.

- Making raised beds the Amish way starts with the craftsmanship and the wood used to construct them, how you fill them, and the plants you choose to grow. Like your entire garden, growing food the Amish way implies respect for nature, using no chemicals, and trying to not harm wildlife and insects so that all is in harmony. Used like this, your Amish raised beds will bring good tastes into your kitchen to use for fresh salads, vegetables and fruit to preserve for the winter, and hopefully to allow you to grow plants in living soil that improves over time.

How the Amish Grow Potatoes in Thin Air

There are many choices you can make when planning your survival garden. One easy-to-grow food the Amish have always depended on is the potato. The potato has incredible utility and can be prepared in many different ways.

The potato can be stored for a tremendous amount of time in a root cellar which is the preferred method of storage for the Amish who do not use electricity. In a root cellar, with consistent temperatures, potatoes can last 6-8 months!

The average boiled potato contains around 90 calories. Potatoes vary in size, but this is a pretty good estimate. Potatoes are a great source of energy. They are also a decent source of vitamin C and with the skin on they can be a good source of potassium.

Potatoes don't take a lot of space to grow, and they can even be grown up instead of out because the potatoes form along the rootstock of the plant. It is pretty common for people to grow potatoes in wooden or plastic towers where they add dirt over time, so the plants continually grow upward, and the potato roots are encouraged to get longer and longer creating a greater and greater yield.

Growing potatoes off-grid in thin air is not as complicated as it sounds. The process is all about using drip technology and gravity to feed our potato plants. The plants and roots are sustained inside a 5-gallon bucket.

The stems and leaves of the plants will grow outside of the bucket while the roots and potatoes grow inside the bucket receiving consistent moisture. We used the irrigation drippers embedded in PVC pipe to create a slow drip system that will keep our potatoes and roots moist.

Water, compost tea, or some other liquid plant food solution is poured into the PVC build and is regulated by the irrigation drippers. It all happens because of gravity and no electricity is required.

THE AMISH WAY *of Gardening*

Tools

Circle saw set
Power drill
¾ inch drill bit
PVC cement
Hacksaw

Materials

6ft of 1 ½ PVC pipe
2-1 ½-inch 90 degree elbow fittings
1-1 ½-inch T fitting
1- 1 ½-inch cap
5 gallon bucket with lids
Grow baskets
2 gallon per hour irrigation drippers

Instructions

To start the build you are going to cut yourself a 10 inch length of PVC pipe and place the cap on the end of it. Then you will cut two small circles of PVC around 1 1/2 inches in length. These will connect your elbows to your T fixture.

You can fit all of these pieces together and seal them with PVC cement to keep them together and assure you do not have leaks from the water.

Fully assembled, the main part of the building is going to look almost like a field goal post that is missing the posts. This piece will be drilled and studded with our irrigation drippers later in the project.

What's most important is that this build must be able to fit into your 5-gallon bucket with the lid on. If it does not than cut your straight length of PVC a little shorter.

Then you are going to need two more lengths of PVC pipe that are 24 inches in length. These will become your goal-posts in the build. More importantly, these are going to be where you add water or compost tea to feed your potatoes.

The tops of these pipes will not be capped. They will stay open to allow you to pour water directly into the tubes.

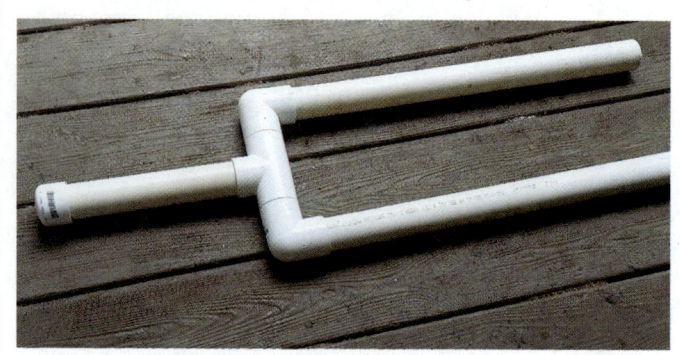

This is what the completed PVC assembly will look like. I did not cement the longer posts in because we have some drilling to do first. Moving the build around and drilling it when it is shorter is much easier.

The Amish Way of Gardening

Using the PVC T build that you have built so far, flip it upside down and mark two circles on the lid where each side of the elbow fittings rest on the lid. This will give you the proper distance to cut your holes.

Using a 1 1/2-inch circle saw you are going to cut out two holes to fit the 24-inch lengths of PVC through. The holes should easily fit the 1 1/2-inch PVC pipe. This lid will have to eventually slide down the 2 goal posts and seal the bucket.

Before you go any further be sure that the lid fits accordingly.

Now, use the 3/4-inch drill bit to bore holes on both sides of the PVC. I drilled 4 holes across the top of the build and 4 holes on the underside and 4 on the opposite side. Then I drilled 3 on both sides of the bottom length of PVC.

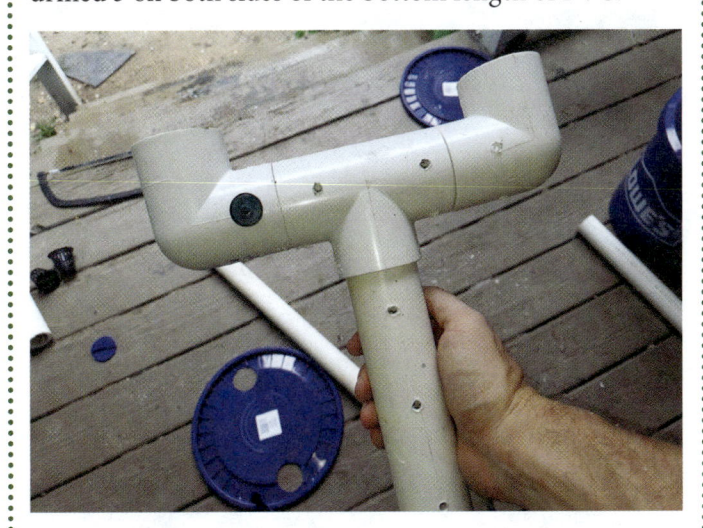

Once all the holes were completed, I applied a small bit of PVC cement to each irrigation dripper and then slid them into each hole.

The 4 holes on the underside of the T spilled water out a little too fast so I would not recommend those for this build as you will get much more out each time you fill the tubes with water.

Here is a look at the build with all of the drip irrigation plugs fitted into the PVC pipe. As you can see, these drippers will hit the long roots of potatoes at many places throughout as the drippers deliver your chose growing solution.

Next, we are going to use the circle saw to cut two locations for grow baskets. These baskets are where we can place sprouting seed potatoes or a cut of sprouting potatoes. You can cover the potatoes with clay pebbles or another substrate.

I placed the length of PBV over the 2 holes that we already cut out of the lids. This will give you the ability to cut your holes for your grow baskets as close to the drip system as possible. If you cut your holes too far from the drip system, the roots will never get enough water.

Don't forget to measure your grow baskets before cutting the holes. My baskets were just a little smaller than 1 1/2 inches so my circles had to be a little smaller than the holes drilled for my PVC.

The Amish Way *of Gardening*

Once you have all your holes drilled into the lid you are going to place the irrigation PVC build into the bucket and then add the 24-inch PVC pipes to extend the build. At this point you are ready to place the lid on and test your system.

Test by pouring water directly in the 24-inch lengths of PVC pipe. You should see the irrigators begin to drip. The drips should be frequent but small.

In time this water will fill your bucket, as you can see. So, you will have to drill a few drainage holes into the bottom of the bucket.

With the build inside the bucket, you are going to fit the lid of the bucket over the two holes drilled for the PVC pipe. Do not confuse these with your grow basket holes.

You may need to shift the PVC build a bit to get it positioned upright. Then you can snap the lid on completely. At this point your build is ready to use.

You can pour water, fish emulsion, plant food solution, or compost tea into the tops of both PVC pipes. This will create that slow drip of moisture to coat the roots of your plants.

The Amish Way of Gardening

Tips For Growing Potatoes in Thin Air

This system is designed to saturate the roots through drip irrigation. Your PVC creation will gradually let the water drip over your potatoes as they grow. However, there are some things you can do to help this whole process along.

1. In the early stages of growing, your plants will need some help developing. Similar to hydroponics you will need plants that have sprouted. This is easy to do with potato plants, sometimes the roots even begin to sprout in storage.

2. Another tip is to use fertilizers on your plants. Things like compost tea and fish emulsion will help your potatoes grow faster. Since this process is void of soil you will also give your plants much-needed nutrition.

3. Monitor the health and growth of your potatoes each day. To ensure the process is working you can remove the lid of the bucket setup and look at how things are growing. If your roots look dry, then you need to water the system more often.

4. Beware of too much direct sunlight in hot temperatures. The captured water in the bucket from the drip irrigation will create a moist environment for your plants. However, in too much direct sun and heat the temperatures in the bucket could get too hot and steam your roots.

How to Sprout Potatoes Quickly for Your System

Since sprouting potatoes are going to perform best in this system, we need to sprout some quickly so you can start the growing process. What is the best way to sprout potatoes quickly?

Potatoes are in the nightshade family just like tomatoes, peppers, and eggplant. They need moisture, warmth, and sunlight to sprout. You can achieve all this by wrapping a potato in a damp paper towel and sitting it on a windowsill that gets light.

Once you start to get eyes or sprouts on the potato you can expose that part to the sunlight by removing the damp paper towel from that area. Once your sprouts are a couple of inches long you can cut the potato to fit your grow basket, keeping the sprouts intact, and begin to grow potatoes in thin air.

Not only is this process an interesting way to grow food but it also can be used in a situation where soil might be unavailable, contaminated, or void of essential nutrients. By building a simple system like this you can turn an apartment patio, a rooftop, or even a basement with grow lights, into agriculture.

This is a system that can also be used to grow numerous types of plants. It takes principles from things like aero gardening, and hydroponics. So, many of the same plants that do well in these systems will do well in this system where we are growing potatoes in thin air.

THE AMISH WAY *of Gardening*

How to Build a Year-Round Underground Food Garden

In a worst-case scenario, underground year-round food gardens are essential because they can provide a stable food supply, especially in harsh environments.

So, here's how to construct one using the most efficient and economical design at home.

Tools

A mattock
A shovel
Pickaxe (if necessary for hard ground)
Wheelbarrow
A ladder
Wood saw
Utility knife
A measuring tape

Materials

4x3 feet wooden pallets (for the underground garden walls)
8x1 inch wooden planks (for joining the pallets) side-by-side
3 rolls of clear plastic sheeting (for insulation)
3x1 inch wooden planks (for constructing the roof)
Nails (different sizes)
Metal brackets or joist hangers for roofing
6-7 oriented strand board (OSB) for the door and wall
A packet of wood screws (different sizes)
4 heavy-duty hinges
1 door latch and lock
4 rolls of 3mm reflective (foil) insulation
Additional support beams (2x4 inch lumber) for supporting the roof

Choose an Ideal Location and Orientation

Ideally, you want it built into a hillside or dug into flat ground. I chose an ideal spot with well-drained soil and avoided low-lying areas prone to flooding.

Also, ensure your greenhouse will be oriented with the longer side (roof) facing the sun to maximize solar intake, even during the cold months.

This positioning helps trap and retain heat.

Instructions

Step 1: Mark and Excavate the Trench

In this step, I measured, marked, and started digging the trench. But note that you can choose different dimensions, based on your preference.

I dug an 8-foot-wide, 15-foot-long, and 3-foot-deep pit with a mattock, hoe, and shovel. I factored in some additional space for adding insulation (which I will demonstrate below).

Use a pickaxe to break the hard ground if you encounter one.

Here's what the pit looked like after removing all the soil: My focus was to insert one-third of the height of the pallets to provide stability.

The Amish Way *of Gardening*

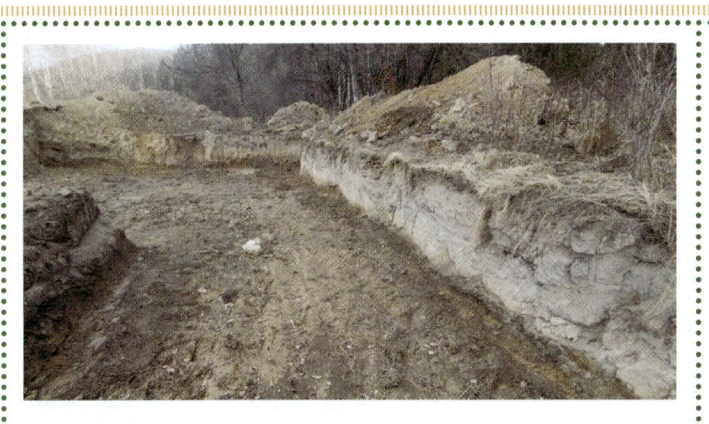

Step 2: Gather the Wooden Pallets and Join Them

I will use wooden pallets to build the walls and frames for my underground food garden. However, you must ensure the trench is deep enough to support the pallet wall as you can see here:

Joining the pallets

Now, join the pallets (side by side) using 8x1 inch sturdy wooden planks. Cut the planks to the precise size using a wood saw and secure them with nails.

Attach the reinforcement across the joints where two pallets meet using a hammer and nails.

Make sure you hit the nails from both ends of the wooden plank to create a firm joint. Here's how I did it:

Always check and ensure the frame is level on both sides.

For additional strength, reinforce the pallets using another wooden plank. Like this:

Positioning Pallets

Carefully lift the pallets and place them vertically along the sides of the trench.

41

The Amish Way of Gardening

Join other pallets (side by side) to form a continuous frame along the walls of the trench. Like this:

Add an extra layer of wooden pallets to create a taller frame around the top perimeter of the pit. This will increase the stability and make securing the sheeting easier.

Here is a picture to illustrate more:

Here is a better view of how the wall is slowly taking shape:

Step 3: Installing Insulation for Heat Retention

After the frame is secure, install a plastic sheeting lining on the outside of the pallets for thermal insulation. Note that this should be done before backfilling the trench.

Here is a picture to illustrate more on how I did it:

Slowly add other pallets along the pit's wall as you fix the plastic sheeting.

This is how it should look like:

Using a digging bar, I dug and excavated a few narrow 3-foot deep holes at regular intervals along the perimeter of the trench into which I will insert 3*2 inch wooden planks horizontally to support the structure and ensure its overall stability.

I started by digging one hole at the end of the structure where I would create the entrance or doorway.

The Amish Way of Gardening

Add other holes strategically along the perimeter of the pit. You can add three holes on the longer side of the trench and two holes on the shorter side.

Slowly insert each wooden plank horizontally into the holes and backfill to ensure stability.

Use nails to attach adjacent pallets.

Here's what it should look like:

Step 4: Backfilling the Trench

Once the pallets are properly aligned and insulated, use a shovel and gradually backfill the trench with soil.

Inspect the trench for any gaps or voids and fix them before backfilling.

Lastly, ensure you compact the soil to add stability and more insulation. Like this:

Step 5: Building the Underground Garden's Roof

Using a measuring tape, get the exact length and width of the garden to determine the roof's size. I chose the gambrel roof design for my structure because it increases the interior space and is easy to construct.

Next, cut and prepare the 3x1 inch wooden planks to the required lengths using a hand saw.

I used nails and a hammer to join different sections of the roof. This picture is a section of the roof rafter construction:

Next, join the upper and lower rafters at the appropriate angles using wood joinery to secure the roof sections.

The Amish Way *of* Gardening

Next, I used metal brackets and cross supports between the upper rafters to secure them. Like this picture below:

Join different sections of the roof to form a complete roof panel. Here is a picture I took of how the roof was slowly taking its shape.

Here is another picture of how I reinforced the roofing frame with additional nails to ensure it is stable.

Continue with the same steps (as discussed above) until you complete the construction of the roofing frame.

It should now look something similar to this:

Next, prepare the frames once more by reinforcing the joints with screws and nails before securing them on top of the structure. This step is important because the roof needs to be sturdy to avoid collapsing.

Next, strategically install vertical pillars inside the dug-out trench for additional support. Typically, the pillars should be at the corners of the structure and evenly spaced along the perimeter of the underground food garden. I installed three 3x3-inch wooden pillars to support the roof of my structure.

Step 6: Building the Door and Its Frame

After the roof is set, it's time to build the door. So, measure the doorway of your greenhouse using a measuring tape and determine the size of the door.

Using the 3x2 inch wooden planks, mark and cut the pieces for the door frame. You need two sturdy vertical and horizontal pieces.

The Amish Way of Gardening

Carefully lay out the vertical and horizontal pieces of the frame on a flat surface to assemble. The frame should be 4x8 feet to match the standard OSB dimension. Here is how it looks like:

Use nails or screws to secure the joints for additional strength and place the OSB board on top of the frame, as I did here.

After the door's outer face is complete, turn it to the other side and cut additional 3x2 inch planks to create cross supports.

In the picture shared below, I cut additional planks for building the door's cross-support.

Place the diagonally across the frame (in a "Z" shape) to add rigidity and prevent the door from warping. Also, don't forget to mark the locations for the hinges on the door.

Step 7: Attaching the Roofing Material

After the door is complete, measure the transparent roofing material to fit the roof decking. Starting from the lower end of the slope, attach the polythene paper to the frame using nails as I did here:

Note: Ensure the material slightly overlaps to create a continuous, weatherproof surface and seal rainwater from entering the structure.

Step 8: Constructing the Walls

Once the roofing is done, measure the length, width, and height of the greenhouse to determine the size and layout of the walls.

Measure the frame, cut, and prepare to assemble the OSB sheets to fit the frames.

Next, fix the wall frames and secure the joints with screws and nails, as seen here:

Continue adjusting the structure, laying, and aligning additional OSB sheets to the frame until they fit correctly. Position the door in the doorway and mark the correspond-

The Amish Way of Gardening

ing hinge locations on the door frame. Next, attach the hinges to the door frame, ensuring the door is level and swings freely.

Here's how I did it.

After managing the front of your greenhouse, go to the back side and install polythene paper with nails to secure it firmly. This will allow sunlight into the underground food garden from the back side.

It should look like this:

Step 9: Installing Insulation

The earth's natural thermal mass helps to maintain a favorable temperature within the greenhouse. During the day, for instance, the sun heats the interior, and the surrounding earth prevents excess heat loss at night.

Even with that said, you must still insulate the garden's interior to assist in heat retention.

I decided to use 3mm reflective (foil) insulation because it was easy to install and was efficient at limiting thermal transfer by radiation. Also, we only need to insulate the walls.

Cutting and Fitting the Insulation

Using a utility knife, measure and cut the insulation foam to fit between the wall studs.

Place the insulation snugly between the studs to ensure no gaps or wrinkles. Start at the doorway and work your way across the room. Also, use nails to attach the insulation material every 6-8 inches along the edges and seams of the frame.

Optional: You can use insulation tape to seal the seams, ensuring an airtight fit.

The Amish Way of Gardening

Step 10: Wrapping Up

Check the entire structure for gaps, loose connections, and areas that need adjustments.

Overall, an underground year-round food garden provides an innovative and sustainable solution for food production in various climates. In a prepping scenario, these easy-to-construct structures leverage natural resources to create a controlled growing environment.

Some Tips and Tricks on Underground Year-Round Food Garden Maintenance

Maintaining an underground greenhouse involves regular inspections, cleaning, and addressing any issues promptly. This ensures optimal growing conditions.

Here are some tips and tricks for effective maintenance:

- Always regulate temperatures inside your underground greenhouse by increasing ventilation during hot summers and adding an extra layer of mulch around the base of plants to guarantee additional insulation during the cold winter.
- Always inspect ventilation holes and covers to reduce condensation inside the underground garden Use hygrometers to monitor the humidity levels.
- Periodically check the roof and walls for tears or punctures, especially after a storm.
- Regularly maintain installed irrigation systems to ensure they provide adequate water to your plants.
- Practice crop rotation to maintain soil health and prevent diseases. Also, check your plants for signs of pests and diseases.
- Regularly prune nearby trees or shrubs to avoid casting shade over your underground greenhouse.
- Uproot weeds to prevent them from competing with your plants for nutrients and space.
- Keep the inside clean by removing dead plants, leaves, and other debris.

Using Plants
The Amish Way

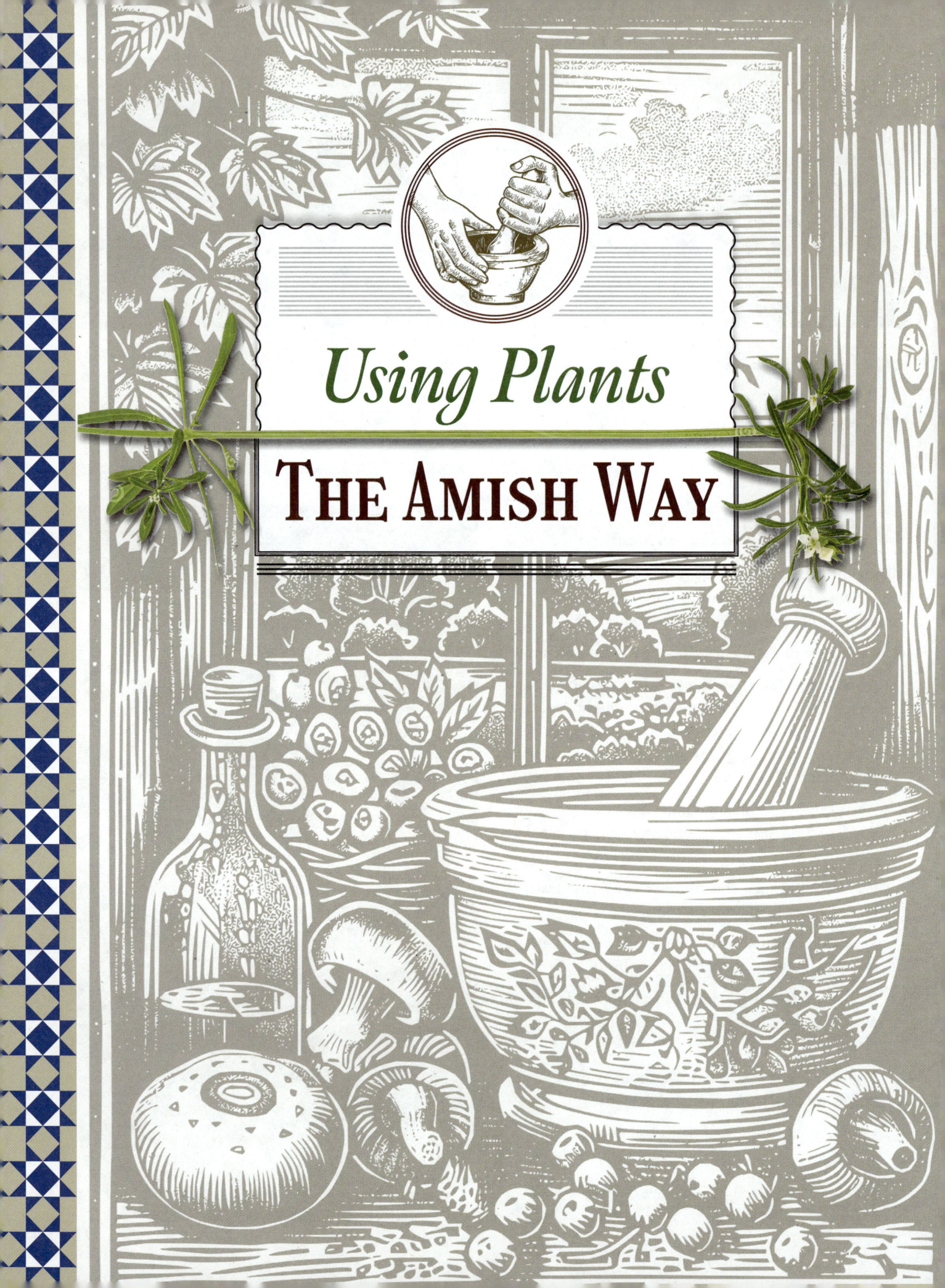

How to Forage the Amish Way

Foraging like the Amish means respecting nature while you pick. When collecting plants, make sure they can continue to grow in that area, so that your footprints leave just a tiny mark on the soil, not destroying the habitat, as often happens on land that the Amish do not protect. It is best to use wicker baskets not plastic bags to emulate the Amish way, use wool gloves and certainly no powered saws, only sharp scissors, deft hands, and simple methods. Collecting food to preserve for the cold winter months and then preserving it for long-term use is a crucial part of Amish food collection. In this chapter, we'll take a look at how to find plants the Amish collect, how to identify them, and then how to preserve them so you can eat your preserved food until the summer arrives again, or even longer.

General Foraging Guidelines

Treat your foraging environment like a cherished, loved space, and visit it often. That way you will see the flowers on fruit trees and bushes in spring, and notice the pollinators visiting them, and also the unripe fruit or seeds that you wish to collect later. Look at the soil too but try not to disturb it. It is illegal to uproot wild plants in many states so if there is a plant you want to grow, do your research first. If it is not allowed, try to source seeds and grow them in your own garden. American Ginseng was over-collected so much it is almost extinct and endangered now so remember to pick just a little of whatever you collect. Nut trees are a rarity but if you find one, you will be competing with squirrels and wildlife for them so take some for your personal use but not all of them. If you want to pick mushrooms, check that it is permitted in your area and the quantity allowed, as this is often stipulated in many states. Only pick some of any plant material or fruit available so that you pick enough for you but also to allow the plants to survive and thrive.

Mistakes to Avoid When Foraging

- **The Amish will never strip an entire patch of plants**, because they believe that nature will provide if they look after the land. Be aware that digging up roots will kill that individual plant so only take a few, and never all of them. Cover up the roots of any plants dug up by accident, replacing the soil to ensure it keeps growing after you leave.

- **Check the ID carefully before you pick**, particularly if there is a poisonous lookalike. Learning when a plant is in flower or when the fruit should be ripening will help you to identify it. If there are instructions about the shape of the leaves or the shape of the stem, check and make sure this is the case before you pick. Some plants may be known to cause irritation or dermatitis so wear gloves. Know the poisonous plants to avoid and if possible, have a way of checking this before you eat anything.

- **Before picking in any new location, do some research first.** Check if the neighbourhood is sprayed from municipal edge weed spraying and if you do not want to eat pesticides, then only forage from wild sites. If plants are from a natural background, you do not need to wash them too much if you are confident the habitat is free from municipal spraying or pesticides. Check also that you are permitted to collect plants from this area. For example, it is not legal to forage roots from state parks or national parks in many states.

- **Discard any slug-eaten leaves and bruised fruit that will not store well.** Diseased fruit may spread to other food in your storage area, so do not store it. Bruised fruit can be eaten fresh if possible or cooked in pies. Just compost it if it is gone too brown or too bad to use.

PLANTS YOU CAN FORAGE

In each section, you can find a description of the plants to forage and possible mix-ups in identification with poisonous plants. For each plant, there will be information on how to preserve it.

1. AMISH GOOSEBERRY *(Ribes grossularia)*

This plump, oval-shaped fruit is delicious in puddings and pies or eaten fresh off the bush when ripe. They look green when unripe, and some varieties of gooseberries remain green but Amish Gooseberry plants have a distinctive pink or red color later in the season and have a little tail at the end of the fruit.

How to Identify Gooseberry

The berries are less than 1 inch (10-15 cm) wide and they have stripes from the tip to the base so they are easy to identify. The fruit is sweet and soft, with seeds inside. They can grow into a shrub 3 feet wide and 3-4 feet tall in the wild. The leaves have curly edges and feel quite soft to the touch. The whole plant is hairy with thorns on the canes and branches that support the leaves and fruit, so wear gloves when picking.

The fruit grows on branches and fruit develops from flowers, that first turn green and form a plump oval shape that gradually turns pink or red once ripe in midsummer from early to mid-July. They are about 3-4 feet tall and the Amish grow them in groups.

In the wild, they are less common but you may be lucky. Learn how to identify this plant in a fruit nursery and then if you spot the canes and the leaves when walking in spring, return to watch the fruit develop and come back to pick them when ripe. Birds love this fruit too so leave some for them.

All gooseberries are edible so even if you find a different variety in your neighbourhood, you can be confident it is gooseberry. Check the soft leaves, thorns on the stem and branches, and the stripes on the fruit.

You can eat gooseberries cold in a summer pudding or preserve them for winter use.

How to Preserve Gooseberries

The best method is canning. This preserves whole fruit in sugar and the processing will kill any germs. Canned fruit will last 2 years at least. Gooseberry jam or preserves are other options, and these will save for several years. I have eaten gooseberry jam after 5 years so this is a good one for longer-term storage.

Clean and sterilize glass jars or mason jars with lids before you start. A simple way is to pour boiling water into them and allow them to dry. You will need a cold plate to test the setting of the jam and I like to use sealing covers directly on the jam before adding the lid. These can be made of greaseproof paper or recycled paper secured with an elastic band.

Use 3 cups of gooseberries, 3 cups of sugar, and 1 cup of water in a saucepan. Some cooks like to add lemon juice to aid setting but gooseberries are high in pectin, which is the substance that makes jam set, so add a little lemon juice if you like but it usually sets without this. You can vary the quantities if you do not collect this many gooseberries too. Cook the fruit for about 20 minutes on low heat, and allow it to come to a boil, then reduce the heat further and allow it to simmer for another 5-10 minutes. Then test the mixture on the side of a plate. If it sets, then it is ready. If it is runny, allow it to cook for another 5 minutes and test again. Once it sets on the plate, allow the jar to cool a little, and then pour it into the sterile containers and seal it with lids. The Amish like to tie a cloth over the top and secure this with string or ribbon. Make sure you add a label with the date made and place the newest jars at the back of the shelf so you use up the oldest jars first.

Spread this on breakfast toast, add a spoonful to natural yogurt for a healthy snack, and use its distinctive sweet taste to add body to cooked desserts.

2. ANGELICA *(Angelica sylvestris, Angelica archangelica or Angelica atropurpurea)*

The pictures show the seed heads, the flowers and the leaves.

This plant has edible leaves, stems, roots, and seeds so this is a useful plant in all seasons for the forager. It has many variants in the US, the sylvestris variety is also known as Wild Angelica. All Angelica smells sweet and has been used in making puddings for centuries. Try cutting a stem and you will learn to identify this distinctive feature.

How to Identify Angelica

This wild plant has a clue in its scientific name. Sylvestris means from or of the forest, and the pinkish-white flowers of Angelica enjoy damp paths close to streams, or growing in woods and forests, wherever the seeds land.

These are very noticeable plants with thick stems, usually with a pink stripe on them.

The leaves have a pointed one at the top and then 2 leaves directly opposite, and the leaves form opposite each other after these top three. The edges have tiny teeth with points. The thick stem is unique, often with pink stripes, the leaves are dark green with a shiny surface, and the flowers are in pretty bunches that stand high above the foliage on a thick stem. The flowers can be yellow, as in the case of the archangelica variety, and in Minnesota and Wisconsin, you can find the pinkish-white flowers of the atropurpurea variety. You can pick the whole flower buds at the stem and steam them gently to eat as a spring vegetable.

Once you learn to identify one variety, you can recognize the stem and the leaves easily and the scent of the leaves is another clue. The seeds are often described as having a licorice smell so go close, touch them in your hand, and sniff. Finally, the seeds when they arrive, are almost black and they hang in bunches as the plant dies back in the fall. In your garden, these seeds will spread and cover up almost any other plant so if you decide to grow it, make sure to cut off the seeds before this happens.

What to Forage

In spring, you can pick leaves and stems, and the flowers are edible too. The seeds arrive in the fall and these can be picked and dried for use in cooking later in the year. It is best to pick young stems as the older ones become quite thick and hard to cut as well as more stringy in texture. When picking leaves, wear gloves because some people find the sap an irritant. It is fine when cooked as a soup or served like young spinach. The stems can be candied. The roots are often candied as well so this plant is a great find for the forager.

Poisonous lookalikes

Be aware that Cow parsley, Cow parsnip, and Hemlock all show some resemblance to Angelica but the scent of Angelica leaves is the clue. If you pick one and smell it, the sweetness tells you that it is Angelica.

How to Preserve Angelica

Pick fresh leaves, stems, and flower buds in spring as a sweet vegetable to welcome the spring. Leaves can be cooked like spinach and frozen (if you use a freezer). Leaves can be dried and made into soup in months when fresh leaves are not available and the distinctive taste makes a warming broth in winter.

The stems should be cut young to eat fresh because older stems are tough, but you can candy the older stems.

To candy stems

Pick young stems, chop them into small pieces 1-2 inches long, and cook them gently over low heat in water. Strain away this water but keep it for the next stage, remove the stems, and peel the skins. Cook the stems for 10 minutes more in fresh water, and then strain.

Next, you need to use the same amount of sugar as the stems, so weigh them when cool, then add the same weight in sugar to a bowl and leave the stems for 2 days. Make sure the stems are completely covered by sugar as this preserves them. Cover the bowl with a clean cloth.

After 2 days, cook them again for 5-10 minutes until the stems turn light green. This tells you they are ready.

Make syrup

The thicker stems can make an excellent syrup to use in colder months as a sauce on puddings and cakes. Pick larger stems and cook them until soft. This can take 30 minutes or more. Add the same weight of sugar and simmer this mixture for a further 15 minutes. The sugar preserves the syrup well if you keep it in a cupboard for up to 2 years.

The seed heads can be picked, dried, and stored in jars with lids out of direct sunshine. Add them to bread toppings, grind them into powder, and use them like cinnamon or cook them in casseroles of meat or fish. The slightly sweet flavor will complement poultry and game too.

Using Plants THE AMISH WAY

3. BERRIES (such as Blackberries, Blackcurrants, and Red Currants)

For the forager, the variety of berries available in the US is wonderful. Depending on where you live you may find blackberries, black currants, red currants, dewberries, or Pacific blackberries. All these berries can be dried or processed to make a valuable source of vitamins in the winter and you can rehydrate them for fruit crumbles, like the Amish do. They call it Bumbleberry pie, which means any berries you can find can go in as long as you are confident about identifying them.

How to Identify Berries

The common blackberry has many hybrids, up to 350 worldwide but the form of the fruit is unmistakable, with white flowers that become a soft berry, that turns from green to red and eventually black with tiny little segments, each containing a seed. *Rubus Rosaceae* is the generic name for blackberries and California has its own version, known as *Rubus ursinus*. These berries are ripe in late summer or early in the fall when they are black. Do not eat red or green berries.

You can tell it is a blackberry if the plant spreads widely, has sharp thorns, and veined leaves that feel quite rough to the touch. They form dense patches in wild areas and continue to spread little runners that settle in new soil further away from the parent plant. The thorns hurt if you try to walk through a thick bush so come prepared with long sleeves and trousers and use gloves when collecting. This plant colonizes sunny positions on the sides of mountains, the edges of farmland, any disturbed ground where a bird drops a berry, and they grow at most heights and even up to 8,000 feet so you are bound to have one of these bushes close to you, wherever you live in the US.

Wild Currants are native to North America and they come in different colors – blackcurrants, white currants, golden currants, and red currants. The scientific name *Ribes americanum*, is a wild red currant, but there is also a bush called *Ribes sativum* which bears sour, red berries. Black currants are known as *Ribes nigrum*. The shrubs can grow up to 4 feet tall. Red currants can be identified by the small clumps of hanging berries, that form as almost white but gradually ripen in the summer sunshine to a bright red color. Black currants form one berry and this gradually changes from green to blue and finally black by July. These swell in size as they grow and you will find them all over the bush in single berries, not clumps. Currants are fabulous in fresh juices and if you freeze them you can have a good winter supply of vitamins too. Some Amish communities do not freeze fruit because it uses electricity but you can freeze them if you have that option.

My advice is to speak to a local foraging group and learn to identify these berries before you go out on your own. Remember that the scientific name for blackberries is rubus and for currants it is ribes, and before you start foraging, you can check the pictures for local bushes that you find. Never eat any berry unless you have positively identified it as there are lookalikes that can cause serious gastric upset or even death.

What to Forage

The berries.

• Poisonous lookalikes !

Deadly Nightshade has smooth, black berries, not bumpy ones. Its berries are shiny with a thick skin and they are as the name says; deadly. Do not consume these. Currants are normally ripe in July not September when Dealy Nightshade berries appear. It is a member of the potato family and the flowers are purple and the smooth skin on the berry may convince you that you have found a currant. So check the month, and check again before eating anything that looks like this plant.

How to Preserve Berries

Make redcurrant jelly in a similar way to the Amish Gooseberry recipe above, but you need to strain the mixture through muslin at the end to make a clear, rich, red-colored jelly. This can be time-consuming but this is a delicious accompaniment to cooked pork or game traditionally and well worth the effort. You can also make blackberry preserves, can fruit whole, freeze them, make juice, and add them to desserts such as fruit crumbles.

4. CORN SALAD / PURSLANE *(Portulaca oleracea)*

This plant is often called "pigweed" by farmers because pigs like to eat it and it is regarded as a weed. In the American Midwest, the Amish reportedly used to call it "meisdreck" which translates roughly as mouse dirt. However, this useful plant is often used nowadays in Amish spring salads, sometimes chopped up and served with chicken or meat, or with cooked sweetcorn. It is full of vitamins, and minerals such as magnesium, potassium, and iron, and a great winter food if you find it growing fresh.

How to Identify Corn Salad/Purslane

4 leaves grow opposite and from the center, so that new leaves show as small ovals inside the first 4 leaves, growing from the center as the plant grows in size. The leaves are round and almost look like a child's drawing. In the wild, they clump together in bunches, with a thick stem, and the clumps are low-growing and compact. You will often find them mixed in with grass. The leaves are a deep green and the flowers, if present, are yellow which eventually turn to black seeds. They spread easily across wild areas.

What to Forage

Use leaves and stems in winter salads and sandwiches when out foraging. You can also cook it lightly like spinach and add it to scrambled eggs to get your vitamins.

How to Preserve Corn Salad

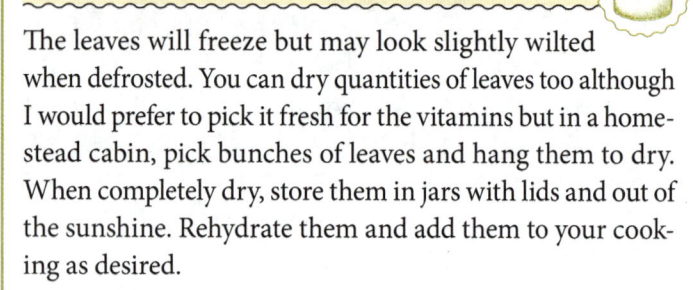

The leaves will freeze but may look slightly wilted when defrosted. You can dry quantities of leaves too although I would prefer to pick it fresh for the vitamins but in a homestead cabin, pick bunches of leaves and hang them to dry. When completely dry, store them in jars with lids and out of the sunshine. Rehydrate them and add them to your cooking as desired.

Although widely regarded as a weed, you can forage it fresh in winter months with the roots attached, and save the seeds to sow wherever you like in sunny soil. It is used as a green manure in agriculture, which means the plant keeps soil intact in winter while growing to prevent soil erosion but in spring it is dug up and turned over to rot back into the soil to add nutrients for the crop that follows on afterward. So you can incorporate its great taste into your palette, then sow seeds and use it as a green manure to benefit your soil. What more can you ask of a plant?

Using Plants THE AMISH WAY

5. CLEAVERS *(Galium aparine)*

These are a welcome splash of green leaves in the spring countryside and I love using them fresh, like spinach. However, the Amish use them as a refreshing tonic. They just pop them into a jug of water and leave them overnight, then drink a cup in the morning and it gives you a boost of nutrients.

How to Identify Cleavers

Cleavers sprout as soon as the soil temperature and the air warm up in February or March, depending on your climate zone. Look for them on the edges of gardens, growing in wild areas, and under tree cover. 5, 6, or 7 leaves are arranged in a circle around the stem, which usually has a line of darker green or even pink or brown running vertically to the base of the stem. The stems and leaves feel hairy and you can feel little hooks on them. Its name comes from its ability to stick to animals, birds, or human clothes as they walk past and its round seeds can decorate any jacket in a minute, as you notice when you come home from a walk in the forest.

What to Forage

The leaves, the stems, and the flowers are all edible. Some people find the hooks cause skin irritation though, so wear gloves when you pick them and try a small sample first.

How to Preserve Cleavers

Put them directly into a jug of cold water and allow the herb to settle overnight. Then drink a cup full in the morning as a tonic. You can cook the leaves slightly in a knob of butter and eat it like spinach. You can make Cleavers pesto by adding some pine nuts and a cup of oil and mixing the mixture like Basil pesto. This will keep for several months and if frozen, it can be stored for 1-2 years.

The Amish probably would not use a freezer or an electric blender, but it does make the next idea easier. You could use a hand whisk or blender too. Chop the pieces as small as you can and make Cleavers juice from the freshly picked herb. If you use a refrigerator or freezer, place it in small containers and defrost whenever you need it.

If you want to dry the leaves, allow them to wilt on a clean cloth and then store them in a clean jar with a lid. You can pop that into the water whenever you need that tonic! They should be fine for a year but check to see if any mould occurs and discard any that look musty. By then it will be spring again and you can pick them fresh.

Using Plants THE AMISH WAY

6. ELDERFLOWER AND ELDERBERRY TREES *(Sambucus nigra)*

These trees provide the Amish with elderflowers in spring and elderberries in the fall. The only thing to remember is that if you pick all the flowers in spring, you will have no berries in the fall so pick some blooms from different trees to ensure the berries arrive later in the year. Bees adore elderflowers too so you can often find the tree in the wild because of the buzzing and the scent of the flowers. The berries are known to keep colds at bay and you can make elderberry syrup by mixing berries with sugar and take a spoonful when you feel a cold coming on.

How to Identify Elderflowers

The trees grow up to 32 feet (10 m) in height and the scent of fresh elderflowers will stop you in your tracks in late April, or early May. It is sweet and distinctive and the flowers come in clusters of creamy white bunches. From a distance, the tree looks white at flowering time.

What to Forage

The creamy white flower clusters in late April or May, but remove the stalks before using.

The black berries in the fall but do not eat green or red berries, just black. Remove the stalks before using them.

As a **mosquito repellent**, you can pick a small branch with leaves anytime, and place this in a vase of water an hour before your garden party and this should discourage them and keep the mosquitoes at bay. The insects dislike the smell intensely.

How to Preserve Elderflowers and Elderberries

How to make fresh elderflower cordial:

First, remove the stalks from the flowers and use only the petals. Then mix 3 cups of flowers with 2 cups of sugar and stir well, then add 2 pints of boiling water to fill your jug or container and leave this to brew. Add the juice of a lemon and some people like to add a tablespoon of apple cider vinegar. Allow this to cool, and bottle it in clean sterile bottles. Use it as cordial by adding water to suit your taste, and it makes a refreshing drink in late spring and throughout the year. This will last indefinitely but I like to check the bottles every few months and use any that may turn cloudy or darker in color.

How to dry bunches of flowers for elderflower tea: Just cut several flower stalks and tie them together to dry in a shady area hanging upside down. To make tea, just drop a teaspoon into a cup and add boiling water. The tea will last for a long time if you seal it in a jar with a lid out of direct sunlight.

How to Make Amish Bumbleberry Pie: Use any available mixed berries picked from the wild or any leftover from picking (including blackberries, blackcurrants, gooseberries, plums, or elderberries). Pick a few bunches of fresh elderberries and remove the stalks. Add them to any berry mixture and add honey or sugar to sweeten the dish if you like. You can top elderberries with crumble or put them in a pie and add a dash of cream or ice cream to suit.

Using Plants THE AMISH WAY

7. HAZELNUTS *(Corylus avellana)*

All nuts are valuable to the forager as a good source of protein, and in the US you can find a large variety depending on your local climate and soil. The list includes almonds, black walnuts, chestnuts, macadamias, hazelnuts, peanuts, pecans, and pine nuts.

In this section, I will describe how to find hazelnuts because these are commonly used in most Amish communities, but if you research your local foraging websites, you can discover which nuts grow wild in your neighbourhood, and where the nuts are growing. If there is no information, you can even plant some yourself so you can be sure no chemicals are used anywhere near them.

The Amish enjoy hazelnuts in Friendship bread, mixing the chopped nuts with oatmeal, dried fruit, and flour, cooked together.

How to Identify Hazelnuts

Hazel trees can easily be spotted in spring because they have beautiful long, dangling, yellow catkins among their pointed green leaves. Single trees grow as tall as 10-16 feet and seem to have several trunks that continue to expand widthways if they are not pruned or coppiced. You may find a planted hazel hedge on the outskirts of farms or in local gardens, which the owner prunes annually to keep in check.

Once you find a wild hazel tree you can be sure that there will be a good supply of nuts by the fall so make note of where it is and return to check when the days are getting shorter. If you find a tree in summer, look for the nut forming (see pic above), and by the fall, it will turn brown so that you know it is ready to pick or may even have fallen to the ground. The trick is to watch it develop, learn where the nuts form, and then remember to go back to pick some before the squirrels have buried them all for winter food supplies.

In spring, look for long, yellow catkins, and in summer look for the nut forming (see pic above) surrounded by green crinkly leaves. By the fall, the leaf surround and the nut case will turn brown so that you know it is ready to pick, or sometimes if you look at the foot of the tree some may have even fallen to the ground. The trick is to watch the nuts develop, learn where the nuts form, and then remember to go back to pick them up before the squirrels have buried them all for winter food supplies.

What to Forage

The nuts. You will see the nut in its hard shell, encased in the leaves that have turned brown by collecting time. Separate the nut (top) by peeling away the leaves (right) and exposing the hard nut case (left).

Check them carefully and discard any nuts with a hole in them; these have been bored by pests so you should not store them.

How to Preserve Hazelnuts

Nuts should be stored in their natural case because if you open them from their shell they last less time and the nut often goes mouldy in jars so keep them in the case that nature provided until you need them, and they will be fine for at least 12 months. Make sure to store them in a cool place out of direct sunlight, and check them regularly by opening a few to eat.

You will need a nutcracker (or a large stone in the wild) to open the hard brown shell, and the pointed brown nut is inside. You can grind these into hazelnut flour, chop them and eat them fresh, add them to energy bars with oats, or make them into delicious protein-filled snacks using hand-milled hazelnut flour. All of these can be vacuum-packed to extend their shelf life too.

8. SWEETCORN *(Zea mays)*

Sweetcorn is grown on almost all Amish farms because it can be eaten fresh, canned, and dried for winter food supplies and early sweetcorn is sold to provide income in early summer, while a different variety of corn is sown later for animal feed throughout the winter. Popcorn is also grown on many Amish farms and saved for healthy snacks throughout the year.

Many Amish recipes use sweetcorn at big family celebrations like Thanksgiving, and it is also an essential ingredient for casseroles, which can be adapted by adding some extra to feed a few extra mouths.

Corn is wind-pollinated so you will see blocks of these plants waving in the wind on Amish farms rather than single rows because planting in square formations means fertilization is more secure.

The Amish sell early sweetcorn as a boost to their income early in summer and you will find it on sale in Amish stores everywhere by June, alongside Amish strawberries. Most other types of sweetcorn cultivated in the US ripen later in the year, in September or October, so this early corn is a treat and worth a visit to the nearest Amish store.

How to Identify Sweetcorn

It is unusual to find sweetcorn growing wild nowadays apart from in very remote locations, but early settlers to the US were shown sweetcorn growing by Native Americans from the Iroquois tribes, recorded in 1779 so this is a native plant, a type of grass that is now grown by farmers all over the US. It is a type of grass that grows very tall up to 7 feet, higher than the average person, with a grain type of growth at the top of this stalk, and a pouch (or two) lower down, holding the growing cob. The central stalk can be as thick as an inch wide, and it is a sturdy stem able to hold one or sometimes two cobs of corn. The leaves are long and dark green but as the summer progresses, the leaves start to fade in color to cream or even brown. Do not pick anything except the cob, which can be located about halfway down the stem. You can hear the wind whispering through a cornfield as the plants grow quite closely together and their leaves rustle with any wind.

When cobs are growing you will see a small swelling first and then as they ripen, you will notice wispy hair-like tassels that are green to start with, but these turn golden yellow and eventually brown, as the corn cob inside starts to ripen. This is most likely in late August or early September through to the fall in the wild. You may find some growing at the edges of fields where sweetcorn was planted agriculturally the previous season.

If you find corn, test the ripeness of the cob by gently pressing a fingernail into the yellow flesh of one kernel. If it's soft and easy, the corn is ready to pick. A milky white sap often emerges and you can eat the cob fresh off the plant or take it home to cook or store it.

What to Forage

The ripe, yellow cobs. Remove the tassels, the brown covering, and the stem. Just eat the yellow kernels although the stem is handy for barbecues, if you want to hold them to munch directly off the cob. Make sure to add the cobs to the compost bin or better still, feed them to the chickens who love to pick any flesh remaining off the cobs.

How to Preserve Sweetcorn

The Amish enjoy eating sweetcorn fresh and also value it for adding to casseroles in the cold winter months with chicken or meat. A wonderful way to preserve it for the longer term is to vacuum-pack the sweetcorn to exclude air.

Some good advice from Amish cooks is that blanching the corn cobs first helps to retain the sweetness of this crop. Blanching means dipping the cob into a saucepan of boiling water for a few seconds and then immediately start preserving it. Picked sweetcorn cobs start to convert the sweetness to starch almost immediately so this partial cooking stops the sugar converting. After blanching you can cook, can, freeze, mill or vacuum pack your corn to preserve it.

Using Plants THE AMISH WAY

Canning sweetcorn

Cut away the kernels from the cob and then spoon these directly into your sterile canning jars. You need to prepare boiling water to cover the kernels but make sure you do not fill the jars to the top. Leave about ¾ of an inch to an inch of room at the top of the jar, then close the lids and place them in a pressure canner to ensure the contents will last for longer. Allow about 50 minutes for jars that hold 1 pint and slightly more time for larger jars.

This is a great way to conserve leftover corn from a barbecue or a family celebration.

Freezing sweetcorn cobs

Blanch them in boiling water for about 30 seconds because this partial cooking stops the sugar from converting to starch. Place them in bags or containers for the freezer. Frozen corn is usually good for 1-2 years, although I prefer to grow my own and replace last year's crop for the new harvest.

Making flour

All you need is a hand grinder or any sturdy hand mill that can cope with grain like sweetcorn. Electric grinders are easy and produce tasty, yellow-colored flour in seconds. You can also grind corn using a hand mill or give an energetic teenager looking to earn some pocket money a job!

Extending their shelf life a bit further

You can vacuum-pack sweetcorn first and then freeze it. Make sure you date the bags or containers so you know which to eat first. Vacuum-packed food keeps the contents in a stable state, not open to the air, and also removes any moisture that can damage stored food too.

Using this vacuum-packed sweetcorn

Remove it from the freezer and allow it to defrost. Then you can decide whether it is for immediate consumption or if you prefer to make it into flour. You could make several Amish Friendship loaves with the flour and re-freeze the cooked loaves if you want to make sure your freezer is full for a longer period.

This is a great way to have corn sealed in a pest-proof bag and you can pop these bags straight into the freezer. The frozen bags are safe for 2 years and if you mill it into flour, that extends the life even further as it will last as long as any typical flour. This way, you can use your sweetcorn milled into flour whenever you need it.

A final tip about sweetcorn is that if you cannot find it growing wild, source some Amish sweetcorn seeds from a store and try growing your own. Most homesteads have large gardens and you can grow enough corn for a family of 4 in a space 10 x 10 feet. Sow the cobs directly into the ground when the spring soil warms up in an area that gets direct sunshine, and then plan on harvesting by September. After tasting fresh homegrown sweetcorn, you will never look back and you are assured that the crop does not contain pesticides or any chemicals.

Using Plants THE AMISH WAY

9. MUSHROOMS

The first piece of advice about foraging mushrooms is to do so safely and only when you are completely positive that your identification is correct. Learn by going on a course and learning the edible fungi in your immediate area. Visit your local Amish food store or your local market and chat with the vendors about the mushrooms they pick and sell. Then, wherever you forage, go with a list of edible and poisonous fungi in your neighborhood.

The second piece of advice with mushrooms is that you need to ascertain whether their collection is permitted in your state or the site where you intend to pick, and in what quantities. Some states place restrictions on picking any mushrooms at all in parks, whereas other states (like California) allow you to collect five pounds of mushrooms per person, provided you have bought a permit.

If you are in a state where picking is not permitted, then you can copy Sam Peachey, an Amish farmer resident in New York, who is famous for cultivating shitake mushrooms on logs on his farm that he sells at local markets. His greenhouse is based on Amish design too, that allows air to circulate freely and encourages hot air to rise to achieve even growing temperatures. He even uses a wood-burning stove to keep the interior warm in winter so that temperatures rarely dip below 70°F inside while the freezing New York winter chill never enters.

What to Forage

1. Chanterelle mushrooms

Chanterelle mushrooms can be collected underneath hardwood trees or conifers in the wild and they have a long stalk that gets thicker where it joins the small cap. The edge is wavy, not straight and it seems to turn upwards towards the sky. The cap is concave too and often yellow in color, but as they grow old they lose the intensity in color so avoid very pale-looking mushrooms. They are best collected in spring too, so that solves any yellow mushrooms found in the fall.

2. Chicken of the Woods and Hen of the Woods

Both of these mushrooms are found in forested areas, often in the Eastern states of the US but they can be found in various locations. They are not to everybody's taste so try a little piece of one if you are successful in foraging plant if it does not disagree with you, you can cook a little bit more next time.

3. Morel mushrooms

These are often found in Colorado on mountainous areas and they can be black or yellow. A clue is that they are found above 10,000 feet so check this before you pick anything.

Using Plants THE AMISH WAY

4. Oyster mushrooms and Shiitake mushrooms

Oyster mushrooms and Shiitake mushrooms are often grown on logs by commercial mushroom growers who use spawn to start them and then continue to harvest the mushrooms knowing that they are safe. You can find these in Oklahoma, Illinois, Pennsylvania, Tennessee and also in California, sometimes in Texas.

5. Parasols

Parasols are a delicious wild find and very edible, but they have a very poisonous cousin in the US so if you cannot identify with 100% certainty, leave this one alone. Parasols are named for the shape of the cap, which closely resembles something that shades you from the sun! Their patterns are hard to mistake, they look brown and resemble a snake skin marking. They also have a ring that can be moved up and down the stem, which is one of the recommendations for not picking so do not pick unless you are sure that it is the one you are looking for.

• *Lookalikes are the Shaggy Parasol or the False Parasol*

Shaggy parasols are edible but the False Parasol has a much smaller cap so if you pick larger mushrooms, you can be more confident that it is the Parasol. Foraging tips are only to pick parasol mushrooms whose cap is 8 inches (20 cm) or more because the poisonous False parasol (*Lepiotas*) does not grow such a large cap.

Another tip for positively identifying a parasol site is that this is one mushroom that can be transported to a new site provided that is legal in your state. If you are lucky enough to find a parasol on your own land, remember where it is and go back early in the fall each year. The Amish will throw a layer of compost on the area in the spring after harvesting to encourage further growth the next year.

To move a piece of the mycelium root, you simply dig carefully around the base of the stem and remove the mushroom with a whole spadeful of the mycelium, (the root system) attached and take the mushroom and this earth to a new site, where you can wait with bated breath to see if it takes. Try not to remove a huge amount and make sure you pat the earth back into place before you leave. Plant the mushroom in a sunny location with rich soil and keep your fingers crossed. Water it well in this first season so it does not dry out.

6. Porcinis

These mushrooms grow in pine forests and also close to spruces and firs and they are a tasty forager's find in early fall. However, if you live in a more mountainous area you may find them earlier in the summer months too as they prefer to grow in cool conditions.

Using Plants THE AMISH WAY

7. Puffballs

These mushrooms grow near footpaths and walking trails in shady woods and their unmistakable shape is a great treat for a forager in the fall or the winter. A forager's tip for these mushrooms is that older mushrooms may have turned yellow or even brown inside and are not edible any longer. If you are in doubt, use a clean knife to cut one open once found and if it is discoloured, not white, then do not collect it.

How to Identify Mushrooms

A good checklist for the forager includes ticking off a list from a foraging guide for your area. What is the environment? What trees are growing close to this mushroom? Is that correct in the identification guide? For example, if you find a yellow-capped mushroom under a conifer tree in spring, you can start by saying this could be a Chanterelle but to to be absolutely sure you need to see the spore print, the shape, and so on. However, if you find a yellow-capped mushroom growing under an oak tree in July, then your identification is probably not going to be a Chanterelle.

Other things to help with identification are:

- **Avoid white gills.** Many mushrooms with white gills are edible but Amanitas are the deadliest mushroom known to man in the US and you do not want to eat these ever. Amanitas have white gills.

- **Do not pick red mushrooms** because many are poisonous, and it's not worth the risk if you're not an expert.

- **Avoid a ring around the stem.** Some mushrooms have a ring around the stem and they are edible (e.g. Parasols) but many of the mushrooms with rings are poisonous. Unless you are sure, then do not pick mushrooms with this second ring around the stem.

How to Preserve Mushrooms

The Amish like to eat their mushrooms fresh, making soup and adding them to hearty breakfasts to feed the farmers and laborers. However, the Amish also like to dry mushrooms for winter use, including Oysters, and Shiitakes.

Cut them into smaller pieces and place them on a clean cloth or piece of greaseproof paper, out of direct sunlight. Some mushrooms can be dried whole but it takes a long time and mold can set in so the Amish will place them on a wire tray and place this in an oven on low heat to dry them quickly.

Once dried, these mushrooms can be rehydrated, preserved in clean jars with lids, vacuum packed, or frozen and when you want to, they can be added directly to casseroles or soups for winter meals.

Once you identify a site where you have picked mushrooms, remember the patch and visit every year at the same time. That way you can collect fresh mushrooms and stock your larder with mushrooms for years to come too.

Now you know where and when to forage for food to store in your winter larder. You know the way the Amish forage and how to preserve the plants you find. You can ID the plants successfully, forage mindfully, and not over-pick and ensure that the plants survive. Having a healthy environment to forage from means you can preserve these 9 plants to make dried foods, boost your canned supplies, and make good use of "weeds" in your local environment. Use the tips to check and enjoy eating from your larder regularly, knowing the food comes straight from the field. It is also a good idea to check everything in the larder when you remove any product, and continue to check for mold or pests.

Using Plants THE AMISH WAY

Medicinal Plants You Can Forage

The Amish try to deal with illness by prevention, living a healthy life, growing and eating home-grown food, and using natural and alternative remedies handed down for generations in preference to visiting a doctor. In this chapter, you can make remedies for aches and pains, learn how to soothe wounds, burns, sore throats, lower cholesterol, and ease a migraine. You will also learn the centuries-old methods of the Amish for preventative care, like poultices, infusions, and herb-infused oils. The plants commonly used by the Amish include American Ginseng, Burdock, Comfrey, Echinacea, Feverfew, Garlic, Goldenseal, Mullein, Peppermint, and Plantain.

Using Plants THE AMISH WAY

1. AMERICAN GINSENG *(Panax quinquefolius)*

Description

Native to Missouri and Eastern regions, American Ginseng used to be found abundantly in woods and tree-covered areas. Over collection of ginseng has meant it is now almost endangered and some states now forbid picking it from the wild. In Pennsylvania, to export a root, you need a license. However, the Amish are careful to cultivate a patch of ginseng within their gardens, and only dig up sufficient for their immediate use, ensuring that nature thrives where they grow plants.

Identification

Quinquefolius means 5 leaves and this will help to identify this plant. The Amish leave plots of wild areas under trees for it to grow, as this maintains the habitat over time. Look for pointed, oval-shaped, veined green leaves with five separate leaflets to each leaf growing around a central stem. The leaf size can vary too with some larger than others. It grows in shaded, rich soil, and has green flowers that appear in warm weather from June onwards, gradually turning to red berries by September at the tip of the flower stalk.

Foraging Period and Methods

This plant is killed by removing the root, so the Amish are careful to only dig up a few plants at a time, allowing the rest of the patch to continue growing. You will know when to pick it because the leaves begin to die back, and the red berries are very bright in the fall. Dig very carefully with a small stick around the base of the plant and choose just one root, digging deep to extract it. Try not to dig up surrounding plants. Work like the Amish, carefully protecting the environment and taking the minimum. Do not dig in the same area the following season; move a little away from the previous site to take another root.

Parts Used

The root. It extends deep into the earth, with small roots and knots which appear cream in color when washed.

Traditional Use

The Amish use ginseng for coughs and congestion, or as a tonic in convalescence to boost the appetite and reduce exhaustion. Make an infusion of the roots and sip it.

The Amish also use it as a poultice to extract materials from boils and to clear oily skin and acne.

Modern scientific tests show that it can also reduce inflammation, and reduce tiredness.

Any Motable or Poisonous Lookalikes?

Poison Ivy (*Toxicodendron radicans*). Although the leaves of this plant may be confused with Ginseng, they are much shinier with a dark green gloss and there are usually only 3 leaflets, whereas Ginseng usually has 5, arranged in a circle around the stem. Check the base of the plant. Ginseng has a stalk while Poison Ivy has a vine root that can be pulled out easily, and you will see roots on the segment that can sink into soil to create a new plant. Ginseng root stays underground and digs deep. The flowers are very different and the ivy berries are black whereas the Ginseng berries are red. Ginseng leaves become pale yellow in the fall but ivy leaves change color from yellow to red.

Using Plants **THE AMISH WAY**

Warning

American ginseng is endangered in some US states and wild harvesting is only possible in these 19 states; Alabama, Arkansas, Georgia, Illinois, Iowa, Indiana, Kentucky, Maryland, Minnesota, Missouri, New York, North Carolina, Ohio, Pennsylvania, Tennessee, Vermont, Virginia, West Virginia, and Wisconsin.

The Amish strive to work with Mother Nature and always ensure that some areas are kept wild to allow Ginseng to thrive.

Remedy

To make an infusion:

- Wash, and then chop a small portion of root (1-2 tablespoons) and add it to a small saucepan with enough water (1 cup) to cover the roots.
- Heat it gently, but do not allow it to boil because this retains the goodness in the liquid, and then strain before serving into a cup. Drink this up to 3 times per day.

Do not waste any excess; it can be stored in an airtight jar and stored in a refrigerator. For convalescence, it tastes better warm and will stimulate the appetite too. Sip this infusion to increase energy levels, soothe earache, and boost your energy levels.

To make a poultice:

Amish healing relies on this plant as a wound covering, that eases pain on skin wounds (or any part of the body that is sore).

- Chop a small part of the root (1-2 tablespoons) into pieces, and simmer in enough water to cover them, for about 20 minutes. Do not boil, just warm the water.
- Place roots and liquid over the affected area, using a clean cloth to cover it, and secure it with pins, ribbon, or string. Allow time for it to soothe the area, for at least 30 minutes. Compost the waste to allow it to return to the earth.

Any unused excess root is precious. It can be dried and used as required.

THE AMISH WAYS

Using Plants THE AMISH WAY

2. BURDOCK (*Arctium lappa*)

Description

Burdock is also known as Bardane, Beggar's Buttons, Gobo, and Snake's Rhubarb and it grows in most states, often in the wild but it is cultivated to be used as a remedy by Amish communities. It has large, heart-shaped, soft green leaves and pink or purple flower bracts, protected by burs. The "bur" in the name refers to the seed heads with little hooks attached, that catch on animal fur or human clothing (often unnoticed) as they pass by. This drops seeds further away from the mother plant allowing them a better chance to germinate and thrive.

Identification

Burdock is a biennial plant, meaning only its leaves appear in the first year whereas in the second year, a flower stalk appears and the plant then goes to flower and seed. It grows from 3 to 10 feet (90 and 300 cm) tall. If you feel any heart-shaped leaf, it is hairy on the underside, and the largest leaves grow at the base of the plant and get progressively smaller as you move up the stem. The stem is thick and green and the unusual purple flowers appear on stalks. These "flowers" have no petals, but bracts and you can see little hooks around the edges if you look closely. These close around the fertilized flower head, go to seed and then the burs can easily attach to animal fur or people's clothes walking by so that seeds can grow in a place further away from the parent. These burs change to a brown color in the fall.

Foraging Period and Methods

Forage leaves for eating in spring when they are tender. Older leaves can taste stringy. Make sure your scissors are sharp or you can damage the plant and the Amish work carefully with nature avoiding this by sharpening tools well before harvesting and only cutting one or two leaves from each plant.

The root is typically harvested in the fall after the end of its first year of growth or in the second year of growth in spring before it sends up a shoot. If the root is allowed to become too large, it becomes very difficult to harvest. A shovel or a gardening fork can be used to dig out the root but remember that this will kill the plant so only dig roots as required, ensuring there are other plants to continue the natural cycle for the year to come.

Parts Used

The root. It extends deep into the earth, with small roots and knots which appear cream in color when washed.

Traditional Use

Burdock leaves give the Amish community one of its best burn and wound treatments, often sold in Amish stores as B&W, Burn and Wound Ointment. The traditional method uses honey directly on the cleansed wound, or an ointment prepared with honey, followed by wrapping the wound in steeped burdock leaves.

The Amish prefer to treat burns and wounds at home, but an admission to hospital for a serious burn often means a doctor will suggest a skin graft. Generally, Amish families prefer to use herbal preparations rather than allow the wounded person to have a skin graft.

Dr Stewart Wang, M.D., Ph.D., Endowed Professor of Surgery at University Hospital in Michigan and Director of U-M's Burn Coordinating Center, experienced first-hand how reluctant Amish parents can be about accepting skin grafts and hospital procedures when he met his first Amish patient whose parents were members of the Plain Community, who are a self-sufficient group of Amish farmers with stores selling leather goods, and construction all done by the community. *https://www.med.umich.edu/surgery/icam/seeking_common_ground.html*

Using Plants THE AMISH WAY

The child was unconscious, being kept alive by a heart-lung machine, at C.S. Mott Children's Hospital and she had open wounds on her legs, but Dr Wang could see that they were not infected. In an interview with Sara Telpos, https://www.med.umich.edu/surgery/icam/seeking_common_ground.html, he explained the skin graft procedure to her parents who refused this treatment. They asked instead to use herbal preparations (B&W), accompanied by prayer to allow healing to take place. Dr Wang admitted initially that he was unimpressed but agreed to allow them to try the use of the herbal treatment supervised by him. B&W is considered an herbal treatment and if the physician involved agrees, it can be used but Dr Wang was an exception in that generally herbal supplements were not utilized at the hospital.

The child recovered and since then, further scientific studies have examined B&W's ability to reduce pain, help prevent infection, and accelerate wound healing. Dr Wang compared B&W to conventional medicine and noticed that the wound remained moist so that dead skin and living tissue separated easily, whereas grafting meant that wound areas needed to be scrubbed. The B&W allowed tissue separation to occur easily removing the need for scrubbing a wounded area and permitting new growth to begin.

Burdock Leaves. Other medicinal uses for Burdock leaves include Burdock root tea, which can be used as a facial wash to treat acne when cooled. Herbalists conclude that Burdock leaves are diuretic and a blood purifier (Khan et al., 2013).

Burdock roots have anti-oxidant and antidiabetic benefits too, according to a study by Chan et al. (2011).

Any Notable or Poisonous Lookalikes?

Deadly Nightshade (*Atropa belladonna*) is a highly toxic plant that can look similar to Burdock. The two are sometimes confused because their roots have similar appearances and they both can have purple flowers. You can tell them apart because Deadly Nightshade flowers do not have the thistle-like bracts that Burdock has, and Burdock does not have the shiny, black, poisonous berries that are typical of the Deadly Nightshade plant. Because of the risk of harvesting Deadly Nightshade instead of Burdock, it is important to only harvest Burdock from the wild when you know for a fact that the plant you want to forage from is Burdock.

Warning

Avoid Burdock if you are pregnant, trying to be, or nursing.

Do not touch or pick the burs without gloves because they can irritate the skin.

Remedy

Using the traditional method involves cleansing the wound and applying honey first. After this, the cooked burdock leaves are wrapped around the wound and secured with a clean, sterile cloth, and pins.

Wound and Burn Poultice

You will need: honey, water to cleanse the wound, water to boil the leaves, and Burdock leaves.

Instructions:

- Add 1 cup of fresh Burdock leaves (or several large leaves big enough to cover the wound if it is a large area) to a saucepan full of water, (enough to cover the leaves completely) and place it on medium heat.

- Bring the water to the boil, and then remove from the heat. Allow it to cool to a temperature so that the injured person feels it will not burn them.

- While the leaves are coming to a boil, cleanse the wound with water and then gently dab the wounded or burned area with some honey, taking care not to hurt the patient. Honey is a natural healer.

- Apply the leaves directly over the honey on the burned or wounded area. Use a long sterile cloth for wrapping the affected area, and secure it with 1-2 pins.

- Repeat the process 3 times daily as required until the wound begins to heal.

3. COMFREY *(Symphytum officinale)*

Description

This plant provides the Amish with a wonderful plant for use in the garden that attracts bees and pollinators with its delicate tubular flowers, and its leaves can be added to soil as an improver, but it can also be used in wound healing. The plant is not native but was introduced by settlers but now grows all over eastern states. It is also known as Knitbone, and Bruise wort, reflecting its healing qualities.

Identification

Comfrey typically grows to a height of 1 to 3 feet (30 to 91 cm) tall. Its dark green leaves are oval-shaped, veined, pointed, and large. If you touch a leaf, you can feel bristly hairs on it that may irritate the skin, so wear gloves when picking. The leaves at the base of the plant are larger (about 8 inches in length) than the leaves toward the top of the plant. Its stems are green and upright. The stems are branched and covered in sparse, bristle-like hairs. Comfrey plants flower from mid-spring to early Summer. Clusters of flowers are bell-shaped, and they hang downwards in white, pink, or purple shades.

Foraging Period and Methods

Comfrey grows all year round and even survives snow and cold temperatures well. Harvesting is best done early to mid-September before the first frost. To harvest Comfrey, you can pick small leaves or use sharp scissors to make a clean cut at the leaf stalk near the base of the plant. Only pick the larger, unfurled leaves toward the base of the plant, leaving the smaller leaves will continue to grow beyond the first frost. Sections of root are easily pulled from a plant; just dig the area and cut off a section using sharp scissors. Wash this well and use it fresh or dried.

Parts Used

The leaves and roots. Comfrey leaves can be used as a wrapping on injuries if outdoors, for emergency care. Comfrey root powder reduces pain and inflammation and has been used for healing bone fractures, bruises, joint and muscle pain, and ankle sprains. Comfrey used to be consumed internally historically but this is not recommended.

Traditional Use

Comfrey leaves are applied topically to treat injuries, burns, and wounds. Comfrey leaves and roots are used to treat sprains, strains, fractures, bruises, and pulled muscles and ligaments. The Amish use it as a pain reliever, but only for external use because it contains pyrrolizidine alkaloids, which can be harmful to the liver.

Any Notable or Poisonous Lookalikes?

Foxglove (*Digitalis purpurea*) is a medicinal plant that is commonly mistaken for Comfrey before flowering. It is used to make a powerful drug in the laboratory but can be poisonous if eaten by humans. The flowers of both comfrey and foxglove are very distinctive, so if you are unsure of the ID, best to wait until the plant flowers. Foxglove has a single tall stalk, with purple or pink tubular sections, dotted with pretty black or white dots inside. Comfrey flow-

Using Plants THE AMISH WAY

ers are much smaller, and there are huge numbers of them per plant. They are pink, white, or purple shade, and they hang downwards like little bells.

Both flowers are adored by bees which is another reason the Amish grow them. Foxglove contains cardiac glycosides that can be toxic to the heart and even cause death if they are consumed in moderate or high doses. You can tell the difference between the two leaves because Comfrey leaves are usually larger than Foxglove, and feel soft but hairy to touch, while Foxglove leaves have many soft hairs that make them feel as soft as velvet.

Warning

Do not eat comfrey leaves or roots. Use on wounds topically but do not consume.

Remedy

Comfrey Compress

You will need: 1-2 Comfrey leaves large enough to wrap around the wound, and water to warm the leaves in a saucepan.

- For emergency care out in the open, simply wrap leaves around the injury or sore part and secure them with string, ribbon, or whatever means available.

- If you have access to a saucepan and water, soak the leaves in water to extract the healing substances, by adding them to the pan and covering them with water. Warm them for up to 10 minutes on low heat but do not boil. Then remove from heat and keep covered.

- If the wound is small, wrap the warm leaves around it, cover it with gauze or sterile cloth, and use pins to keep it in place.

Comfrey Soak

- You can also soak sore feet or wounded arms in a basin of the liquid, covering the sore part with the leaves. Soak for up to 20 minutes for pain relief and help with healing.

- Any unused excess root is precious. It can be dried and used as required.

4. ECHINACEA (*Echinacea* spp.)

Description

This plant has colorful flowers that the Amish love to plant in their flower gardens, which attract bees and pollinating insects and are also a joy to observe as they go about their daily tasks. It is also known as Coneflower and Purple Coneflower, due to the shape of the blooms. It is native to the south-eastern United States, extending from Ohio to Michigan to Iowa, and as far south as Louisiana and Georgia.

Identification

Echinacea grows between 2 and 5 feet (61-152 cm) tall. It has hairy, rough, oval–shaped leaves, attached alternately to the stem. The stem itself is upright and usually unbranched, holding a single flower that blooms in

Summer. The flowers of cultivated Echinacea come in a variety of colors, but wild Echinacea flowers are typically white or pinkish purple. The head of each flower can be orange, green, or mahogany-brown in color and has a distinct cone-like appearance. When the flower opens, its petals tend to point downward, contributing to its cone-like appearance.

Foraging Period and Methods

Harvesting Echinacea when the flower buds begin to open. The flower heads and leaves should be cut using a sharp instrument like scissors or a knife. The flowers and leaves can be used fresh or dried. Roots can be dug up at the end of the season and used fesh or dried during winter months.

Parts Used

Echinacea leaves and flowers. Echinacea root can also be used medicinally.

Traditional Use

The Amish use Echinacea to improve immunity and to prevent and treat head and chest colds. They also use Echinacea topically to treat minor wounds, stings, and insect bites by adding flowers to honey or oil to make ointments to dab onto affected areas.

Any Notable or Poisonous Lookalikes?

Black-Eyed Susan (*Rudbeckia hirta*) is in the same family as Echinacea and it can sometimes be mistaken for Echinacea. This plant has cone-shaped flowers like Echinacea, but its flower heads are bright yellow with a dark brown center. However, if you touch Echinacea cones, they feel quite prickly, whereas Rudbeckia flower petals feel soft. While the roots of Rudbeckia hirta can be used medicinally, the flowers are mildly toxic to livestock and should never be consumed by humans. Like other plants in the Asteraceae family, Rudbeckia plants can cause asthma attacks and allergies in people who are sensitive to the plant.

Warning

Taking caffeine at the same time as Echinacea can lead to headaches so avoid coffee and cola while using this plant.

Remedy

Echinacea Ointment

You will need: freshly picked flowers and some honey.

- Pick a cup of fresh Echinacea flowers and leaves. Cut the flowers finely on a chopping board into small pieces and then add small amounts of honey gradually, stirring the plant material until the mixture has a paste-like consistency (5-10 minutes).

- Cleanse the wound with water, and then use a spoon to transfer a small amount of the paste to a piece of sterile cotton cloth. Fold the other half of the cloth over on itself and apply it to the sting, insect bite, or wound without pressure to avoid hurting the person more. You can use a pin to secure the cloth. Allow this to remain on the wound for at least 24 hours, then remove it using warm water if it sticks.

- Store any unused paste in a glass container and store it in a cool cupboard out of direct sunshine.

Echinacea infusion

Use: flowers, leaves, and roots.

- Chop the plant material into small parts and then add boiling water.

- Allow the mixture to sit for 5-10 minutes and then strain it into a teacup and sip.

Using Plants THE AMISH WAY

5. FEVERFEW (*Tanacetum parthenium*)

Description

The leaves are delicate and formed like lace with curly edges and a vibrant green color. They catch the rain when it falls too and make a pretty picture. The flowers look daisy-like, with a curved center and white petals. The stalk is thick and supports the blooms well. This plant is a pretty addition to any flower or herb garden as appealing to look at as useful for medicine.

Identification

The delicate, white-petaled blooms have a curved yellow center but the smell of this plant is unmistakable so when you know it, you can smell it from several feet away. Pick a leaf and rub it between your fingers as a test.

Foraging Period and Methods

It depends on your climate but for many Amish communities, the leaves are almost evergreen so a fresh supply can be picked almost all year round. In extremely cold climates, dig up a plant and take it indoors to use fresh in winter.

Parts Used

The leaves.

Traditional Use

Historically, as the name implies, Feverfew was prepared in infusions to bring down fevers but the Amish also use it just when a migraine strikes. Sipping an herbal infusion of the leaves at the first sign of a headache can often relieve it and medical research has demonstrated its ability to reduce pain and ease other symptoms such as disturbance caused by daylight. This plant offers an alternative to aspirin, which so many people routinely take for pain. An Amish gardener working in the fields or flower garden, can pick a few leaves and eat them directly. The Amish report that these leaves ease headaches, toothache, and even arthritis.

Be warned that some people have allergic reactions in their mouths though, so it is best to try a tea first, and if that feels ok, then add a few leaves to a salad and try them mixed with other food to determine if you can eat this plant. You can also save the leaves – dry them by hanging a small branch upside down with string out of direct sunlight, and use them later in dried tea preparations.

Any Notable or Poisonous Lookalikes?

American Feverfew (*Parthenium integrifolium*). This plant is often called Wild Quinine and is used similarly. These stems are topped with white flowers, without the yellow center of Feverfew flowers. Its leaves are not as curly at the

Using Plants **THE AMISH WAY**

edges either. Leaves from both plants have a similar effect and you can use American Feverfew to make a leaf poultice to soothe burns because this leaf does not irritate skin. This plant can be used to ease fluid retention and bloating by drinking a hot infusion of a few leaves.

Warning

Touching or eating the leaves of Feverfew can irritate some people. Do a test first by trying an infusion of leaves as tea, to see if your mouth is affected. Before eating a leaf, try rubbing just a little piece on a small patch of skin on your arm or hand, and if no irritation occurs, then try a few leaves in a sandwich. Dried leaves do not usually irritate so either pick and dry your own or buy them dried from a health food store.

Remedy

A leaf or two keeps the migraine away!

This could be made for the Feverfew plant because people who consume it regularly are less likely to suffer from migraines so it cannot hurt to eat a few leaves a few times per week if you are prone to them. The leaves can be made into an infusion or hidden among other ingredients in a salad. The remedy is to eat a few leaves every week or put them into a sandwich.

Feverfew Tea

You can pick fresh leaves most months of the year unless your climate is deep snow in Winter. If this is the case, dry some leaves when the flowers are in bloom and then use these to make tea. Just add a few leaves to a cup, add boiling water, and allow to brew for 5-10 minutes and sip when the taste is to your liking.

6. GARLIC (*Allium sativum*)

Description

It is not only the Amish but the whole of humanity all over the world that recognizes garlic as a healthy ingredient in meals. The Amish have used garlic for centuries in kitchens to keep their families healthy. Also used as medicine, the bulbs of cultivated and wild garlic offer the Amish a plant that is known to reduce high blood pressure, lower cholesterol, and offer many health benefits to keep families happy and healthy.

The strong oniony smell is very obvious but you will also be attracted by the purple flowers, that offer the harvester a wonderful burst of color in late spring, and early summer.

Identification

A single clove of garlic is planted in the fall to make whole new cloves by the following summer and Amish gardens have rows of bright green spikes of this plant growing. There are many different varieties but all share the spiky green leaves and the oniony smell, and all the flowers are purple providing bees with pollen early in the summer. When the green leaves die back, the stem turns brown and you can gently scratch away at the root to harvest a round bulb of garlic. The root is covered in white skin, bulb-like, and cylindrical.

Foraging Period and Methods

Garlic bulbs can be harvested in the summer. You will notice that the leaves turn creamy brown and wilt and then the bulbs are plump and ready to pick. After the flowers begin to appear, the bulbs become more fibrous so it is a good idea to harvest before that or to chop the flower off and use it in bouquets. To harvest Garlic, dig the earth around the bulb and pull sharply so the bulb is unearthed. If you want to save bulbs for planting, hang them upside down in a cool shed out of direct sunlight. By spring some cloves will develop small green shoots and these can be planted directly into the soil.

Using Plants THE AMISH WAY

Parts Used

The Amish use the bulbs/cloves of garlic in their medicinal remedies. The leaves and flower buds are edible and possess medicinal value as well.

Traditional Use

The Amish use garlic to reduce high blood pressure, to lower cholesterol, as an aid to keep colds and flu at bay, and as a welcome, healthy addition to the food that keeps Amish families well. Prevention is better than cure, you will hear in Amish kitchens.

garlic with herbs being used to improve immunity and to prevent and treat head or chest colds and chopped garlic is also used in healing poultices.

In a community assessment in Polk County, an Amish mother described using garlic in a wound treatment oil, prepared for her daughter who ran about barefoot in the summer months. The child had stepped on a manure pitchfork, and the wound was described as deep, dirty, and very painful. The mother reported steeping the foot in available natural Epsom Salts to cleanse it first, and then making an ointment from garlic, burdock, comfrey, and plantain leaves that grew in the backyard. All these ingredients were fresh, picked on the spot, and prepared in the kitchen. The mother used olive oil to bind the ingredients together. The wound was soaked in Epsom Salts three times per day and the garlic oil mixture was gently dabbed on the wound. With time, the child recovered completely and no infection was noted.

Any Notable or Poisonous Lookalikes?

The most notable poisonous garlic look-alike is Lily of the Valley (*Convallaria majalis*). This medicinal plant contains powerful active constituents that work on the heart muscle and can lead to death if it is unintentionally consumed. The leaves of Lily of the Valley and Wild Garlic can appear very similar; however, Lily of the Valley has white or pink bell-shaped flowers that are grouped together in clusters of 6 to 12 and confined to one side of the stem whereas garlic and wild garlic flowers are always purple.

Warning

Garlic is very obvious on the breath after eating it but a few leaves of parsley can counteract this smell.

Remedy

Garlic Tonic

Apple vinegar is widely used by the Amish and this tonic uses it as a base, with chopped garlic and ginger roots and honey to taste.

You will need: 3 tablespoons of organic apple cider vinegar, 3 fresh cloves of garlic, grated, 1 inch of fresh ginger root, 2 teaspoons of honey. Water can be added if you prefer a more liquid tonic.

- Press the garlic cloves and place them in a clean jar. Remove the skin of the ginger and cut or grate it into the jar. Add the apple vinegar and the honey and then shake vigorously. Add water if desired. Take 2 teaspoons of tonic before meals once a day.

Using Plants **THE AMISH WAY**

7. GOLDENSEAL (*Hydrastis Canadensis*)

Description

Goldenseal is part of the Amish healing collection basket for its properties that can soothe soreness and also build the immune system to make it stronger when sore throats and mouths are the problem. This plant is commonly known as Orangeroot and Yellow Puccoon and when you dig it up, you can see why. The root has a strong yellowy-orange glow and it is this part that is used most in Amish remedies.

Identification

Goldenseal is a small plant, growing to a maximum of 12 inches (23 and 30 cm) tall. The stem is hairy and unbranched and you will notice two jagged leaves, with five lobes. The greenish flowers arrive in April or May and these are small, with multiple stamens and pistils. They do not have petals and they transform into a green berry-like circular fruit that is not edible. This eventually ripens to red, and you will notice its bright color from mid-summer to the fall. These are worth collecting for the seeds they contain, although they take their time germinating, the Amish always say that patience will produce the plant eventually. It can take three years so your patience will be tested. When digging up the root, be aware that this will kill the plant so give thanks before you harvest, and use every piece of the root well. It can be dried for winter use and stored in an airtight jar if you do not use it all for one remedy. Be careful and mindful when removing roots and use them well.

Foraging Period and Methods

Goldenseal can be found growing wild in rich, deciduous woodlands. It is commonly seen growing close to Tulip Poplar, American Beech, White Ash, and Sugar Maple trees. You can find it growing wild in woods from Vermont to Georgia, and west to Alabama, Arkansas, and Minnesota. The Amish are aware of how popular this plant is for foraging among the general population, and its detrimental effects, so they allow it to grow in soil in the backyard garden, where it can thrive. This supports the use of plentiful supplies of root to be used in herbal remedies without totally destroying the habitat where it grows.

To harvest Goldenseal, one root should be gently unearthed and harvested in the fall, after the leaves have begun to die. Keep in mind that harvesting Goldenseal means removing the root which kills the plant. So the Amish harvest mindfully, only taking one root where others can fill the gaps left and allow the growing patch time to grow back.

To plant Goldenseal, you can start it in a pot in compost or just sprinkle the seeds in a suitable patch of ground outdoors. Water them well and wait, sometimes for as long as 3 years.

Parts Used

The roots.

Traditional Use

The Amish use Goldenseal to make a tonic for sore mouths or throats and to support the immune system generally. The excavated root can be dried and ground into powder as colds and sore throats tend to occur in winter when the roots are unavailable.

Goldenseal root powder is also used topically on skin sores caused by Poison Ivy to encourage healing.

Any Notable or Poisonous Lookalikes?

Wild Geranium (Geranium maculatum), can look similar to Goldenseal to the novice and this plant is also known as Cranesbill, Spotted Geranium, Spotted Cranesbill, and Alum Bloom. The leaves are similar in appearance to those of Goldenseal, but Cranesbill has flowers with purple pet-

Using Plants THE AMISH WAY

als whereas Goldenseal's flowers are greenish-white and do not have petals. Cranesbill is not poisonous; it is used medicinally to address gastrointestinal issues like diarrhea, cholera, indigestion, irritable bowel disease.

Remedy

Goldenseal Throat Tea

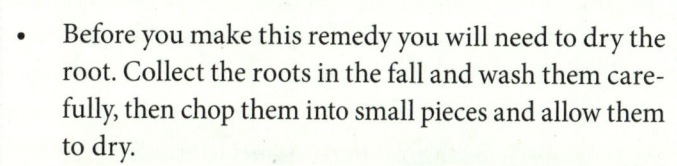

- Before you make this remedy you will need to dry the root. Collect the roots in the fall and wash them carefully, then chop them into small pieces and allow them to dry.
- Once dry, you can chop them further, add them to some water, and warm them over a gentle heat to soften them.
- To make tea, simply strain the pieces away using a sieve and give the cup of tea to the person with the sore throat. The sieved root can be added to the compost bin.

To grind the pieces into powder to soothe sores and wounds

- Chop the dried root pieces into small parts, and then use a mortar and pestle. This is hard work but it is worth the effort when your throat hurts in winter or somebody in the family needs an ointment to heal sores from stings or poison ivy.
- Shake the powder onto the affected area, cover it with gauze or sterile cloth, and secure it with pins.

Warning

Only use Goldenseal for the time it takes your sore throat or mouth to heal. This plant should not be taken daily or regularly, only when needed.

8. MULLEIN (*Verbascum thapsus*)

Description

Mullein is not native to the US, but it has been naturalized here for centuries, as seeds were taken to the New World by settlers, most probably by the Amish too because it has proven uses in Amish alternative medicine. There are 5 different types of Mullein in Ohio alone and this plant has many variations. The one to collect has bright yellow flowers, on a single thick, tall stem with yellow flowers, and a set of green leaves arranged in a rosette at soil level.

Identification

Sometimes this plant is known as Great Mullein, referring to its tall flower spike. It is a biennial plant, meaning it starts to grow in the first year but flowers in the second. The leaves begin in a rosette shape, with wide, soft leaves with a slightly grayish tinge. These are the medicinal part and can be used in a variety of ways although some of the

Using Plants THE AMISH WAY

Amish also collect the flowers to steep in oil for earache.

It can reach up to 8 feet tall depending on the richness of the soil. In its second year the delicate yellow flowers open from buds on this stem which open to reveal bright, yellow blooms adored by wildlife.

Foraging Period and Methods

Pick leaves fresh during spring and summer months and dry some leaves for use in winter. Pick leaves when the plant is flowering.

Parts Used

Leaves and flowers.

Traditional Use

The Amish use it for bronchitis, chesty coughs, and lung infections. Mullein tea will act as an expectorant, and the person will clear phlegm from a chest or lung infection by drinking 2-3 cups per day. Be warned that the leaf is hairy and these may irritate a sore throat so it is best to strain the tea after steeping the leaves. The tea is also a gentle natural sedative, which is useful when children are ill.

The soft leaves can be used topically on wounds and the tea is used to relieve arthritis pain because of its anti-inflammatory properties. It has a delicate, fresh taste.

Remedy

Mullein tea improves arthritis pain and drinking it regularly may help with asthma symptoms. It can be drunk warm or cold.

Use fresh leaves if available or dried leaves from the fall onwards.

- Gently tear the leaves into smaller sections and drop these into a jug or teapot. Add boiling water and infuse for at least 10 minutes.

- Strain the mixture into a teacup for immediate use or cool and store in an airtight container and store in the fridge.

Collect some leaves for drying in summer and hang them upside down in an area without direct sunlight. When dry, crumble them into a storage jar and make tea when needed.

Any Notable or Poisonous Lookalikes?

The most common Mullein is Great Mullein (*Verbascum thapsus*) but in Ohio, you may also find Moth Mullein (*Verbascum blattaria*) or Wand Mullein (*Verbascum virgatum*) but these are not as common as Great Mullein. The yellow flower heads of Wand Mullein are completely different from the single flower stem of Verbascum thapsus, because they spread widely with several stems and the leaves do not have the soft texture of Verbascum thapsus. Neither of these mulleins can be used as substitutes, so check the flowers and leaves carefully in Ohio.

Warning

The leaves have a soft touch but the tiny hairs can be an irritant, so some people prefer to dry them, pour hot water over them to soak and infuse them, and then strain this infusion before drinking.

9. PEPPERMINT (*Mentha piperita*)

Description

On a hot summer's day, peppermint tea cools you down and this plant also has antiseptic qualities. There are many varieties of mint and they all share that characteristic taste. Worldwide this is the flavour of toothpaste but pepper has its place in the Amish remedy book too.

Identification

The minty smell of Peppermint will identify it for you every time. Pick a leaf and roll it between your fingers or taste it. Although it grows well in a sunny location, its preference is for some shade in the hottest part of the day so in Amish gardens you can find it under trees or close to larger herb bushes that offer some shade. A square stem indicates mint, and four leaves grow opposite each other at right angles in a cross shape, attached to this stem.

The square stem helps to identify a mint. Pick a little bit of the stem and observe its shape. If it looks square and not circular, then you are almost positive it is mint, provided you can smell the fragrance as well.

Leaves are pointed at the end, oval-shaped and 1-2 inches long with very obvious visible veins Both stems and leaves have tiny hairs visible.

There are almost 200 species of mint but they all have that smell. The flower spike appears from late June onwards and it is pointed at the top, about one inch long, and flower colors vary depending on the variety, from white to pink to blooms with a tinge of purple. Bees adore peppermint flowers too.

The whole plant is low-laying and tends to expand in width rather than upward. A typical plant grows between 18 and 36 inches (45 and 91 cm) tall.

Foraging Period and Methods

The Amish prefer to harvest Peppermint before the plant blooms, usually in June or midsummer because the flavor is at its most intense. You can easily pick or cut fresh leaves fresh. The buds of the flowers form a vertical spike and gradually the white blooms open. Another clue for foraging in the wild is that there will be an expanse of the herb because this is a spreader and in your herb garden, you will probably want to restrict it to a pot or a raised bed. The minty flavor of the raw leaves provides a useful ingredient in the kitchen too.

Parts Used

The leaves, flowers, and stem. They are all aromatic and smell unmistakeably of mint. You can pick stems to dry the herb for winter use too.

Traditional Use

The Amish use peppermint for respiratory illnesses, such as cold and flu but it is also used to provide topical pain relief for muscle cramps, muscle aches, and pains as well as being a useful summer drink to cool the body when drunk as tea. The Amish use it in cases of anxiety to calm nerves and to soothe an upset stomach.

Any Notable or Poisonous Lookalikes?

Pennyroyal (*Mentha pulegium*) is a plant in the mint family that has a similar appearance to Peppermint. This plant is used medicinally in small doses, but it contains an oil that is damaging to the liver when consumed internally

Using Plants THE AMISH WAY

and can also lead to miscarriage in pregnant women. You can tell the two apart because Pennyroyal plants are much shorter than Peppermint and other mint plants. It typically grows to a maximum of 12 inches (30 cm) in height. Pennyroyal also has a different aroma; it smells more like wintergreen than Peppermint. Also, Peppermint stamens are as long as the petals, while Pennyroyal stamens extend well beyond the petals.

Remedy

Amish Peppermint Tea

Collect some fresh Peppermint leaves and pour boiling water over them in a teapot. Allow to cool and add ice cubes if required. Strain into teacups and drink. This makes a cooling drink on a hot summer's day.

Decongestant Peppermint Steam

To ease decongestion, use warm steam and some fresh herb leaves. Dried leaves can be substituted in winter for cold symptoms.

- You will need 2 teaspoons of peppermint leaves, dried or chopped fresh. You can also add thyme and rosemary leaves if these are available.
- Boil a quart of water and add it to basin, and then sprinkle the herbs into this water. Cover the basin with a towel and breathe in the steam for 5 minutes. Repeat 2 or 3 times per day as required.

10. PLANTAIN (*Plantago officinalis, Plantago major, Plantago lanceolata*)

Identification

The leaves are long, pointed, dark green, and with a distinctive rib pattern of long lines from the pointed tip of the leaf to the base. When you know that some Amish communities call it Pig's Ear Leaves you can see the resemblance.

The leaves form a rosette at soil level around a central stem. Plantain is a low-growing plant, between 6 and 8 inches (about 15-20 cm) in height, although it has been known to grow up to 24 inches (61 cm) tall. Each leaf is typically between 2 and 8 inches long (5 and 20 cm) and 2 to 4 inches (5 and 10 cm) wide. The upper surface of each leaf is medium green, while the underside is light green. Each leaf has five to seven prominent stringy veins. Small cones with brown "flower" buds appear on the stems in the Spring and early Summer. The flowers are densely grouped together in a spike, and their stamens are white or cream in color.

Description

This pretty "weed" can be found growing wild everywhere in the US and there are three varieties that can be used in the same way. The Amish know its benefits as a medicinal plant. Pilgrims use leaves in shoes to reduce foot soreness. The first Amish settlers arrived with this knowledge of the medicinal qualities of Plantain, and Amish healers continue to use it as a medicinal herb to this day.

Using Plants THE AMISH WAY

Foraging Period and Methods

This plant grows everywhere, as the seeds are blown by wind to any available site. However, it is important not to pick from paths or road edges where they may be sprayed with pesticides or weed killers. The Amish grow their plants in gardens and can pick them fresh whenever they are needed. Young leaves offer the most nutrients and you can pick or cut them from spring through to the fall in most states.

Remember not to pick a whole bag and to leave some seed heads intact because this encourages the plant to spread for future harvesting. The seed heads are valuable winter food for birds too so leave a few for them. Leaves are edible and nutritious, high in calcium, and a source of vitamins A, C, and K.

Parts Used

The leaves and seeds.

Traditional Use

Plantain is in plentiful supply and both the leaves and seeds are antibacterial and antiseptic so they are useful for wound treatments. The Amish use it to make an ointment or oil to spread on cuts, bites, and stings, and also to ease dry skin problems. Placing leaves directly on the skin reduces fever and you can wrap a bleeding wound to stop the blood. Infusions of leaves can be used as an eye wash to soothe sore eyes from hay fever or eye infections.

The Amish harvest some leaves in summer, dry them, and use this to make an ointment or herb-infused oil for wound relief in winter.

Any Notable or Poisonous Lookalikes?

Very few plants resemble Plantain and its unique seed head, so this is a great plant for beginners. Luckily, plants that do look similar, like Hostas, have edible leaves too. In fact, these plants are sometimes known as Plantain lilies. *Hosta plantaginea* smells very fragrant, unlike Plantain, so if you sniff you know you have the wrong plant. Hostas are bigger plants too, with a very different flower stalk shape, so you are unlikely to make a mistake.

Warning

Plantain leaves are edible and the seeds too. However, eat in small quantities because over consumption can lead to a dramatic drop in blood pressure.

Remedy

Emergency first aid

- Pick fresh leaves if you cut yourself out in the open. Apply them directly to the wound. The leaves are antibacterial and antiseptic. Tie them on with a blade of grass if nothing else is available.

- If you are walking a long distance without socks, pick a few plantain leaves and line your shoes or sandals with them. When you arrive, rub the leaves on your feet and feel how refreshing it feels after a long day working or walking. It also works well if you have a cut and want to stop the bleeding.

Plantain eyewash

- Pick enough leaves to fill a cup and then rinse off any dirt before chopping them up.

- Add 3 cups of water to a small pan and gently heat the leaves so that the essential oil will transfer to the water. Simmer for 20 minutes, then remove the pan and strain the mixture into a jar or cup. Allow to cool.

- Fill an egg cup or a small glass with the cooled mixture and wash out eyes affected by pollen or hay fever. Store any leftover liquid in a cool place and use it daily to ease hay fever eyes.

Using Plants THE AMISH WAY

Amish Medicinal Garden You Should Have in Your Backyard

It's amazing how many medicinal plants are likely growing right off your front porch or in your backyard. Most of us are not trained to notice these unassuming plants, and rather than use them we walk right past them every day. Many Amish understand how to identify and use these plants, and as a result, they are able to stay healthy without spending a dime.

Some common medicinal plants used by the Amish include chicory, yarrow, marshmallow, chamomile, evening primrose, lavender, calendula, and California poppy. The majority of these plants can be found growing in the wild. However, these plants can also be cultivated rather easily.

In the Medicinal Garden Kit you will find 10 packs of 4,818 high-quality, NON-GMO seeds packaged in the US. Even if you've never planted anything before, you'll have no trouble growing these 10 plants. With your kit, you will also receive the FREE Herbal Medicinal Guide: From Seeds to Remedies, with all the guidelines on how to grow, harvest and prepare each plant. Your backyard or windowsill pharmacy will come back year after year, without you having to replant it, providing you with a reliable source of natural remedies.

https://medicinalseedkit.com/taw-qr/

Of the aforementioned plants, lavender, calendula, and California poppy are cultivated most often, and the others can be found growing in the wild (often prolifically). They can be grown in pots (calendula is called the "pot marigold" because it does so well in containers) or raised beds. Due to the invasive nature of some of these plants, it is best to grow them in contained areas where they cannot escape cultivation. Most will take off by just spreading seeds on fallow ground. In this chapter, you will discover the incredible healing powers of these plants, how to use them, how to identify them in the wild, as well as how to prepare them in medicinal formulations.

Traditional Uses

There is a reason the Amish use these particular plants the most. First, they are incredibly effective and have a long history of medicinal use. Second, they are often easy to find and thus can be readily utilized in remedies. Let's take a look at each of these special plants to learn more about why they are used and how they may help you and your loved ones.

Using Plants THE AMISH WAY

1. Chicory *(Cichorium intybus)*

Chicory is a common sight along roadsides in the summer. You have likely viewed it while driving or taking a walk, and once you know how to identify it, you will be thrilled at how much you find! Chicory isn't really native to North America, but is now widespread thanks to European settlers introducing it here hundreds of years ago. Today, not only is it native to Europe and widespread throughout North America, it can also be found all over Australia.

Chicory is fairly easy to identify. It can grow quite tall, up to five feet in height. It can have many branching stems with unlobed lanceolate leaves and daisy-like purple flowers. These flowers can have a light blue or lavender hue depending on many factors. The flowers grow up the stems and are often open at dusk and close back up during the daytime hours.

Chicory has an interesting history of use that even dates back to the Civil War. It is said that soldiers blended roasted chicory root into their coffee rations to make them last longer. There is a reason why so many people have utilized chicory root like coffee! It tastes just like coffee when you roast the roots in the oven and grind them up to infuse in hot water. Not only is chicory useful as a coffee substitute, it has several medicinal properties that can bring healing to the gut, liver, and even help with occasional constipation. It should also be noted that the leaves and flowers are edible and can be added to salads, etc.

Chicory roots contain inulin. This compound is a wonderful prebiotic that can support a healthy microbiome. In addition, chicory roots can protect the liver from damage and soften stools for those who suffer from constipation and need a gentle remedy to bring on a bowel movement.

Oftentimes, the simplest way to prepare a remedy is the most effective. This is especially true for Amish remedies. When it comes to chicory, the recipe below is a simple yet effective way to prepare the roots for maximum benefits.

Chicory Root Gut and Liver Support Tea

The best way to get the most from chicory roots is to prepare them fresh in a tea. This keeps most of the inulin intact. For this recipe, you will need one to two teaspoons of freshly chopped chicory roots, one cup of hot water, and a tea bag/tea infusion device to infuse the plant material into the cup of hot water.

Heat water on the stove until it is almost boiling. While the water is heating, fill a bag with one to two teaspoons of chopped chicory root. Put the hot water into a cup and place the bag inside for 15-20 minutes. Add raw honey to taste.

For constipation, drink one cup and wait two to three hours. You may drink a second up if you have not had a bowel movement after three hours. For daily liver and microbiome support, drink one cup in the morning.

Using Plants THE AMISH WAY

2. Yarrow *(Achillea millefolium)*

It is said that the Greek warrior Achilles used yarrow on the battlefield to help heal his soldier's wounds. In fact, this is how yarrow got its Latin name which is Achillea millefolium. There is a lot of truth in this interesting historical tidbit! Yarrow does in fact have wound healing and styptic properties. Not only is it an astringent plant that can help tighten and draw tissues back together, it is also styptic and can stop bleeding. Additionally, yarrow has antimicrobial and antibacterial properties to cleanse wounds and prevent the onset of infection. Aside from using yarrow externally for wounds, it also has a history of internal use for lowering fevers (it can induce sweating to cool the body off) stopping internal bleeding (such as heavy menstrual flow), and even supporting immune health to fight off viral illnesses like colds.

Yarrow is native to temperate regions throughout the world, such as Europe and North America. It can often be found growing in fields, roadsides, and ditches. It is sometimes mistaken for wild carrot, but if you look closely, you will notice several distinguishing factors that separate it from wild carrot. First, yarrow has fernlike leaves and wild carrot has carrot-scented leaves that are indicative to plants in this family. Not only are yarrow's leaves fernlike, but they also have a very distinctive medicinal/herbaceous smell that can greatly help with identification. Both yarrow and wild carrot have clusters of tiny white flowers. However, wild carrot flowers are often a uniform circle shape with one or several tiny dark flowers in the center. Yarrow flower clusters are not uniform circles. All aerial parts of the yarrow plant can be used medicinally in teas, tinctures, and salves.

Styptic Wound Powder

The Amish love to use yarrow in a simplistic way for the treatment of various wounds. One of the most effective and easiest ways to prepare the plant is to create a styptic wound power that helps staunch blood flow, cleanse the area, and promote faster healing.

To make this powder, first harvest yarrow leaves and allow them to fully dry by placing the leaves on a towel or drying rack. When they are fully dried out, grind them into powder using a mortar and pestle or a heavy-duty food processor (many blenders or food processors require a "dry blade" to grind plants into powder, so be aware of this). Make sure the powder is as fine as possible before filling a sterile glass jar for storage. Place a lid on the jar and store this in a cool, dark place to use as needed. Place this powder directly on cuts, scrapes, and minor bleeding wounds to stop bleeding and help aid in faster healing.

Using Plants THE AMISH WAY

3. Marshmallow *(Althaea officinalis)*

The best way to utilize the root is to make an infusion. Heat is not something that goes well with marshmallow root and can render it less effective. Make a cold infusion the Amish way by following these steps:

Soothing Marshmallow Infusion

An infusion is not the same as a tea. Infusions are a wonderful and gentle way to extract the mucilage properties from marshmallow root while keeping the medicinal properties intact. To make one, start by filling a sterile glass jar with two to three tablespoons of chopped marshmallow root pieces. Next, gently cover the plant material with two cups of lukewarm water (spring water is best). Place a lid on the jar and place it in the refrigerator overnight. It takes several hours for the mucilage properties to diffuse into the water and thicken.

The next day, remove the jar from the refrigerator and give it a good shake. Strain out the liquid and discard the root pieces into the trash or compost. Drink ½ cup of this liquid every few hours to find relief from ulcers, digestive discomfort (such as IBS or Ulcerative Colitis), or to coat the urinary tract to soothe burning. Refrigerate between uses, where it should last 3-5 days.

Marshmallow is another plant with a history of interesting uses. The name "marshmallow" may bring to mind those sticky campfire treats, and you may be surprised to learn that the roots of this plant were once used to make marshmallows. Today, most marshmallows are made using other ingredients, but the thick mucilage produced by marshmallow root can still be used to make marshmallows the old-fashioned way if you ever get the urge to try it!

The marshmallow plant can get quite tall, with many reaching up to six feet in height. They prefer moist ground, but gardeners usually have luck growing them in a variety of soil types. The leaves are large and hairy, with three to five shallow lobes. The flowers are quite noticeable, with pink/lilac/white petals and purple stamens.

While herbalists often use the leaves, flowers, and roots medicinally, the most potent part of the plant is in the roots. Dig up marshmallow roots to make powerful infusions that can soothe sore throats, coat and soothe an upset stomach and digestive system, and even coat the urinary tract to provide relief from urinary tract infections and interstitial cystitis symptoms.

Using Plants The Amish Way

4. Chamomile *(Matricaria chamomilla)*

Chamomile is a very useful plant that is native to the Europe and the Mediterranean areas. There are multiple "chamomile" species, but the one most often used is Matricaria chamomilla. In addition to this species, there is a prolific and easy-to-find North American species called pineapple weed (Matricaria discoidea) that can be used in its place.

German chamomile (Matricaria chamomilla) only grows up to two feet tall, and that is in ideal conditions. Its flowers are noticeable, with a bulbous yellow center surrounded by white petals. Leaves are wispy, thin, and bipinnate or tripinnate. Use your sense of smell to aid in identification! The plant smells strongly herbaceous and medicinal, with notes of apple. Pineapple weed is similar but lacking all white petals. You will only see the yellow bulbous centers at the top of the plant. It smells very strongly of pineapple.

Chamomile can help calm frazzled nerves, aid in sleep, soothe spasmodic coughing, and aid in a variety of digestive complaints from upset stomach to gas and bloating. It can be used topically in salves and oil infusions to calm skin irritations from redness to rashes. However, do not use this plant if you are allergic to plants in the aster family.

Chamomile Tincture

One of the best ways to utilize chamomile is by making a tincture. Tinctures are excellent for extracting the beneficial medicinal compounds in plants- plus they have a very long shelf life! To make a tincture, start by using fresh or dried aerial parts of the chamomile plant.

Fill a sterile glass jar with the chopped chamomile and then completely cover this with at least 80 proof alcohol. Place a lid on the jar and put it in a cool, dark place to infuse for 4-6 weeks. Shake your jar daily to aid in infusion. After 4-6 weeks is up, strain out the liquid using a strainer or cheesecloth. Place the liquid into dropper bottles for easier usage.

Take one to two droppers full as needed to help ease digestive woes, reduce anxiety, aid in sleep, or stop spasmodic coughing (and other spasmodic conditions).

Using Plants THE AMISH WAY

5. Evening Primrose *(Oenothera biennis)*

Evening primrose can be found in both temperate and subtropical regions, so it has a wide distribution area. For this reason, it also has a long history of use by Native Americans and European settlers. The yellow flowers growing on spikes are a great identification feature. You may notice them growing along roadsides, in ditches, and throughout fields in spring, summer, and even fall months. The yellow flowers have four bilobed petals and the leaves are lanceolate. The whole plant can grow to over five feet in height. A tight rosette forms the first year and a stalk the second.

This is one plant that you won't need to grow, as it is common throughout most of the world. It gets its name due to the fact that the flowers open in the evenings. This is a good time to take a walk and look for the plant to harvest for medicinal use.

All parts of the plant are used for medicinal purposes. The seeds are one of the most famous parts of the plant, having a long history of use to make evening primrose seed oil. However, the leaves have been used to treat sore throats and digestive upset and the flowers are an effective skin remedy for bruises, rashes, and other skin irritations.

Evening Primrose Oil Infusion

Create a powerful skin-healing remedy using the open flowers and leaves of the evening primrose plant. Collect as many as you wish and wilt them overnight on a towel or drying rack. Try using an even amount of leaves and flowers (feel free to use seeds as well). Next, fill a jar with the plant material and then completely cover this in a carrier oil like olive oil, jojoba oil, coconut oil, or avocado oil. Meanwhile, fill a pan with a few inches of water and place this over low heat on the stove. Sit the jar of plant material and oil in the water bath, making sure no water spills over and inside the infusion jar. You may loosely place a lid or cover over the jar as it infuses, but do not tighten it.

Allow this to infuse for eight to ten hours. The longer it is allowed to infuse under low heat, the better. Finally, strain out the plant material and bottle the oil in dropper bottles for easier usage. Massage this oil into contusions, bruises, rashes, irritated skin, psoriasis, eczema, and more.

6. Lavender *(genus Lavandula)*

Lavender is originally native to the Mediterranean region. However, its popularity as a medicinal plant has made it quite famous all over the world. Today, it is commonly grown in temperate regions all over the world. It can be grown in containers, raised beds, or straight in the ground. Because it is native to the Mediterranean region, it tends to prefer less water and is somewhat draught tolerant.

Lavender has been extensively studied and found to help lower blood pressure, calm the mind and body, and evoke feelings of peace and wellness. Lavender is enjoyed in many forms, from essential oil to tinctures and teas. It can help ease digestive upset and has antimicrobial properties as well. Many people swear by lavender for headaches and migraines.

Soothing Lavender Headache Poultice

The potent aroma of lavender can help ease the nerves and relax muscles that cause issues with tension. For this reason, it is often utilized to help with headaches and migraines. For many people, simply inhaling the essential oil from the plant can help take the edge off a bad headache. However, if you don't have the essential oil sitting around, you can make an effective (and fast) remedy at home with lavender that is sure to help ease the pain of a migraine or headache.

Headaches can be debilitating, so it is important to have a quick and simple remedy on hand if you feel one coming on. If you grow lavender, harvest the flowering tops and allow them to dry on drying racks or towels so you always have some on hand to make this remedy. Store your dried lavender in an airtight glass jar out of direct sunlight.

When you feel a headache coming on, take one to two tablespoons of dried lavender, grind it up, and make a paste with a small amount of water. Apply this poultice to the forehead and temples and lie in a dark room for 20-30 minutes, trying to relax. Practice deep breathing and inhale the aroma of the lavender as you relax. You will emerge ready to take on the day!

Using Plants THE AMISH WAY

7. Calendula *(Calendula officinalis)*

Calendula, or "pot marigold" as it is often called, is a very useful medicinal plant to have around. Try planting seeds and growing calendula in containers throughout the summer months. Collect the flowering tops as they emerge (make sure to get the resinous bracts under the flowers as well). Place the flowers on drying racks and then store them in an airtight container to use as needed in remedies.

Calendula is not the same plant as marigold, even though it is referred to as a pot marigold. It has flowers that are more daisy-like in appearance, with less petals than common marigolds. Both calendula and marigold share a beautiful, bright orange hue. These plants don't get very tall, with most reaching two feet in height. Leaves are spade shaped.

This plant has a history of use for skin irritations, lymphatic support, and digestive support. Try the remedy below for use in lymphatic massage or for skin irritations.

Calendula Salve

Calendula salve is a cheery, bright orange remedy made from the flowering tops of the plant. These flowers contain medicinal resin that can promote soothing and healing. To make it, you will need eight ounces of calendula-infused carrier oil, one ounce of beeswax pellets, and a double boiler.

Start by infusing the flowers into a carrier oil. Choose from any carrier oil you like and whatever works best for your skin type. Fill a glass jar with the dried flowers and then completely cover these in a carrier oil. Try to use around 8 ounces of oil, as this is an optimal amount to make salve with. Sit this in a bath of water on the stovetop on low heat and allow this to infuse for 10-12 hours. The longer it is allowed to infuse, the better.

Strain out the oil and set it aside in a jar. Discard the infused calendula pieces in compost or trash. In a double boiler, melt the beeswax pellets and then gently add the infused oil to the beeswax, stirring carefully. Once this is fully blended, remove it from heat and pour into jars to cool. Avoid using plastic jars, as toxins in plastics can seep into your remedy.

Massage this salve into wounds, bruises, contusions, rashes, and other skin irritations for relief. It will stay in place well and not become runny or messy thanks to the beeswax acting as a binding agent.

Another great way to use this salve is during lymphatic massage. It can help clear lymphatic stagnation and help the lymphatic system function more efficiently. In turn, this helps the immune system work more effectively.

Using Plants THE AMISH WAY

8. California poppy *(Eschscholzia californica)*

California poppy is known for its ability to calm the nerves, ease anxiety and stress, and more. It is a classic nervine plant, so it can help if you have trouble falling asleep at night.

The easiest way to get the most from this plant is to make a tincture to take as needed for anxiety, stress, and help falling asleep.

Don't be fooled by the name. California poppy may be a member of the poppy family, but it does not contain any opium. It is a gentle, yet effective remedy for adults and children alike. California poppy is native to western North America, where it grows in large, orange, clusters throughout meadows, hillsides, and more.

This species of poppy is not as big as its relatives. It is a rather small and unassuming flower, growing up to a foot in height. The bright orange flowers with four large petals are sure to catch attention and help you identify the plant. One of its most distinguishing identification characteristics is its blue-green foliage. Leaves are alternately divided.

California poppy may be native to California, but you can grow it in just about any climate. Spread seeds in the spring on fallow, well-draining ground to enjoy summer flowers. Harvest aerial parts and hang them to dry or place them on drying racks/towels to use in remedies as needed.

California Poppy Nervine Tincture

To create a tincture with this plant, harvest aerial parts and chop them up well. Fill a sterile glass jar with the plant material and then completely cover this in at least 80 proof alcohol. Place a lid on the jar and sit it in a cool, dark place for four to six weeks. Shake your jar daily to help it infuse more effectively.

After four to six weeks, strain out the liquid and discard the plant material. Store the liquid in a dropper bottle for ease of use. Start by taking one dropper full as needed for anxiety, stress, and help sleeping. Move up to two droppers full if you feel like you need a higher dosage. You can also take one to two droppers full for headaches, especially if they are stress-related.

Using Plants THE AMISH WAY

AMISH COUGH SYRUP AND THROAT DROPS

Not even the Amish are immune to the occasional bout of illness, be it the common cold or the dreaded flu. Yet, unlike the majority of society, they do not refrain from seeking traditional medical treatment, unless it becomes absolutely necessary. So, for things like cough and sore throat, a homemade cough syrup or throat drops will usually do the trick.

You will be learning how to make two remedies for coughs and colds. One is a honey-based "cough syrup," which resembles a soothing syrup for people with a persistent cough. The other is natural honey "cough drops." If you don't have blackberries on hand, tart cherries or tart cherry 'juice' can substitute for the blackberries in the cough drops. The other thing you can do is opt for blackberry brandy instead of the blackberry juice in the "cough syrup."

Amish Cough Syrup Recipe: *"Snake Juice"*

Dosages

Adults 1 Tbsp.

Children 1/4 tsp.

Ingredients

3-4 lemons sliced
2 large onions sliced
1 cup honey to pour over
1 ½ cup juice from 1 c blackberries & water (*see step 1*)
1 pint of peppermint schnapps

Instructions

Step 1

Put the kettle on to heat up your water. Once heated, pour the water over the blackberries and let it sit for 10 minutes. Then, strain the berries through a cheesecloth to extract the liquid. Make sure you squeeze the cheesecloth to get all of the liquid out.

Step 2

Alternate between layers of lemons and onions in the jar until you have equal amounts.

Step 3

Pour the honey over the top of the lemons and onions.

Step 4

Add the entire bottle of peppermint schnapps and the liquid from the berries. Cover with cheesecloth and place in the refrigerator for two weeks so that it has to macerate.

Once the meticulously crafted batch of homemade cough syrup has undergone full maceration, it is ready to be stored in the refrigerator. With its soothing properties, this remedy stands ready to offer solace to those ensnared by the relentless grip of an incessant cough or aching throat. In the realm of wintertime remedies, this humble yet remarkable elixir serves as a rugged defender against the relentless onslaught of winter bugs. When kept within reach, it guarantees our homes remain sanctuaries of health and well-being. This recipe is reported to last over a year in the fridge and has no more alcohol than cough syrup, but it is still not intended for children under the age of six years old.

Using Plants THE AMISH WAY

AMISH COUGH DROPS RECIPE

Dosages

Due to their inherent chewiness, it is strongly advised against administering these delectable drops to children under the age of six. From their initial firmness, these drops gradually soften into a supple consistency comparable to taffy in your mouth. They can be taken out of the refrigerator as needed and eaten like lozenges whenever someone has a sore throat or persistent cough. You can have as many as you want; just remain cognizant of the substantial sugar content that honey possesses.

Ingredients

1 ½ cups honey
¾ cups scalded water
½ cups frozen blackberries
3-4 drops of food-grade essential peppermint oil
¼ cups lemon Juice
Powdered rose hip, corn starch, or sugar for dusting

Instructions

Step 1

Put the kettle on to heat up your water to scalding. Once heated, pour the water over the blackberries and let them sit for 10 minutes. Then, strain the berries through a cheesecloth to extract the liquid.

Step 2

Scrape the honey into a saucepan. Add the lemon juice and blackberry liquid. Make sure to squeeze all you can from the cheesecloth. Turn the heat on to medium-low. Cook the mixture while stirring often until it reaches about 300 degrees Fahrenheit on a candy thermometer or until it turns completely hard when dropped into a bowl of ice water (30-40 minutes). It'll be very frothy right before it's ready.

Step 3

Add the peppermint oil and mix one last time before removing from the heat.

Step 4

Cool mixture for 5 minutes. Meanwhile, prepare a nonstick paper or mat by greasing it with coconut oil. You can use a pan to prevent overflow.

Step 5

Pour the mixture onto the middle of the paper and let it sit until you can touch and mold it by hand. It doesn't take long, so you'll have to work quickly, but please be aware that the candy mixture will burn you if it gets on your skin while it's still super-hot.

Step 6

Pull small chunks of mixture from the outer edges where it cools faster. Roll into balls or chunks and cool on another part of the greased paper.

Step 7

After the drops have cooled, dust them with powdered rose hip for a little extra vitamin C or some kind of starch so they don't stick together. You can also wrap them in wax or candy paper for storage in the refrigerator.

Using Plants THE AMISH WAY

Amish Plasters

Introduction

The Amish understand something that many of us outside of their community often don't, and that's that everything we need to be generally well and live a good life has already been given to us. A lot of this can be attributed to the level of faith the Amish have in God and the natural abilities to heal ourselves given by God. They know that every component of a plant or seed has some superpower to heal the body and that the body is specially designed to receive these plant components as nourishment. We buy their natural cures in droves because they've done a fantastic job identifying which plants have which effects—having to pay a pretty penny for them, too.

But what happens if we have the same faith in ourselves and our abilities? Can we not make effective cures using the same plants and natural materials in our environment—just as the Amish do? Many Amish cures are made from simple kitchen ingredients we already have on hand. We eat them and drink them without knowing their true potential. We, too, can learn to listen to our inner wisdom and play a more significant role in our healthcare. Here are three simple yet potent plaster treatments from the Amish that you can whip up in your kitchen with just a few everyday household items.

Making and Using Plasters

- To avoid skin burns, rub olive oil onto the place where you'll be putting the plaster.

- Never wear them for more than twenty to thirty minutes, and check under each one regularly to prevent blistering or burning.

- Plastic wrap may be used instead of doubling up on towels. This will keep all moisture inside the plaster as well, but it won't be as potent.

- You can add water when cooking down onions and garlic to keep them from sticking.

- If you don't want to use a mortar and pestle, you can use an electric grinder to grind your mustard seeds. This will create a finer powder.

- Plaster is only good to use once.

- Do not store them in the refrigerator. Use them right away.

- If your skin starts to turn red or feel like it is burning, remove the plaster immediately.

Using Plants THE AMISH WAY

Amish Mustard Plaster

Mustard stimulates blood circulation wherever you apply it, which is why it will turn that area red. By boosting blood circulation and opening up capillaries, the mustard plaster will help expand the lungs, which can aid in coughing up mucous and phlegm. It works to relieve muscle pain in a similar fashion.

A mustard plaster can be used as a topical muscle relaxer or expectorant.

Ingredients

1 tablespoon of mustard seeds
¼ cup of flour
Warm water (until consistency of pancake batter)

Instructions

Step 1
Grind the mustard seeds into a powder using a mortar and pestle. Add that to a bowl.

Step 2
Add the flour to the mustard powder.

Step 3
Add a small amount of the warm water and mix again. Continue adding water until your mixture reaches the consistency of pancake batter. If it gets too thin, add more flour.

Step 4
Lay a cotton towel flat. On top of that, lay a piece of cheesecloth or a second towel.

Step 5
Add the plaster. Spread the plaster evenly with a spoon until it covers an area large enough to cover whatever you're putting it on.

Step 6
Next, fold in each corner to make a square or rectangle. Flip it over and do that again with the second clean cloth.

Using the Mustard Plaster

Apply a thin layer of olive oil to the affected area of the skin and then set the plaster "packet" on top with the flat side down. Applying the plaster on the chest or back, over the lungs, can help with congestion and coughing.

Place a heating pad or warm water bottle on top of the plaster and let it sit for up to twenty minutes to help loosen congestion and phlegm.

Using Plants THE AMISH WAY

Amish Onion & Garlic Plaster

Amish onion and garlic plaster helps with colds and flu, stubborn coughs, and bronchial inflammations. Place it on the front or back of the body over the lungs to relieve persistent coughing.

Ingredients

1-3 onions (save the juice from the cutting board if possible)
3-4 cloves of garlic
¼ teaspoon of dried thyme
2 tablespoons of apple cider vinegar
A little flour

Instructions

Step 1
Dice the onions and mince the garlic. Add both to a pan.

Step 2
Sauté the onions and garlic on low until golden brown. After about five minutes, add the thyme so that all the juices and herbal components can combine.

Step 3
Sauté until golden brown, adding the vinegar for a minute or two. Shut it off and let it cool to room temperature.

Then, add enough flour to make a spreadable plaster.

Step 4
Spread the mixture onto a piece of cheesecloth placed over a cotton towel, making sure it covers an appropriately sized area.

Step 5
Fold the cloth in on itself to make a square or rectangular "pack." Flip it over, then do it again with the towel.

Using the Onion and Garlic Plaster

Lie down and place the pack onto the area over the lungs, either on the front of the chest or on the back.

Place a heating pad or hot water bottle over the plaster and let it sit for up to 30 minutes. Check the area periodically to ensure it's not getting too hot. If it begins to burn, remove the plaster.

Note: Some people experience instant relief, while others notice a temporary increase in phlegm, which needs to be expelled. You can repeat this process up to three times daily and switch between the back and front of the body.

Using Plants **THE AMISH WAY**

Warming Plaster for Pain:
Ginger, Cinnamon, and Cayenne Pain Relief Plaster

If you're experiencing pain or cramps in your muscles, joints, back, or neck, try using this Amish warming plaster. The combination of these ingredients provides a warming effect that helps reduce inflammation and discomfort by improving blood flow to the affected area.

The effects of the herbs utilized to make this plaster are detailed below.

Cayenne Pepper

Capsaicin is an ingredient in cayenne pepper with anti-inflammatory and antispasmodic qualities. The capsaicin in cayenne pepper blocks the transmission of pain signals from nerve endings to the central nervous system, which is why it is so effective in alleviating pain in muscles and nerves. A wide variety of painful conditions, including neuropathy, back pain, muscular spasms, cramps associated with menstruation, and arthritis, can improve with the help of cayenne pepper.

Ginger

Ginger's anti-inflammatory properties have been studied in clinical trials for a number of pain conditions, including arthritic and muscular discomfort. Warming ginger aids circulation and eases tension in aching muscles.

Cassia Cinnamon

When used topically, cinnamon's warming properties can alleviate aches and pains thanks to the chemical molecules cinnamaldehyde and cinnamic acid. These substances have a natural anti-inflammatory and pain-relieving effect.

Ingredients

1 whole dried cayenne pepper or 1/8 teaspoon of cayenne pepper powder
¼ cup of flour
2-inch piece of fresh ginger
2 tablespoons of cinnamon bark or 1 tablespoon of powdered cinnamon
1 tablespoon of whole flax seeds
1-2 tablespoons of cornstarch
1 cup of water

Materials

A piece of cheesecloth
A clean kitchen towel
A saucepan
A wire mesh (optional)

Instructions

Step 1
Smash the ginger with a mortar and pestle.

Step 2
Toss the ginger, along with the rest of the herbs, into the saucepan. Pour in the water and bring to a simmer over medium heat. Then, turn the flame to low and simmer gently for ten minutes.

Step 3
Turn off the heat and strain the liquid through cheesecloth or wire mesh to remove all large particles. Lower the heat and add the liquid back to the pan. Gently simmer until it decreases in volume by half.

Using Plants THE AMISH WAY

Step 4

Once the mixture has been reduced by half, you can add in the flax seed. Stirring consistently, continue to heat for one minute. Then, shut it off and let it cool to room temperature.

Step 5

While the plaster cools, you'll want to get your towel and cheesecloth ready by laying them out flat, first the towel and then the cheesecloth.

Step 6

Even after it cools, your plaster will be a bit soupy. Add the cornstarch one teaspoon at a time to create a consistency that pulls away from the sides of the bowl.

Step 7

Spread it out onto a sizeable enough area to cover whatever you plan to put the plaster on. Afterward, carefully fold in each corner of the cheesecloth. Then, turn it over and repeat the process with the towel. At the end, you should have the towel's flat side facing the surface you're working on.

Using the Warming Plaster for Pain

Place the plaster pack on the area of pain for up to twenty minutes. If it doesn't get too hot, place a heated water bottle or heating pad on top of it. If it gets too hot, remove the heat source immediately.

Using Plants THE AMISH WAY

Amish Antibiotics

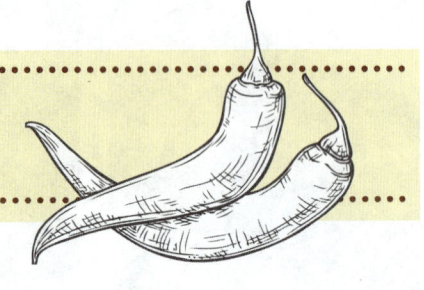

Amish "Super Tonic" – A Potent, All-Purpose Herbal Remedy

Let's recap what we've learned so far about Amish herbal medicine: first, the Amish are quite proactive about protecting their health, often with the help of herbal supplements like garlic and echinacea; second, they have a sophisticated understanding of herbal medicine, passed down orally through the generations; and third, these remedies are often made wholly or in part from pantry staples. Perhaps no Amish home remedy better reflects the spirit of Amish traditional medical knowledge than the so-called "super tonic" that can be found on the shelves of most Amish pantries (at least, we always had it in our household, growing up) – though if you didn't know any better, you might mistake it for a jar of pickles or a homemade salad dressing!

The roots of super tonic can be found in Sauer's Compendious Herbal, which recommends a tablespoonful of apple cider vinegar infused with sea onion (*Drimia maritima*, also called squill) or horseradish (*Armoracia rusticana*), taken each morning, as "an outstanding remedy for maintaining good health" (Weaver, 2000). Nowadays, sea onion is not very commonly used (it can be toxic if not prepared correctly) but fortunately, you can get the same benefit from plain old white onions, along with horseradish and a few other easily obtainable ingredients. As you might guess from the ingredient list, it's strong stuff – especially if you use really hot peppers! – and not necessarily the most pleasant-tasting thing, but there's a reason Amish people still swear by it today!

The recipe that follows is intended to be generic, so don't be afraid to tinker with it: echinacea, dandelion root, and goldenseal are all excellent additions. For my part, I have added one slightly unusual ingredient, namely butterfly weed (*Asclepias tuberosa*). Butterfly weed used to be known as pleurisy root, and was revered by Native Americans and eclectic physicians alike for its potency in treating respiratory conditions. If you plan to take the super tonic year-round, you can skip it – but for a little extra punch during cold and flu season, it's well worth the effort of obtaining some. Not that it's hard to find: you can buy it in most garden stores, and it's quite easy to grow from seed, so consider planting it in your herb garden!

Ingredients

Apple cider vinegar, raw & unfiltered if possible;
Equal parts of:
• Fresh garlic, peeled & chopped/crushed;
• Fresh ginger root, grated;
• White onion, finely chopped or grated;
• Fresh horseradish root, grated;
• Fresh or dried medium-hot peppers (jalapeño, serrano, cayenne, etc.), de-seeded and chopped;
• Dried butterfly weed (*Asclepias tuberosa*) root, roughly chopped (optional, but recommended for treating respiratory infections like colds & flu)

Note: The amount of vinegar, and the size of container needed to prepare the tonic, depends on how much of each ingredient you use. The recipe that follows assumes ½ cup of each ingredient.

Using Plants THE AMISH WAY

Preparation

Combine the fresh ingredients in a quart glass jar, then add enough vinegar to completely cover. Close jar with a tight-fitting lid and let steep, away from direct sunlight, for at least two weeks, and up to six months. Strain and store in a cool, dark place. A cellar is ideal, but your pantry, kitchen cabinet, or laundry room will do just fine!

Dosages:

Take one tablespoonful daily, especially during cold and flu season. If you have a cold or flu, take up to three times daily.

Amish "Amoxicillin"

Amoxicillin is a powerful drug against bacterial infection, and fast-acting too. Generally, the actions of conventional medicines are very specific. That said, amoxicillin targets all types of bacteria – bad or good.

The general side effects of amoxicillin use could include an upset stomach and diarrhea, as it can interfere with gut flor.

Herbal antibacterial remedies are milder, but they come with a wider range of benefits. Garlic, for example, is not only a whole-body antibiotic. It is also an immunity booster, digestive tonic, detoxifier and liver tonic. Getting rid of the bacteria is just one phase of the process. You also need to boost your immune shield and support the good gut bacteria.

The Herbs in My Natural Amish Amoxicillin Recipe

These are but a few from the list of effective herbal antibiotics. These are a good start since most of them are readily available in any kitchen. Some of them are also easy to grow in your herbal garden whenever you need them.

- Garlic
- Onion
- Ginger
- Turmeric
- Citrus fruit
- Cayenne
- Pineapple
- Black pepper
- Honey
- Apple cider vinegar (ACV)

Making Nature's Amoxicillin at Home

It is possible to concoct your own antibiotic using most of these potent ingredients. Keep a jar of this tonic handy and use it to treat infection during a disease outbreak.

Using Plants THE AMISH WAY

The most popular winter drink that is packed with antibacterial and antiviral properties is Fire Cider. It is made up of powerful herbs and spices steeped in apple cider vinegar and honey.

Fire cider is versatile and you can use any herbs, fruits and rhizomes. For this recipe, we use all the potent natural antibiotics to make a delicious fruit punch. Unlike fire cider tonic which needs a couple of weeks to ferment, this fire cider punch can be used immediately.

You may also store it in the fridge, for a handy natural antibiotic whenever you need one.

Ingredients

½ cup fresh pineapple, washed and cut into half-inch cubes
2-inch ginger, peeled
1-inch turmeric root, peeled (or ½ to ¾ tsp turmeric powder)
2 to 3 cloves garlic
1 medium-sized onion
¼ organic lime or lemon with peel, chopped
1 ½ tbsp honey
1/8 tsp cayenne pepper
A pinch of black pepper
Blender
Strainer
⅔ cup ACV
Glass jar

Instructions

Step 1
Put all the ingredients in a blender (pineapple, garlic, ginger, onion, lime, turmeric, apple cider vinegar and honey). Of course, we don't use electrical blenders back at home, as we have food mills for this. But if you have anything electrical that can ease your work, feel free to use it!

Step 2
Blend until smooth and consume. If you don't like the texture of this fire cider punch, you may pass it in a fine mesh strainer to extract just the liquid. But, eating the pulp will get you the most benefit out of this delicious and spicy blend.

Step 3
Transfer the juice to a glass mason jar and store it in the fridge. The fire cider shot can last for 2 weeks.

How to Use

Take a shot glass of the fire cider punch before a meal. You may also use it as an ingredient in salad dressings or marinades. This fire cider shot makes an excellent cocktail, just add some sparkling water for a hot, pungent and health-supportive shot.

Adjust the taste and potency of the fire cider by adding more or taking less of some of the ingredients, your call.

If you don't like pineapple, you can use apple instead (this is what we often add in the recipe back at home). Just make sure to remove the seeds before adding them to the blend.

You can also use fresh cayenne pepper instead of powder for a spicier cider. However, I opted for powdered cayenne in the recipe to make it manageable for children as well.

Using Plants **The Amish Way**

Amish Painkillers

Introduction

These natural painkillers are used in a host of ways in the Amish communities. They are used to treat pain orally (such a cough or respiratory condition), topically (for relief from blisters, rashes, sore muscles., etc.) and as poultices for pain relief from both internal and external wounds and conditions.

Amish Multi-Purpose Pain Relief Elixir

This Amish painkiller elixir helps to reduce not just pain, but also inflammation, which may be the primary or most poignant origin of the internal or external discomfort.

You can use either fresh or dried herbs and plants for this recipe.

Ingredients

2 cups raw apple cider vinegar - preferably with *"the Mother"
½ cup dry dandelion flowers, leaves, and roots or 1 cup of fresh
¼ cup dry rosemary leaves or 1/2 of a cup of fresh

Materials

Mason jar or similar glass jar with a tight-fitting lid
Cheesecloth or a fine mesh strainer
Amber or dark glass bottle for storage (optional, but recommended)

Instructions

Step 1
If you are using fresh herbs or plants, rinse them to remove any insects or debris. Allow them to dry on a towel until they are 100 percent dry.

Step 2
Put the rosemary and dandelions in the Mason jar.

99

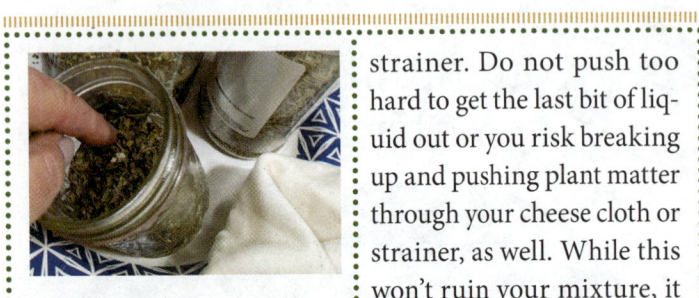

Using Plants THE AMISH WAY

Step 3
Pour in the apple cider vinegar. Make sure to entirely submerge the rosemary and dandelions.

Step 4
Place the lid and ring onto the jar and seal it tightly.

Step 5
Put the mixture in a cool dark place or the refrigerator for two weeks.

Step 6
Give the jar a couple of good shakes each day.

Step 7
Watch the level of the apple cider vinegar, if it bubbles up and leaves the plant matter exposed, pour in just enough more to cover the plants.

Step 8
Strain the mixture through the cheesecloth or fine mesh strainer. Do not push too hard to get the last bit of liquid out or you risk breaking up and pushing plant matter through your cheese cloth or strainer, as well. While this won't ruin your mixture, it will vastly shorten its shelf life because the plant matter will allow bacteria to grow inside. I recommend doing a double staring instead of pushing hard during a single strain. Remember, you are not trying to ring out a washcloth here, folks!

Step 9
Pour the mixture into a dark bottle if you have one, or store in a cool dark place until ready to use. When mixed and stored properly, the Amish elixir may last close to 24 months - especially if you used dry and not fresh herbs.

*Apple Cider Vinegar with "the Mother" is considered the purest form of ACV. It has not been filtered or refined and left in its completely natural state. The good existing bacteria, a.k.a. "the Mother" has not been destroyed during processing. Raw and unrefined ACV will typically boast a thick and cloudy appearance. If you do not have raw ACV, use what you have on hand and stockpile raw ACV when you can.

Topical Use
One of the most popular and possibly the most effective ways to use this Amish painkiller recipe is topically. The all-natural elixir can be applied right onto the part of the body that is suffering from inflammation due to arthritis, joint, tendon, or muscle pain. Just soak a cloth in the Amish elixir and then wrap it around or place it upon the sore area of the body. When treating smaller areas, using a cotton ball of Q-tip is recommended.

Full Body Soak
Run warm bather water and then pound in 1 cup of the all-natural Amish painkilling elixir and stir it in a bit with your arm. Soak in the tub for a good 25 minutes to help reduce inflammation and stiffness - especially in the joints.

Drinking
You can also drink the Amish elixir to help with internal pain and inflammation. Simply mix about 2 teaspoons into a glass or tea or water and drink up to three times a day. If adding to water, consider adding a bit of honey or lemon to improve the taste - the apple cider vinegar can be a bit overwhelming.

Warm Poultice/Compress
Warm the Amish elixir just slightly until it feels cozy warm to the touch. Soak a cloth in the elixir and then apply it to the part of the body in need of pain relief. This method works especially well on sore muscles and tendons.

Massage Oil
Combine the Amish painkilling elixir using a 1-part elixir to 3 parts carrier oil ratio and stir well to combine. Recommended carrier oils include: olive, coconut, sunflower, arnica, or almond. Rub the mixture gently onto the afflicted area for quick pain relief. The massage oil method works particularly well for arthritis pain (especially in the fingers and toes), tendon, and nerve pain. If you have a sore back, this Amish elixir massage oil will likely become your new best friend.

Using Plants THE AMISH WAY

Amish Major Pain Relief Tincture

Wild lettuce has been used not just by the Amish, but also by our ancestors across the globe for major pain relief for centuries. If you or a loved one is suffering significant pain due to a wound, kidney stone, or other affliction, taking wild lettuce tincture, extraction, or tea may bring relief alongside conventional treatment. While wild lettuce is known to bring about potent pain relief by those who take it, the respite does not usually last long. You should expect to achieve a couple of hours of pain-free bliss after taking this natural "sedative" and painkiller.

Ingredients

1 cup of dried or fresh* wild lettuce leaves.

*If using fresh leaves, wash them and allow to completely air dry on a towel before use. You can also use the stem, but the Amish and many herbalists do not find the hard work of chopping the thick stems into small bits (you need a super sharp knife and muscles or a powerful blender to do this) worth the effort.

80 to 100 proof alcohol (vodka is typically used)

Materials

Mason jar or similar glass jar with a tight-fitting lid

Cheesecloth or a fine mesh strainer

Amber or dark glass bottle for storage (optional, but recommended)

Instructions

Step 1
Chop the leaves into fine pieces using a knife or herb scissors.

Step 2
Wash and sterilize the glass jars and firm fitting lids/rings that you are using. Allow them to dry thoroughly - the Amish sterilize them on very low heat in the oven.

Step 3
Place the chopped wild lettuce bits inside of the jar.

Step 4
Pour in just enough alcohol to cover the leaves. 1-part leaves to 5 parts alcohol are the most common ratio used. Leave a thumb's width of head space at the top of the jar.

Step 5
Store the jar of wild lettuce in a cool and dark place for four to six weeks. Shake the jar once a day. If the alcohol level goes below the plant matter, add in just enough to ensure all pieces are again covered.

Step 6
Strain the mixture through cheesecloth or a fine sieve. Do not push so hard that you force plant matter or tiny bits of plant matter, into the tincture collection bowl. I highly recommend straining twice. Putting a plate on top of the folded cheesecloth container the mixture and walking away for half and an hour is the best method to use during straining.

Step 7
Pour the tincture into small individual bottles, amber or dark ones if possible. Label, date, and store in a cool dry place until needed. When prepared and stored properly, the wild lettuce tincture should remain potent for at least three to four years - but possibly quite longer.

Using Plants THE AMISH WAY

*If you opt to use vegetable glycerin to make the maceration more kid friendly, it should last for at least two years, as well. When using a vinegar to also avoid the alcohol content, do not expect the wild lettuce extract to remain potent for more than 12 months.

Dosages:

For adults, wild lettuce tincture is commonly taken as 1 dropper full under the tongue (or 1 ounce mixed in with a strong flavored soft drink to dull its bitter taste) up to four times per day. For intense pain, some users have taken as much as a half to a full dropperful hourly as needed.

If you simply want to make a tea from wild lettuce, or need to use it quickly and there is no completed tincture on your shelf, consider placing up to 2 teaspoons of dried lettuce leaves with a single cup of boiling water poured over it. Allow the mixture to steep at a low simmer for at least 15 minutes before drinking. Wild lettuce tea is often consumed up to 3 times per day for adults who are trying to treat their pain naturally.

None of these Amish remedies are approved by the FDA and the dosages have not been evaluated by a medical professional. Simply because these are natural ingredients, does not mean that will not produce an allergic reaction in some people (either topically or internally) or negatively interact with prescription or over the counter medications. Always consult your doctor before embarking on any type of herbal supplement or remedy treatment plan.

SNAKE JUICE

No, this Amish natural remedy is not made with the venom or any other bodily fluid from a snake. The way it got its name is unknown, but however the moniker came about, this stuff gets the job done!

Amish snake juice is used to treat the pain and discomfort that stems from not just the common cold, but also for combating respiratory related pain provoked by strep throat, the flu, and pneumonia, as well. It is a staple in Amish households across USA.

It is at least typically as effective as Fire Cider, and in the Amish opinion, a lot simpler and quicker to make.

For instructions on how to make it, and for dosage recommendations, **please check page 89.**

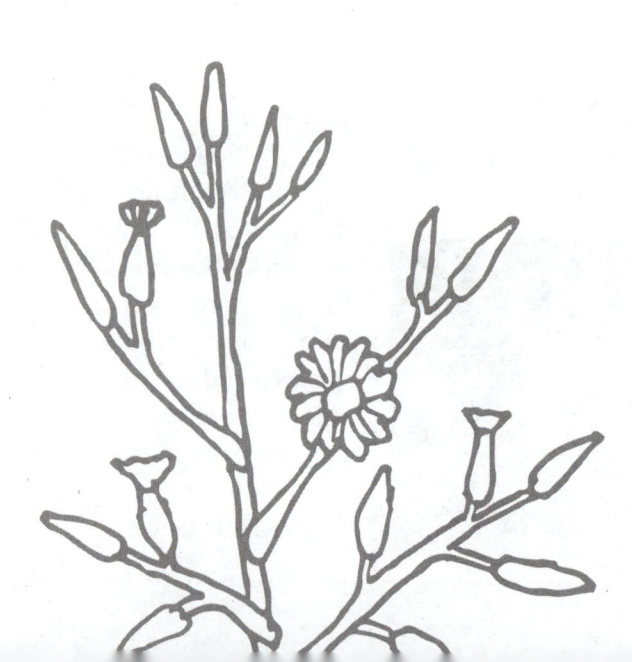

Using Plants THE AMISH WAY

Amish Black Drawing Salve

If you've ever run your hands across a rough-cut piece of wood, you may have ended up with a few splinters buried so deep, you couldn't see them, let alone get them out! Or perhaps you tried to pull them out, but they broke off and built an infection-insulated home inside your skin.

When school began in September, part of our duty as students included cutting wood for the upcoming winter. Grub Hill Schoolhouse is surrounded by woods. During our lunch break, which was 60 minutes long, we went into the woods to cut wood. One day, as I was pushing my hand saw back and forth at a pretty fast pace, my left hand slipped right underneath the saw. The back of my hand was cut open really badly. Blood shot out from the back of my hand as I had cut a vein. As I was running to the schoolhouse, I took my handkerchief and tightly wrapped it around my wrist to slow the bleeding. When I got to the schoolhouse, our teacher helped me clean the wound with water. After the wound was cleaned, the teacher helped me dress it with B & W ointment and wrap my hand with gauze and Petflex wrap. We kept the handkerchief around my wrist until my hand was wrapped in gauze and Petflex. When I came home from school, I told my mom what happened. My mom proceeded to open the bandage and wash the wound with clean water and alcohol to prevent any future infection. She continued to clean it and look for any sign of infection every night. She dressed the wound with new B&W ointment every evening until everything healed completely. Today I have a relatively small scar on my hand compared to the initial cut. Initially, I had lost some feeling in one of my fingers, but as the wound healed, the feeling came back. Going to a doctor never crossed my mind as I knew my mother was always prepared and knew how to take care of an injury like this.

Anyone would be lucky to have a homemade Amish Black Drawing Salve on hand if something similar happens. It is made with ingredients like kaolin clay, activated charcoal, and herbal oils, which not only pull objects and infections from the skin but help soothe and mend the skin. Because this salve is so effective at drawing, it's also used to treat boils and cystic acne.

There is more than one kind of "black salve." Just to be clear, this is NOT the black salve that contains bloodroot (*Sanguinaria canadensis*) or its synthetic companion, zinc chloride. If you search for "black salve" online, you might come across a deluge of horrifying images and accounts of people who tried to use black salve to treat cancerous tumors. This particular type of salve is also sometimes explicitly called "cancer salve," and many people who have used it have been harmed. However, the problem with these salves is the two mentioned ingredients. These substances should not be used casually because they have been linked to major medical issues, mainly the deterioration of healthy skin tissue.

Once again, the recipe that follows IS NOT for that kind of salve. You will not be using bloodroot or any synthetic chemicals. This one is gentler and, honestly, much more effective for a broader set of symptoms. However, some people do use this Amish Black Salve to treat warts, moles, and skin tags. The Amish Black Drawing Salve can be thought of as a versatile medicine cabinet staple that can be used for many things, such as extracting splinters and healing wounds.

Although it is known as Amish Black Salve, many argue that the recipe originated with the Native Americans. It's hard to say. It wasn't that long ago when everyone used herbal remedies as medicine, and there haven't been many conflicts between the Amish and Native American tribes. Interestingly, many aspects of both cultures are similar. It is reasonable to assume some knowledge could have been shared by the two cultures, as many cultures and races have braided their traditions since the dawn of American civilization. Besides, it's common for people from different cultures to share similar herbal knowledge. In any case, this salve is regularly made, used, and sold to others outside the Amish community who value their labor of love. Those who lack the knowledge to make their own herbal remedies and other goods at home flock to Amish-made interests because they recognize the superiority of their craftsmanship and appreciate the quality of the goods they produce. But this recipe isn't hard to make, and anyone with the desire and a little basic herbal knowledge can do it.

I'll demonstrate how to make it at home using a few really basic supplies. Some of them are even growing in your backyard. After gathering the necessary supplies, you'll need to allocate some time to infuse them into a base oil for this recipe (it's just a jar in a crock pot). If you have greater funds than time or energy, you can also purchase herbal oils at your local herb shop or online.

Ingredients

Although the ingredients may vary slightly, the main benefits you want to infuse into this salve are drawing, antibacterial, anti-inflammatory, analgesic, and skin-mending. This blend offers a little bit of each.

Comfrey

This is an herb that has anti-inflammatory properties and promotes wound healing. It is ideal for open wounds because it contains allantoin, which helps new skin cells form.

Plantain

Plantain is an herb with natural antibacterial and anti-inflammatory properties. It acts to prevent bacterial growth while relieving pain. You can use the strong pulling properties of plantain to get rid of skin impurities. Bee stings, splinters, and minor lumps and bumps can also all be effectively treated with it.

Calendula

This plant increases collagen synthesis, speeding up the healing process. It is excellent for rashes and eczema since it has antifungal and antibacterial properties and reduces redness and inflammation.

Lavender Oil

Lavender has antibacterial properties and reduces pain and inflammation. It also increases the production of collagen and speeds up wound healing.

Tea Tree

Warts, fungus, eczema, acne, and psoriasis can all be treated with tea tree oil. It is known for killing numerous viral and bacterial strains, including staphylococcus, which is responsible for acne and boils.

Olive Oil

Olive oil is full of antioxidants and vitamin E. It also has ingredients that may heal skin damage, like squalene and oleocanthal. Olive oil is hypoallergenic, anti-microbial, and non-toxic.

Vitamin E Oil

This is a potent skin antioxidant and preservative.

Honey

Honey is naturally anti-bacterial and moisturizing.

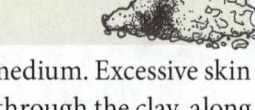

Kaolin Clay

Kaolin clay is an excellent drawing medium. Excessive skin oils can be extracted from the skin through the clay, along with any impurities contained within them.

Activated Charcoal

Charcoal has antibacterial and anti-inflammatory properties. It also helps to remove any impurities in the skin, which keeps your skin healthy and prevents the breakout of acne.

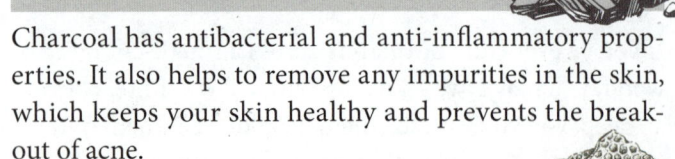

Beeswax

Beeswax moisturizes, conditions, relaxes, and soothes the skin. It repairs damage, encourages skin regeneration, and eases irritation. It also forms a nourishing, protective layer against toxins and solidifies this drawing salve.

What Can Amish Black Drawing Salve Be Used For?

As you can see, many skin-loving benefits come with this salve, which means it can be used for many things. Here are some traditional uses for this salve:

- Drawing out infection or foreign objects
- Removing splinters, slivers, and shavings
- Boils
- Warts
- Extracting venom from insects
- Bee stings
- Bug bites
- Allergic reactions
- Acne
- Rashes
- Healing wounds
- Poison Oak or Ivy
- Sores
- Dry skin
- Burns
- Yeast
- Stings from plants

How to Use Amish Black Drawing Salve

Use your salve by dabbing a bit on the affected area and immediately covering it with gauze or a bandage. The activated charcoal in this salve can be a bit messy, so you'll want a bandage to secure the salve to the affected area for drawing purposes. Allow it to draw out the infection or object for at least a few hours or overnight. Splinters and foreign objects may take some time to work their way out, and the salve may need to be reapplied over a couple of days.

Using Plants THE AMISH WAY

One batch will last quite a while, depending on how much you use it. If any irritation occurs, discontinue use. Although this salve is a fantastic natural remedy, it shouldn't replace proper medical attention. If you have any health issues or concerns, please consult with a healthcare professional.

Using Amish Black Salve for a Splinter

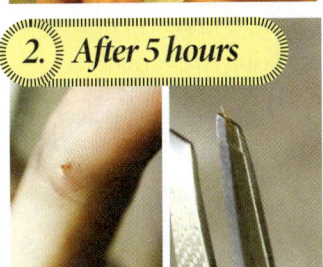

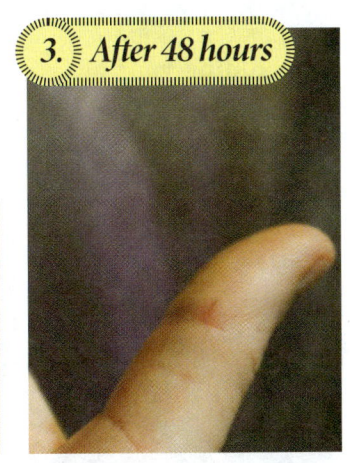

1.
2. After 5 hours
3. After 48 hours

Picking Plantain

In most areas, plantain grows freely, and it really likes to grow around rocks and sidewalks. Finding it yourself and drying it is a pretty easy task.

The Amish dry their herbs without the use of electricity, which is simple to do. All you need to do is let your plants breathe in warm, dry air until all the moisture evaporates. Be sure to place the herbs in a well-ventilated area. You can hang them by their stems or separate them onto a light, dry towel or screen so long as they aren't touching each other. They don't need sunlight to dry.

Before making my herbal oil, I selected a few plantain leaves by hand, washed them, and blotted them with a paper towel before drying them in my dehydrator for about four hours.

Infusing Herbal Oils for Amish Black Drawing Salve

Before making the salve recipe, you'll want to infuse the olive oil. I used plantain and calendula for my infusion and added comfrey herbal oil that I bought and already had on hand. But you can use all dried herbs and make your own oil entirely from scratch, as the Amish would do. Or you can purchase all the herbal oils already made. If you use all purchased oils, measure 15 drops of each oil into your measuring cup before adding the olive oil, so that your measurements come out the same. Herbs should be a 1:1 or 1:1:1 ratio. I used about ¼ cup of each.

You can solar infuse your oil, which is the preferred method of the Amish. To do that, simply add your herbs to a mason jar and cover them with olive oil. Let them sit in a sunny window for 4-6 weeks.

If you don't want to wait, you can extract your oils using the crock pot method, like I have done here. This will speed up the process, and you can have your own homemade herbal oil in as little as four to eight hours. The longer you let it go, the more potent your herbal oil will be.

Here's How It's Done:

Step 1.

Put equal amounts of dried herbs in a pint-sized mason jar, then fill it with enough olive oil to cover them and place the jar in a crock pot. the jar to keep things that don't belong in the oil out. Turn your crockpot onto the "keep warm" setting (about 100 F°) and let it warm for 4-8 hours.

*Please note that you don't want your crock pot to get too hot, or it will fry the herbs. Just a gentle warming will do.

Step 2.

Fill the crock with enough water to completely warm all the oil. You can place a towel in the bottom of the crock pot to protect the jar if you want, but we will not be heating it very much, so this is not a necessary step. Be sure to avoid getting water in the oil jar while filling the crock. You can place a piece of cheesecloth on the top of

Step 3.

Once the oil is done, snap a rubber band onto the ring over the cheesecloth and pour the oil through the cheesecloth into a bowl or separate jar.

You are now ready to make your salve.

Using Plants **THE AMISH WAY**

AMISH BLACK DRAWING SALVE

Essential Ingredients

8 tablespoons of calendula, comfrey, chickweed, and plantain-infused olive oil or a combination of infused oil and extracts—so long as it measures correctly
2 tablespoons of beeswax
1 teaspoon of vitamin E oil
10 drops of tea tree oil, or 5 drops of tea tree and 5 drops of lavender essential oil
1 tablespoon of unprocessed honey
2 tablespoons of activated charcoal
3 tablespoons of kaolin clay

Materials

A bowl
A spoon
A double boiler or pan of water and metal or glass bowl
A pint-size mason jar
A piece of cheesecloth
A crock pot or use solar-infused oils
A container for storing your salve

Instructions

Step 1
Start heating a double boiler on the stovetop with a little water if you're using one. If you're using a bowl and a pan of water, add a little water to the pan first, then set the glass or metal bowl on top of the pan so that the steam from the water can start heating the bowl's contents.

Step 2
Start adding your oils. If using store-bought oils, add those to your measuring spoon first, then top it off with olive oil or your homemade herbal oil.

Step 3
After all the oils are in the pan, add the honey and stir until it's dissolved. This step is essential because if you don't stir it well, you will have clumps of honey in your salve.

Step 4
Now add the beeswax, stirring until completely melted.

Step 5
Add the essential oils and stir again.

Step 6
Now remove the pan from the heat and stir in the remaining ingredients.

It will thicken quickly because of the clay.

Step 7
Working quickly, fill your storage container(s) with the salve and let it sit until it is solid. Be careful with it, as it will stain your linens.

Burns and Wounds Ointment

When school began in September, part of our duty as students included cutting wood for the upcoming winter. Grub Hill Schoolhouse is surrounded by woods. During our lunch break, which was 60 minutes long, we went into the woods to cut wood.

One day, as I was pushing my hand saw back and forth at a pretty fast pace, my left hand slipped right underneath the saw. The back of my hand was cut open really badly. Blood shot out from the back of my hand as I cut a vein. As I was running to the schoolhouse, I took my handkerchief and tightly wrapped it around my wrist to slow the bleeding. When I got to the schoolhouse, our teacher helped me clean the wound with water. After the wound was cleaned with water, the teacher helped me dress the wound with B&W ointment and wrap my hand up with gauze wrap and pet flex wrap. We kept the handkerchief around the wrist until my hand was wrapped in gauze and pet flex. When I came home from school, I told my mom what happened. My mom proceeded to open the bandage, wash the wound with clean water and alcohol to prevent any future infection in the wound. My mom continued to clean the wound and look for any sign of infection every night. She dressed the wound with new B&W Ointment every night until everything healed completely.

Today, I have a relatively small scar on my hand compared to the initial cut. Initially, I had lost some feeling in one of my fingers. As the wound was healing, the feeling came back to my finger. Going to a doctor never crossed my mind, as I knew my mother is always prepared and knows how to take care of an injury like this, and below I will show you exactly how you can prepare this ointment yourself.

How Does B&W Ointment Work?

Keim's ointment recipe looks a lot like spun honey. It is made simply and quickly, typically on a wood burning stove. Ideally, the Amish burn ointment contains honey, olive oil, wormwood, myrh, aloe vera gel, white oak bark, wheat germ, and comfrey, lanolin, and simmered burdock leaves.

Because the Amish are not Amazon online shoppers, they use what ingredients are in season or have been dried and stored to make the B&W Ointment. Keim offers many suggestions for alternatives to the less active and non-primary ingredients. When I made the ointment, I never used comfrey.

Once the ointment is made, the burdock leaves (or broadleaf plantain leaf substitute) are simmered just enough to make them pliable. Typically, the salve is slathered onto the simmered leaves which are then placed upon the burn or wound before the area is covered in gauze. This process is repeated three times per day until the wound is healed enough on its own to stop or simply to merely apply the B&W Ointment directly. Amish users believe that this now highly popular ointment does not kill good bacteria along with the bad ones, just like commercial antibiotic ointments do. This is because the most active and prime ingredient in the B&W Ointment is honey, which has anti-inflammatory and antioxidant properties.

Make sure to gently remove the leaf and any remaining ointment as carefully as possible to avoid tearing the skin or exposing it to air more than is absolutely necessary.

Other Uses of the Amish Burn and Wound Ointment

Members of the Amish community also use the B&W Ointment to treat tissue injuries, sunburns, eczema, chapped lips, and chapped skin.

Using Plants THE AMISH WAY

Ingredients

As with any recipe, be it herbal medicine or food, everyone has their own unique twist and preferences and the same can be said with homemade B&W Ointment. The Amish who make their own ointment instead of buying it from an Amish supply store, use the items they have on hand that produce optimal skin suppleness and pro-biotic results. In essence, it would be rare to find two tubs of homemade B&W Ointment created in the exact same way.

Growing your own burdock plants is the best way to have this valuable ingredient, buying them is princely and because they need to be simmered, they must be fresh and not dried. Broadleaf plantain survives the winter in most climates in the United States, boast healing properties of their own, and are large enough to be used (overlapped, if necessary, on large burns or wounds) in place of burdock. Do not attempt to use mullein or lamb's ear leaves, while large, they are too thick and absorbent and do not work well in this ointment recipe.

Burdock Leaf Benefits

Burdock is believed to have a high content of vitamins and minerals and is often used in herbal pills, tinctures, ointments, salves, teas, or dried roots recipes. The leaves are approximately the same size as an adult human hand when harvested at maturity. When stored in a dark and warm place, they can remain viable for rehydrating and simmering in water for about seven days.

Herbalists have traditionally used burdock leaves as a natural anti-inflammatory, anti-fungal; or toxin purifier are needed. If you cannot use burdock leaves and use broadleaf plantain instead, I highly recommend tossing in a few drops of burdock essential oil - and adding it to your survival apothecary pantry in sizable quantities. Other burdock leaf alternatives include: lettuce leaves, grape leaves, or mixing all of the ingredients together to make a flaxseed paste and not use a leaf at all - if that is your only option during an emergency.

Honey Benefits

Honey is believed to have anti-inflammatory, antioxidant and antibacterial agents - which promote more rapid healing while helping to keep the skin supple. Due to its thickness, honey also prevents exposure to air and debris when being used to cover a burn or wound.

Lemons

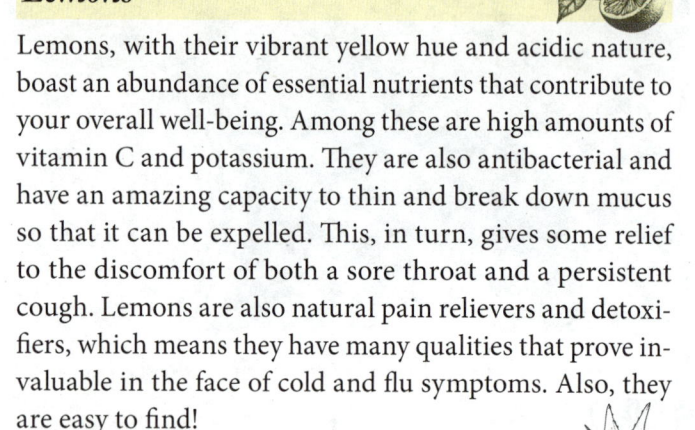

Lemons, with their vibrant yellow hue and acidic nature, boast an abundance of essential nutrients that contribute to your overall well-being. Among these are high amounts of vitamin C and potassium. They are also antibacterial and have an amazing capacity to thin and break down mucus so that it can be expelled. This, in turn, gives some relief to the discomfort of both a sore throat and a persistent cough. Lemons are also natural pain relievers and detoxifiers, which means they have many qualities that prove invaluable in the face of cold and flu symptoms. Also, they are easy to find!

Aloe Vera Gel

This gel also possesses anti-inflammatory, skin protection, anti-bacterial, anti-viral, antiseptic, and wound healing properties. It also helps to keep the skin supple and may provide a cooling sensation when applied to a burn.

Olive Oil

This carrier oil has a high percentage of antioxidants and anti-inflammatory properties. Olive oil also helps to keep the skin supple. Like aloe vera gel and honey, olive oil is a must when making Amish B&W salve because it too is one of the primary active ingredients. Only substitute with coconut oil, almond oil, jojoba oil, or vegetable glycerin if it is an absolute must.

Wheat Germ Oil

Wheat germ is believed to have anti-inflammatory and antioxidant properties. The oil also may help to fight disease and infection. It is wonderful to include in the Amish burn and wound ointment if you have it on hand when it is needed. You can purchase this shelf-stable ingredient so it is handy when needed. If you do not have wheat germ oil on hand, cinnamon oil is a viable alternative.

Lanolin

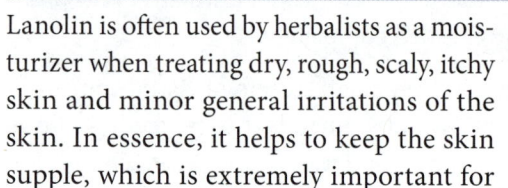

Lanolin is often used by herbalists as a moisturizer when treating dry, rough, scaly, itchy skin and minor general irritations of the skin. In essence, it helps to keep the skin supple, which is extremely important for healing in a burn and wound ointment. While you can render your own lanolin if you keep sheep, it can also be purchased from an herbal retailer or even on Amazon. If you do not have lanolin on hand, jojoba oil or argan oil are viable alternatives.

Using Plants THE AMISH WAY

Myrrh Essential Oil

Myrrh oil is believed to be helpful in many ways, when it comes to dealing with different types of health issues. It is often used topically, as it can reduce eczema or scars and it might help to hydrate the skin. Please be careful with this ingredient, as it is not recommended to be used by pregnant women or by people who deal with serious medical conditions. Always seek advice from a specialist before using the oil topically.

Vegetable Glycerin

This type of carrier oil glycerin has a high concentration of vitamins and minerals and creates a bacteriostatic environment that in turn helps to thwart microbes in and around the burn or wound.

Substitutes for vegetable glycerin include:

- **Geranium Oil** – antiseptic, aids in wound healing, and is anti-inflammatory
- **Frankincense Oil** – anti-inflammatory and helps promote healing.
- **Lavender Oil** – antioxidant, antimicrobial and very soothing for the skin.

White Oak Bark

The bark from the white oak tree has also been a go-to ingredient for natural healers for centuries. The tannins the bark contains an astringent that has been used to address a wide variety of skin issues, to foster enhanced wound healing, and also to decrease inflammation.

To harvest white oak inner bark, scrape off the thin layer of the outer bark first. Use a knife to make a shallow cut through the bark to get to the inner portion that is most regularly used in herbal remedy recipes.

Make an infusion from the white oak bark before using in the burn and wound ointment. Finely chop the bark and then place it in a carrier oil (use olive oil on any of the other above recommended carrier oils) inside of a Mason ja and allow it to stand for at least four or preferably six weeks - strain through cheesecloth or a fine sieve (or both) and use. For a quicker and more modern method, place the finely chopped white oak bark into a crockpot with the carrier oil and warm it through for two to four hours, and then follow these tips above.

Marshmallow Root

The root from the marshmallow plant is believed to support overall skin health and to also promote wound healing. Marshmallow root may also soothe skin redness, relieve inflammation, and infuse moisture into the skin. Marshmallow root substitutes include: Aloe vera, jewelweed, plantain leaves, Althaea officinalis, Calendula, chamomile, Curcuma longa, Eucalyptus, and Jojoba.

Comfrey

Both the leaves and the roots from the comfrey plant contain a substance that may help new skin cells grow, called allantoin. The comfrey plant has also been used by herbalists to reduce inflammation and to help keep the skin supple and healthy. The plant is also used in ointments and salves created to help heal pulled ligaments and muscles, strains, sprains, fractures, to heal bruises, and to treat osteoarthritis. Turmeric, jewelweed and borage are quality substitutes for comfrey.

Lobelia Inflata - *Indian Tobacco Plant*

This plant is often used by natural healers to relax muscles and to treat skin infections, bruises, ringworm, and poison ivy. Chamomile, echinacea, and calendula are good substitutes for the lobelia inflata plant.

Warning

Some people who have used the Amish B&W Ointment have experienced hives, red pimples, overall redness on the skin, skin rashes, and a prickly feeling. It is largely believed that such minor skin reactions are in response to an allergic response to the burdock leaves.

Please note, John Keim states that a fever is a perfectly normal part of the healing process and not necessarily an indication that an infection is growing - just that the body is fighting it off. Keim suggests instead of panicking if a burn and wound patient develops a fever, to instead be on alert for a foul smell coming from the burn or wound to detect infection. Keim gives his patients vitamin C powder to combat a fever during burn and wound treatment - and likely in general.

Using Plants THE AMISH WAY

BURN AND WOUND OINTMENT

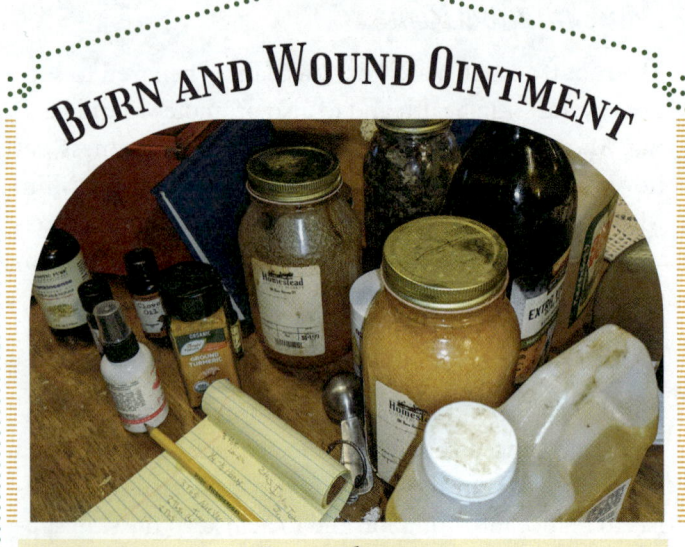

Ingredients

¼ to ½ cup raw honey (start with ¼ of a cup and slowly add more if the texture of the ointment is too runny/liquid-like)
1 cup of olive oil
3 tablespoons *Aloe vera* gel
2 tablespoons of comfrey infusion or substitute
2 tablespoons of marshmallow root infusion or substitute
2 tablespoons of Indian tobacco plant infusion or substitute
1 tablespoon of white oak bark infusion
15 drops of myrrh essential oil
15 drops of burdock essential oil - if not using burdock leaves
15 drops of wheat germ oil
½ teaspoon of vegetable glycerin or 15 drops of essential oil substitute
Beeswax pastilles*

Instructions

Step 1
Gather your ingredients and recipe before starting to make the Amish B&W Ointment.

Step 2
Measure the beeswax pastilles and place them into the crockpot on low. Do not cover the crockpot with the lid, that creates too much steam and will make the wax gooey.

Step 3
Spread the wax out in an even and thin layer so they melt quickly. There is no real need to stir while the wax melts unless you are doing a large batch and have wax that is a few inches thick or more.

Step 4
It will typically take roughly 30 minutes for a single cup of wax to melt completely. Always stir first before assuming the wax is completely melted just to make sure none of the pastilles is still slightly solid.

Step 5
Pour in all of the ingredients except the essential oils and lanolin and stir to combine thoroughly. It will take the honey about 5 minutes or so to melt into the mixture. Stirring helps the process along a bit.

Step 6
Add in the lanolin and stir again to combine. It will also take the lanolin about 5 minutes to melt down into the mixture.

Step 7
Turn off the heat and drop in the essential oils.

Step 8
Pour the Amish B&W Ointment into a plastic or glass container with a firm fitting lid and store in a cool, dry, and dark place until needed. You can use the ointment immediately after it cools down - spread it gently onto your recommended leaf of choice after dipping them into boiling water just enough to make them supple.

*General rule of thumb for wax measurements are: 1 part beeswax with 5 parts natural carrier oil.

A 1:5 wax-to-oil ratio creates a soft, spreadable balm or ointment.

If you use a 1:6 ratio, the recipe will result in a very soft and gooey salve.

A 1:3 ratio will give you a salve consistency which spreads slightly less easily than an ointment.

Using Plants THE AMISH WAY

Deep, Penetrating Ointment for Aching Joints and Sore Muscles

Aching Joints & Sore Muscles Ointment

In case of struggling with knee and joint pain, here's an herbal remedy that has been a go-to for years in the community. This simple yet powerful remedy harnesses the potent properties of rosemary, comfrey, black cohosh, and juniper essential oil – a quartet of scientifically recognized botanical powerhouses for joint and muscle comfort.

Ingredients

½ cup olive oil
¼ cup dried rosemary leaves
¼ cup dried comfrey leaves
¼ cup dried black cohosh root
30 drops juniper essential oil
¼ cup beeswax (you can use pellets or a beeswax bar)

Instructions

Step 1

Begin by combining the olive oil and the dried herbs in a double boiler, gently heating for about two hours. This slow infusion process allows the healing properties of the herbs to fully integrate with the oil.

Step 2

After two hours, strain the herb-infused oil through a fine mesh sieve or cheesecloth into a clean container, discarding the residual herbs.

Step 3

Next, return the strained oil to the double boiler and add the beeswax pellets. Heat gently until the beeswax has completely melted into the oil. Now comes the juniper essential oil. Remove the mixture from heat, add the juniper essential oil, and stir well to ensure it is evenly distributed.

Step 4

While the mixture is still in its liquid state, pour it into tins or glass jars and allow them to cool completely.

As it cools, your mixture will solidify into your finished salve.

How to Use

Using the salve is as simple as it gets. Scoop out a small amount and massage it into your knees or any other joint experiencing discomfort. The warmth of your skin will soften the salve, aiding absorption and driving the therapeutic ingredients to the site of pain.

For minor aches and pains, applying the salve once or twice a day should suffice. In more severe cases, you may benefit from using the salve three to four times daily. Listen to your body and adjust accordingly. Remember, the salve's effectiveness is not merely in its frequency of use, but in the consistency of its application over time. Also, while this salve aims to provide natural relief, it's important to consult a healthcare professional for persistent or worsening symptoms.

Storage

Your homemade salve can be stored in the fridge and should retain its potency for about a year. You'll likely use it up before then, but if you notice any changes in smell, color, or texture, it's time to create a fresh batch.

Amish Parasite Flush

Parasitic infections have been a concern for human health for centuries, leading many traditional cultures to develop natural remedies to combat these invaders. The Amish Anti Parasite Flush is a well rounded herbal tincture that blends herbs and seeds known for their anti-parasitic properties. This tincture combines wormwood, pumpkin seeds, thyme, garlic, fennel seeds, and cloves, each contributing unique compounds that work together to eliminate parasites and support overall health.

This tincture is effective against a variety of intestinal parasites, making it perfect for maintaining intestinal health and flushing out parasites. With its broad spectrum of anti-parasitic action it combats common parasites such as roundworms, pinworms, and giardia, which can cause significant gastrointestinal discomfort and health issues. Additionally, the tincture is effective against tapeworms, hookworms and flatworms. Making this a simple yet very effective go-to remedy!

Amish Parasite Flush Tincture

Materials

Measuring scale
Measuring cups
Blender or pestle and mortar
Garlic press
2 sterilized glass jars or bottles with tight-fitting lids
Fine mesh strainer or cheesecloth
Dark glass dropper bottles
Labels

Ingredients

10g dried wormwood
20g ground raw whole pumpkin seeds
10g dried thyme
20g crushed garlic
10g fennel seeds
10g cloves
350 ml 70% grain alcohol
150 ml spring water, filtered or distilled

Using Plants The Amish Way

Instructions

Step 1
Use a blender or pestle and mortar to grind 20g the pumpkin seeds until the seeds are ground and the shells broken.

Step 2
Use a garlic press or a mortar and pestle to crush the fresh garlic cloves.

Step 3
Ensure all herbs are dried and measured accurately.

Step 4
Place the dried wormwood, ground pumpkin seeds, dried thyme, crushed garlic, fennel seeds, and cloves in a sterilized glass jar or bottle.

Step 5
Pour 350 ml of 70% grain alcohol over the herbs.

Step 6
Add 150 ml of spring water (filtered or distilled) to the mixture.

Note: If using 95% grain alcohol in order to make 500ml of tincture you will need to use 260 ml of grain alcohol combined with 240 ml of water to make your menstruum.

Step 7
Shake the jar gently to make sure all the herbs are covered by the liquid.

Step 8
Seal the jar tightly with a lid. Label the tincture with name and date. Store the jar in a cool, dark place, shaking it gently once a day to help the extraction process.

Step 9
Allow the mixture to steep for 4-6 weeks. This extended period allows the alcohol and water to extract the medicinal properties from the herbs.

Step 10
After 4-6 weeks, strain the liquid through a fine mesh strainer or cheesecloth into a clean jar, ensuring all solids are removed.

Step 11
Pour the strained tincture into dark glass dropper bottles for storage. Label the bottles with the name of the tincture and the date it was made.

Using Plants **THE AMISH WAY**

How to Use

Take two-thirds (2/3) of your weight in kilograms in drops, three times a day. This means each day you should take twice your weight in drops, divided into three doses. Let's say your weight is 60 kg.

Twice your weight: 2×60=120 drops per day.

Each dose: 120÷3=40 drops per dose.

When to take: Before breakfast, lunch and dinner.

Mix the tincture with a small amount of water. Take 20 minutes before each meal. It is often recommended to cycle the use of the tincture, taking it for 2-4 weeks followed by a break of 1-2 weeks if needed. This helps prevent potential toxicity.

The Ingredients and Their Anti-Parasitic Properties

Wormwood (Artemisia absinthium)

Wormwood is a powerful herb used for centuries to treat intestinal worms and other parasitic infections. Key compounds in wormwood, such as thujone and isothujone, are neurotoxic to parasites, causing paralysis and death. Additionally, there are other compounds in wormwood that weaken parasite cell membranes, contributing to their destruction.

Thyme (Thymus vulgaris)

Thyme is a fragrant herb with potent antimicrobial properties, making it effective against various parasites. Its primary active components, thymol and carvacrol, disrupt parasite cell membranes, leading to their death. Additionally, thymol's antifungal properties help maintain a healthy balance of gut flora, while rosmarinic acid reduces inflammation and supports immune function, enhancing the body's ability to fight parasitic infections.

Pumpkin Seeds (Cucurbita pepo)

Pumpkin seeds are renowned for their ability to fight parasitic infections, especially in the digestive tract. The active compound cucurbitacin paralyzes parasites, preventing them from adhering to the intestinal walls and facilitating their expulsion from the body. The fatty acids and amino acids in pumpkin seeds also support gut health and enhance the immune system's ability to combat infections.

Garlic (Allium sativum)

Garlic is well-known for its broad-spectrum antimicrobial properties. The sulfur-containing compound allicin, released when garlic is crushed or chopped, interferes with the metabolism of parasites, causing their death. Another compound, ajoene, disrupts parasite cell membranes, making survival difficult. Garlic also boosts the immune system and promotes detoxification, aiding in the elimination of parasites.

Using Plants THE AMISH WAY

Fennel Seeds (Foeniculum vulgare)

Fennel seeds, known for their culinary and medicinal properties, have mild anti-parasitic effects. The compound anethole has antimicrobial properties and helps expel parasites from the digestive tract. Additionally, fennel seeds support digestion, relieve intestinal cramps, and alleviate symptoms like bloating and gas, common during parasitic infections.

Cloves (Syzygium aromaticum)

Cloves are highly effective in treating parasitic infections due to their rich eugenol content. Eugenol is toxic to parasite eggs and larvae, disrupting their life cycle and preventing reproduction. Cloves' antimicrobial properties cleanse the digestive tract of harmful organisms, and their tannins help heal and protect the intestinal lining damaged by parasitic infections.

Precautions

Thujone, present in wormwood, can be toxic in large amounts and should be avoided by individuals with kidney disorders, seizure disorders, or liver disease. Pumpkin seeds may interact with blood pressure medications. Thyme can slow blood clotting and should be used cautiously by those with bleeding disorders or allergies to Lamiaceae family plants. Garlic can cause gastrointestinal upset, if this occurs discontinue use. Discontinue use before surgery.

Fennel seeds can affect hormone-sensitive conditions and should be avoided by those allergic to carrots, celery, or mugwort. Cloves, rich in eugenol, also increase bleeding risk and can cause allergic reactions or oral irritation in high doses; they should be used cautiously by individuals with bleeding disorders or those taking anticoagulant medications.

The Amish Anti Parasite Flush tincture, while effective for adults, contains ingredients that may not be entirely suitable for children, especially in the concentrations used for medicinal purposes. Wormwood, in particular, should be avoided due to its potential toxicity. Other ingredients like pumpkin seeds and garlic can be used in smaller, food-safe amounts, but thyme, fennel seeds, and cloves should be administered with caution.

This tincture should be avoided by pregnant and breastfeeding women.

Using Plants THE AMISH WAY

How to Treat a Cavity the Amish Way

I remember growing up, I washed my teeth about once a week. I usually brushed my teeth before going to church. We did not use regular toothpaste; we used baking soda. Luckily, we were not exposed to all the sweets and processed food that is available to the outside world. My Dad, who lived his whole life as a Swartzentruber Amish man, I never once saw my dad brush his teeth. I also never heard him say anything about a toothache. Of course, I am not recommending that people stop brushing their teeth. However, I do think there's a reason my Amish father never had oral health issues even though he did not brush his teeth. My Dad was very particular on how our food was raised. He did not allow us to spray any kind of chemicals to kill the never-ending weeds that always grow so fast; instead, we had to cultivate numerous times in order to keep the weeds under control. He was also equally particular about the fertilizer that was used on the plants.

My Dad always used fish oil fertilizer. Whenever we went fishing, we kept the remains in a stainless bucket with a lid, added some sawdust, and let them decompose for about a month before using it. This fertilizer is very stinky after a month, but once we got it onto our plants, it did wonders.

In this chapter, we will explore together the Amish approach to treating cavities, tooth pain, and other issues without relying on modern dentistry.

In some very strict communities, the approach to cavities and overall dental care is incredibly simple… just pull all of your teeth (healthy or not) and replace them with dentures. While that is surely not the route many (or any) of us would chart, especially during SHTF, it does adhere strictly to the Plain People way of life. By pulling their teeth and replacing them with dentures, the Amish believe they are averting oral health problems both current and down the road in the most natural and least expensive manner possible.

Using Plants **THE AMISH WAY**

However, there are other tips and tricks the Amish use, that can help you treat your cavities, but not only:

Clove Oil

Cloves contain a compound called eugenol, which has antimicrobial and analgesic properties. As my Amish friends and neighbors readily attest, applying clove oil topically to the affected area can almost instantly provide temporary relief from tooth pain.

How to Use It

Dilute a drop of clove oil with a carrier oil (like olive oil) and apply it to the affected area using a cotton ball. Avoid using undiluted clove oil directly on the gums or skin, as it may cause irritation.

Saltwater Rinse

A saltwater rinse can help reduce inflammation and kill bacteria in the mouth, promoting faster healing.

How to Use It

Mix half a teaspoon of salt in eight ounces of warm water and stir until the salt dissolves. Swish the mixture in your mouth for 30 seconds, then spit it out. Repeat this process a few times daily.

Herbal Remedies

Healing Tea

One of the cornerstones of Amish oral health remedies is the use of healing teas. These teas, often made from a combination of herbs such as chamomile, sage, peppermint, and calendula, are recommended for their antibacterial and anti-inflammatory properties. Many Amish swear by using herbal teas to help alleviate tooth pain and promote oral health by reducing inflammation and combating bacterial growth. You can start consuming these teas immediately after starting to feel a slight discomfort.

Plantain Leaf Poultice

You can crush the leaves and apply them directly to the affected area for a couple of minutes. However, it is important to note that plantain leaf poultices are best used as a complementary measure and not as a replacement for professional dental care.

Oil Pulling

This practice involves swishing oil in the mouth to draw out toxins and improve oral hygiene.

There are several types of oils that can be used for oil pulling, but two of the most commonly used ones are coconut oil and sesame oil. Many prefer coconut oil because it has a more pleasant taste. It contains lauric acid, which has been found to combat harmful bacteria in the mouth. Sesame oil, on the other hand, is known for its ability to reduce plaque.

When performing oil pulling, it is important to follow these steps for effective results:

1. Start by taking approximately one tablespoon of your chosen oil and place it in your mouth.
2. Swish the oil around your mouth, making sure to pass it between your teeth and around your gums.
3. Continue this swishing motion for about 15-20 minutes. It may be difficult at first, so it is best to start with a shorter duration and gradually increase it as you become more comfortable.
4. Spit out the oil in a trash can or toilet - do not swallow it, as it may contain harmful bacteria.
5. Rinse your mouth thoroughly with water and brush your teeth as usual.

Using Plants THE AMISH WAY

Homemade Dental Care Products

DIY Amish Toothpaste

In the community, store-bought toothpaste is replaced with homemade concoctions free from additives and harsh chemicals. These toothpaste alternatives often contain a combination of baking soda, salt, and finely ground herbs to maintain oral hygiene.

Ingredients

2 c clay powder (bentonite or kaolin)
20 drops of essential peppermint oil
10 drops of clove oil
5 drops of fennel oil
15 drops of tea tree oil
10 drops of cinnamon oil

You will also need a large bowl, a whisk, and a storage container. If you want, you can use frankincense or myrrh essential oils instead of clove or cinnamon. But be aware that the taste may not be as pleasant. Additionally, some people choose to add a small amount of fine sea salt or baking soda to the mix.

Instructions

Step 1
Dump the clay powder into your bowl.

Step 2
Drop the essential oils into the clay one at a time, being careful to distribute them everywhere rather than just in one area.

Step 3
Mix all of the oils into the powder thoroughly with a whisk. Once the oils are fully incorporated, transfer the tooth powder to a lidded storage container and store it in the bathroom, where you normally keep your toothpaste.

To Use Your Amish Toothpaste:

Simply dip your toothbrush into the powder after wetting it with water or peroxide. It will naturally solidify into a paste. Then brush as usual.

Herbal Mouth Rinses

Distinct from commercial mouthwashes, the Amish create their own herbal mouth rinses using natural ingredients such as calendula, clove, and myrrh. These rinses are believed to possess antibacterial properties while promoting healthy gum tissue. These rinses are used both as a preventative measure and as a treatment for oral infections and inflammations.

Plus, do not forget that the Amish consume a lot of nutrient-rich foods, such as fresh fruits and vegetables, whole grains, and dairy products, which provide the body with essential vitamins and minerals necessary for healthy teeth and gums. They also avoid eating sugars or any processed foods that can alter the teeth's health.

Using Plants THE AMISH WAY

Amish Strength Juice

Amish Strength Tincture

Green oats (Avena sativa), otherwise known as milky oats have been harvested and used both medicinally and as foods for many generations. They are basically oats that haven't opened their flowers or produced seeds yet. They are still green in color and have a milky, white sap.

Being wind-pollinated, you will often find wild oats growing on the side of the road or popping up in your garden. In spring, you can use the green, fresh oat tops to boost your energy by turning them into a green-colored juice.

Why Use Green Oats Instead of Dried Oats?

When the oats are developing and are still green, they are higher in antioxidants and dopamine which are closely linked to improving mental health, cognitive function, and energy levels.

You can definitely harvest your green oats and eat them straight away, but this requires de-husking them first which can be a very tedious, but delicious method; just be prepared to 'pop' a large bowl of green oats to make a small smoothie. Of course, the other option is a green oat tea, which avoids having to de-husk them.

However, neither of these are long term methods since there is only a very narrow window of opportunity to harvest the oats in their "green" or "milky" stage; approximately a week.

A tincture, on the other hand, will allow you to benefit from green oats throughout the whole year by infusing the medicinal properties into either alcohol or glycerin.

How to Harvest Green Oats

First, make sure the timing is right: Select a single oat seed that is green, then plump and squeeze it. If it produces a white, milky juice, then it is ready to harvest. You want to harvest before the miniscule flower has appeared out of the tip of the oat.

Then, just like when you were a kid, gently grab the green stalk of the oat plant and slide your hand up the stalk which will pull off the green oats and deposit them straight into your palm. Easy.

Make sure to use your freshly harvested green oats as soon as possible (preferably within 24 hours).

Instructions

Once you have harvested your green oats, put them straight into a jar and cover them with either high alcohol (at least 40% alcohol), or diluted glycerin (1-part pure glycerin with 3-parts distilled water). Use a stick mixer to roughly blend the green oats.

Close the lid and put the jar in a cool, dark location and give it a little shake every day. Leave it for 2 weeks and then strain away the oats so that you are left with a green colored liquid.

Dosage and Shelf-life

Take approximately 1–2 droppers full (1.5 – 3 ml) three times a day.

This tincture should last approximately 1 year when stored in the fridge.

Using Plants THE AMISH WAY

Amish Strength Tonic

Ingredients

½ cup chopped onions
¼ cup minced garlic
¼ cup grated horseradish
¼ cup honey (add more to taste)
A dash of black pepper
A dash of cayenne pepper
1 cup raw apple cider vinegar

Instructions

Step 1: Prepare the Ingredients

Chop the onions, mince the garlic, and grate the horseradish.

Ensure all ingredients are fresh and of high quality.

Step 2: Mix the Ingredients

In a large glass jar, combine the chopped onions, minced garlic, and grated horseradish. Pour in the raw apple cider vinegar. Shake the jar a few times to mix the ingredients well.

Step 3: Add Honey and Spices

Add honey to the jar, adjusting the amount to your taste. Then, add a dash of black pepper and cayenne pepper. These spices will give the tonic a slight kick and additional health benefits. Shake the jar again to ensure everything is well mixed.

Step 4: Let It Infuse

Seal the jar tightly and let the mixture sit at room temperature for two weeks. During this time, shake the jar daily to help the ingredients infuse thoroughly.

Step 5: Strain and Store

After two weeks, strain the mixture using a fine mesh strainer or cheesecloth. Transfer the liquid to a clean jar or bottle. Store the tonic in the refrigerator, where it will stay fresh for up to a month.

Dosage and Use

To consume, dilute one tablespoon of the tonic in a glass of water and drink it in the morning.

This will provide you with an energy boost and support your overall health.

Preserving Food
The Amish Way

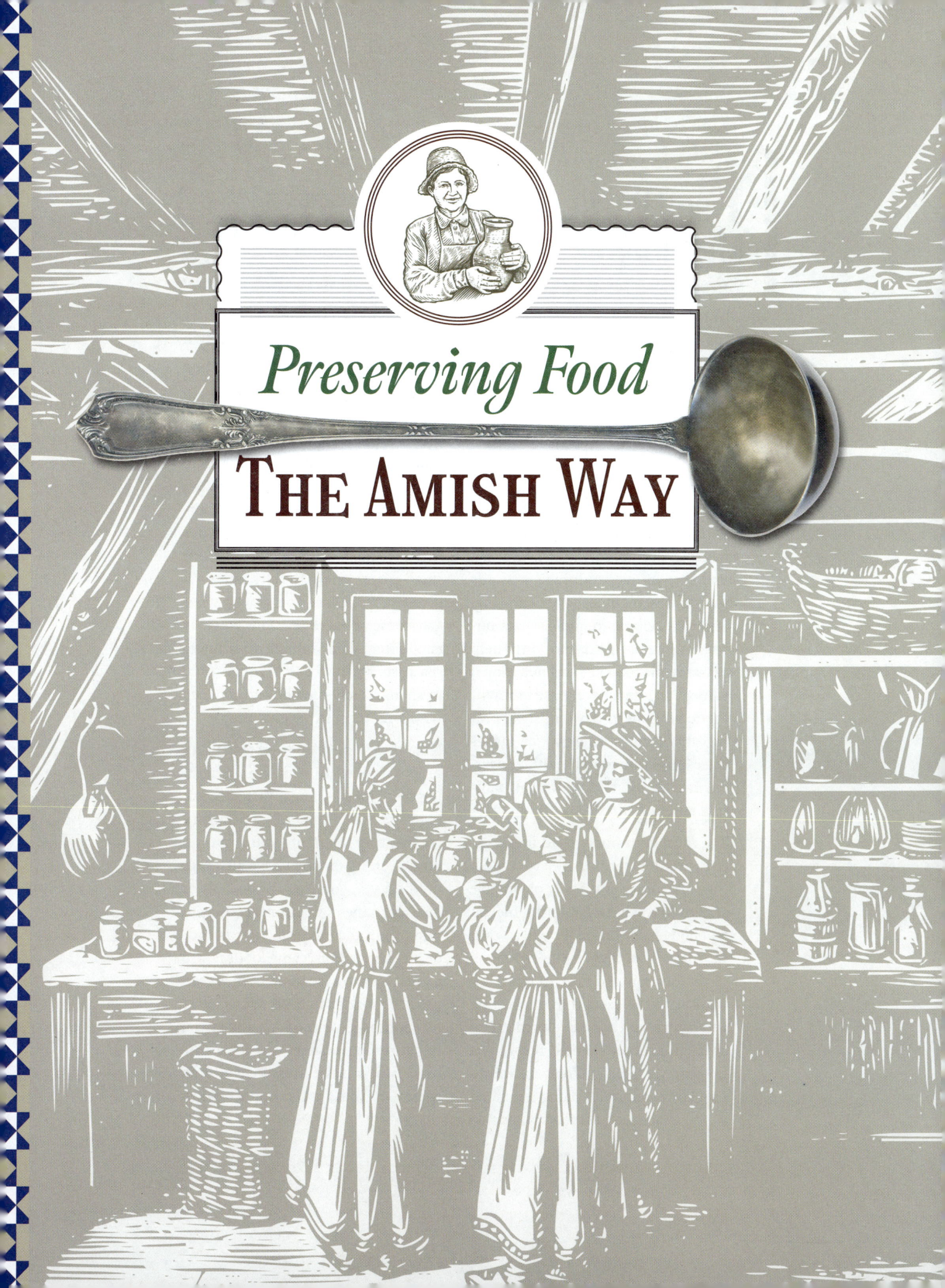

Food Preservation Methods

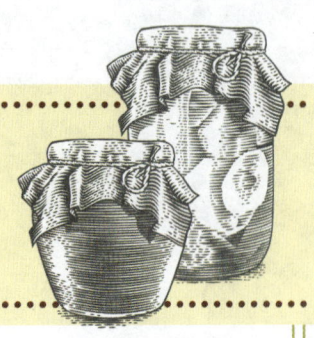

In this chapter, we are going to discuss a wide variety of techniques used by Amish communities to keep their food supplies stable and abundant for all and teach you how to do the same for yourself, your family, your friends, and your community.

There are a variety of components that go into long-term food preservation, from techniques such as pickling, freezing, drying, curing, dehydrating, and fermenting, to storage methods such as basement iceboxes, canning, and root cellars, to high-impact nutritional recipes that not only help preserve the food but add nutritional value. The Amish don't use any synthetic or modern-day industrial preservatives or pesticides, which makes their food cleaner and healthier overall, and we will stick with that tradition herein.

The most commonly used preservatives aren't expensive or hard to find, they are simple and easily obtainable staples like salt, sugar, lard, vinegar, and homemade brine. We will go over the majority of these methods for you in this section and explain how they work with the exception of canning and pantries as they are covered extensively in another chapter. Before you know it, you'll be well on your way to providing yours with a long-term food supply that is as nutritious as it is sustainable, and you won't have to worry about your ability to make it through any future societal hardships.

Another thing we'll be covering in this chapter is how to choose the right preservation methods for your current location and lifestyle and how to adapt techniques, spaces, and recipes to fit your specific needs so this information is applicable whether you live in a large home with a lot of land, or a small apartment in the city, and we'll give you some ideas on how to navigate some of the restrictions you may encounter when you rent your living space, such as how to source clean and fresh ingredients and how to come up with long-term storage solutions.

Note that there is no need to wait for an emergency to start implementing these food systems. Part of building your skills is practice, so start incorporating them into your routines now, even if you don't have a storage method yet, you can always half or quarter recipes for personal consumption or gift the excess to your friends or neighbors. Preserving foods is also a great way to save money since recipes keep foods safely on your shelves for months to years which allows you to gather ingredients when they are in-season or take advantage of bulk specials at your local farmers market.

How Natural Preservatives and Techniques Work

Natural preservatives like sugar and salt have been used by humans for centuries, and most of them work by reducing the water content in the foods you wish to preserve. This osmotic effect keeps bacteria and microbes like salmonella at bay because they can't multiply in low moisture. Let's take a quick look at each of these ingredients and learn a little about how they work.

Sugar

In addition to absorbing water, sugar also works to activate other ingredients that act as preservatives. For example, during the fermentation of foods like miso, sauerkraut, kimichi, and yogurt, sugars convert and produce organic compounds like lactic acid which not only kill bacteria, but help foods keep their natural coloring. It also works as a gelling or curing agent. "Sugaring" is also a common technique used for preserving dehydrated foods, especially fruits and vegetables, by packing them into a jar with either table sugar, honey, or molasses.

Salt

Like sugar, salt absorbs water from cells and can be used a sole preservative or in combination with other ingredients to enhance food longevity. A 20% sodium solution will literally kill bacterial growth all-together, while less concentrated solutions will work much like sugar by inhibiting microbial and bacterial growth. This common ingredient is so effective at removing water, that it is often used on its own to dehydrate or cure meats. Salt also works as a flavor enhancer and can give foods a more palatable texture.

Lard

When rendered properly, lard is an excellent food preservative. It is used mostly to lock-out bacteria and microbes by providing a thick barrier cover over your foods. Grease doesn't allow for bacterial growth so long as it is kept in a dark cool space like a pantry, root cellar, or basement, and it's easy to combine with salt for enhanced preservation properties. It is most often used to preserve meats. Tallow is a good alternative option to lard and works in a similar fashion, but can be harder and more expensive to source today, especially if you plan on storing a lot of meat.

For instructions on how to make it, please check page 132.

Vinegar

One of the most popular, effective, and affordable natural food preservatives is vinegar. When properly stored, it has an indefinite shelf-life. The low PH of vinegar is what keeps bacteria and microbes from growing, and its amazing flavor make it the most popular choice for pickling and extending the shelf life of dressings, sauces, and marinades. There is no shortage of vinegar varieties and it really doesn't matter which flavors you choose as long as you make sure it's a 5% acetic acid solution. This is the acidity level required for safety.

Brine

This salt and water solution is used to season, tenderize, and preserve foods. Brine is used in pickling, canning, as well as curing meats, and can be made easily by using a ratio of 1 cup of water to 1 tablespoon of sea salt, but many variations exist. We will include some traditional Amish Brine recipes in the pickling and meat curing sections of this chapter.

Amish Preservation Techniques

Cold Pickling

Pickling foods is a staple preservation technique in Amish communities that doesn't require canning. This method serves to extend the life of foods for 4 to 12 weeks in an ice-box or refrigerator, and provides a quick and easy way to practice brine recipes and flavor profiles which can later be used in canning as well. You can use this method to preserve vegetables, fruits, and meats, and there are no regional, climate, or space restrictions – and it prevents food waste.

The only special equipment you'll need are hot/cold safe glass containers with a lid, like a Mason or Parfait jar, a pot for boiling your brine, and a decent knife to cut up your foods. It is truly a simple process you can complete in 20 minutes or less. Included are the basic steps taken by the Amish in pickling any food item you desire, and following that are a few recipes and flavor combinations for you to try.

General Instructions

Step 1

Set up your clean empty jars on the counter next to your chopping area. Make sure all lids are accounted for.

Step 2

Chop up your ingredients into bite sizes, thins, rings, or spears so that the brine can soak through them and make it easy to get them in and out of your jar. Fill the jar until there is an inch of space left to the top, that way so there is plenty of room for growth. The brine will need to cover the contents of the jar completely even after the ingredients soak it all up.

Step 3

Make your brine by combining a ratio of 1 cup of vinegar to 1 tablespoon of sea salt into a pot. You may add sugar and other spices here if indicated by your recipe or desired flavor profile. Bring to a boil over medium heat until your salt (and sugar) has fully dissolved. Once your brine has cooled and feels warm, pour it over your chopped foods, close the jars, and put them in the ice-box or refrigerator.

It is best to store the jars for 3 days before consuming your pickled foods, but if you just can't wait that long, make sure you give the brine at least 24 hours to fully soak into your ingredients.

The active preservation agent in pickling is the salt and vinegar brine, but note that if you don't add sugar or other flavor profiles, your brine may be too acidic, salty, or bitter for your liking. Flavors make a big difference when it comes to the satisfaction of your pickled food experience, and adding that bit of sugar can cut down on the strong flavors associated with vinegar and some varieties of vegetables. Of course, if you are going for a sweet pickled flavor you can add more sugar, brown sugar, honey, or molasses too. Just remember to boil it all together.

When pickling raw meats, don't forget to cook them before consumption. This method will not only preserve your meat for a month, but it will also tenderize and flavor it for you. I love using this method when I get a piece of meat that's just too tough, or when I have some random leftover meats that shouldn't be refrozen.

Old-Fashioned Amish Ice-Box Pickles

Makes: 4 Quarts (One Gallon)

Here is a traditional Amish recipe for you to get started. Remember that you can swap out the vinegar for any flavor profile you prefer as long as it has a 5% acidity. When it comes to salt choices, kosher and sea salt are the most recommended because they have no additives or caking agents, but table salt will work in a pinch.

Materials

Large stock pot
Knives
Cutting board
Ladle
Measuring cups and spoons

Ingredients

About 12 medium cucumbers
4 cups of water
2 cups of 5% acidity vinegar
¼ cup of salt
1 ¾ cup of sugar
1 small onion
Handful of fresh dill (or 1tsp dried)
2 large cloves of garlic

Optional Ingredients

Small grape leaf
1 tsp dill seeds

Preserving Food **THE AMISH WAY**

You can begin by preparing your gallon jug or 4 quart-sized jars by washing them thoroughly. On your favorite cutting board, use a sharp knife and cut your grape leaf, peel your small onion and slice it thin, then peel and slice your garlic cloves. Split all ingredients into 4 equal parts and distribute them evenly through your quart-sized jars.

You can start washing your cucumbers now, and be sure to cut-off the edges. You will need around 12 medium sized cucumbers so be sure to adjust quantities if yours are on the smaller size. Large or over-sized cucumbers are not recommended as they are often riddled with large seeds and provide less flavor. Consider your purpose when choosing how to cut your vegetables here. You can slice in thin rounds or long slices for sandwiches, or cut into quarter wedges for a finger snack. Once they're all cut up, fill the jars and remember to leave some space at the top for the brine to cover them.

At this time you can start the brine. Put your water, vinegar, salt, sugar, and optional dill seeds into a pot and bring to a boil over medium heat. This should take about 3 minutes. Stir your mixture until the salt and sugar have fully dissolved, then let it cool down a little before adding it to your jars. You can use this time to clean up cuttings from your counter space. Once your jars are filled, fit the lids on securely and place them in your refrigerator. Although these are ready to eat after 24 hours, the Amish recommend waiting 3 days for best results. These pickles are always refreshing, crispy, and should keep in your ice-box or fridge for around 12 weeks.

This recipe works well with other flavor combinations, such as added celery or peppers. Don't be afraid to experiment.

Sun drying and solar dehydration

In this section we will cover traditional Amish methods of food preservation through direct sun drying as well as indirect solar powered dehydration. The 2 are very similar and often times the terms are used interchangeably. The main difference between these two systems is that one removes more water from foods than the other. Direct sun-drying reduces moisture by about 80%, whereas dehydrating removes up to 95%. Foods that have been dried or dehydrated can be stored for as long as 5 to10 years depending on the food variety and techniques used, and these methods can be combined with others for use in different kinds of recipes at a later date. For example, you can sun-dry a large amount of your tomato harvest, then store half of them dry, and choose pickling on canning for the rest.

Sun-drying foods is very simple, requires little equipment, and can be adapted to your specific living situation easily as it can be done in small or large batches in your garden, yard, porch, balcony, or even through one of your windows. Some people even use their cars!

The simplest form of direct sun-drying works best when the temperature is above 85°F/29.4°C and the relative humidity is below 60%. You just set your sliced fruit, vegetables, or herbs on a drying rack, cloth, or netting, cover with a cheesecloth or muslin and set it to dry. Fruits can take several days to dry fully, so be sure to bring it inside overnight and set it out again in the morning. If you don't have a drying rack you can make a simple one by stapling some mosquito netting, mesh, or tulle to a wooden frame. Any perforated material will do the trick. You could also use a cooling rack such as those used for cooling baked goods and cover them with a breathable material to keep bugs away. Herbs and vegetables like peppers can be placed in a simple netting and hung out to dry.

The best foods for DIRECT-SUN-DRYING

- Tomatoes
- Dates
- Figs
- Apricots
- Pears
- Peaches
- Apples
- Peppers
- Hot peppers
- Chilies
- Grapes
- Plums
- Kiwi
- Mushrooms
- Summer squash
- Zucchini
- Garlic
- Leafy greens
- Herbs

Preserving Food THE AMISH WAY

This method is NOT suitable for meat, but don't worry, we'll be covering that later in this chapter.

Here are some step-by-step tips from the Amish on how to prep your food for direct sun-drying.

Instructions

Step 1

Gather foods you wish to sun-dry and prepare your cutting area. Choose a well sharpened knife so that you don't damage or bruise your foods in the process. Wash everything thoroughly. Don't worry about letting it dry, just shaking it off is enough.

Step 2

Slice or wedge your food of choice as evenly as possible. Thinner slices and smaller wedges will dry faster, so keep that and your expected weather in mind. Peeling isn't necessary. For tomatoes, peppers, kiwis and cored apples, slicing works great. Wedges work better for apricots, pears, peaches, and apples that haven't been cored. Plumbs can also be wedged or cut in half, but can be left whole if you don't mind the process taking a little longer. Mushrooms, grapes, garlic, and herbs don't really require any special cutting style as they will dry out pretty quickly.

Step 3

If you are drying fruits and vegetables set out a bowl with lemon juice or vinegar (red wine or apple cider varieties work best), and soak your food in them for 5 minutes. Which you use depends on what you are drying and your preferred flavor profiles. For example, you can use lemon for kiwis, tomatoes, and apples, or vinegar for mushrooms, zucchini, and summer squash.

Step 4

Arrange your food on your chosen racks in one single layer, and make sure you keep your foods together in groups (tomatoes with tomatoes, zucchini with zucchini) because they have different water contents and drying times. Set your racks in your chosen area and let the drying begin. Don't forget to cover your food to keep insects away.

Step 5

Once a day, use a spatula to flip your food on the rack. This allows for more even drying and keeps food fresh on the underside.

The drying process often takes three to five days depending on both the food type and the relative humidity. Fruits and vegetables that are properly dried will look like all typical dried foods and should be movable (not brittle). You can test it by cutting a piece and giving it a good squeeze. If no liquid comes out, it's done. They should be soft and dry like the inside of a raisin or a prune.

Extra Amish Tips

- Sprinkle fine kosher salt on your mushroom, zucchini, tomato, and summer squash after they are arranged on your rack.

- Foods like peppers, hot peppers, and chilies can be hung instead of placed on a rack. If sliced into rings, just loop them on a string and hang it from both sides so they can't slide off. If cut in wedges, you can thread them with string, twine, or fishing wire. Just be sure to leave space in-between them so they dry from every angle.

If your region gets plenty of sun but also tends to be more humid, you can make a simple solar dehydrator with a mesh floor and add the screen mesh frame or cheesecloth over-the-top, creating a mini greenhouse effect that will give your foods the needed heat, control the humidity, and keep them safe from bugs.

To use this method you have to make sure your food has plenty of breathing room.

Preserving Food THE AMISH WAY

WATER GLASSING EGGS

Water glassing, or sodium silicate preservation, is a simple and efficient method of storing eggs for long periods without refrigeration. Historically, the technique originated in Germany in the 1600s and was widely popularized in the early 20th century, especially during the World Wars when food shortages were prevalent.

Water glassing allows eggs to be stored for up to several months, significantly extending their shelf life beyond the usual recommended time frame.

One of the drawbacks of this technique is the fact that the bulkiness of containers required for water glassing may limit the number of eggs you can store. Also, regular checking is necessary to make sure that no air has entered the container and the eggs did not spoil in the meantime. Another limitation is the fact that the availability of sodium silicate may be limited in certain areas in US (especially during hard times), which makes it quite challenging to continue preserving eggs using this method.

Tips and Tricks for Successful Water Glassing

- Use freshly laid eggs for water glassing to maximize their longevity.
- Rotate the eggs regularly by placing new eggs on top and using the previously preserved ones.
- Mark the date of preservation on the container to easily track when the eggs should ideally be consumed.

WATER-GLASSED EGGS

Ingredients

Fresh, unwashed eggs (preferably within a week of being laid)

Sodium silicate solution (food-grade quality)

A clean and sterilized storage container with a tight-fitting lid

Instructions

Step 1: Prepare the Eggs:

- Ensure the eggs are clean and intact without any cracks.
- Do not wash the eggs, as this removes the thin protective layer (bloom) on the shell, making them more permeable to bacteria.

Step 2: Mix the Sodium Silicate Solution:

- Follow the recommended ratio of sodium silicate to water provided on the packaging instructions.
- Stir the mixture until completely dissolved.

Step 3: Place the Eggs in the Container:

- Carefully arrange the eggs in a single layer at the bottom of the container, avoiding direct contact with the walls.
- Pour the sodium silicate solution over the eggs, ensuring they are fully submerged. Add more solution if needed.

Step 4: Seal and Store the Container

- Secure the lid tightly to prevent air and moisture from entering the container.
- Store the container in a cool, dark place away from direct sunlight and extreme temperature fluctuations.

Preserving Food **THE AMISH WAY**

WATER BATH CANNING THE GARDEN HARVEST

This process creates a vacuum seal, preventing the growth of harmful bacteria and extending the shelf life of your favorite foods.

Unfortunately, many folks are needlessly intimidated by the concept of home canning - especially pressure canning. While water bath canning is a simpler process and does not require the investment in a pressure canning pot, neither process is difficult to either learn or master.

The basic process for water bath canning vegetables is demonstrated below using tomatoes as an example.

Safety Measures and Recommended Equipment

1. **Always follow safe canning practices:** Ensure your workspace is clean, use proper utensils, and adhere to recommended processing times and altitudes specific to your location.

2. **Use a water bath canner or large pot with a rack:** This will allow for proper water circulation and even heat distribution during the canning process.

3. **Invest in essential canning tools:** Essential equipment includes jars, lids, bands, a jar lifter, magnetic lid lifter, canning funnel, and a bubble remover/headspace tool. These tools will make your canning process easier and safer.

4. **Be cautious of altitude:** Adjust processing times to account for altitude differences to ensure safe preservation. Consult reputable resources for specific guidelines.

CANNED TOMATOES

How It's Made

Step 1: Gather Fresh, Ripe Tomatoes

The first step to successful water bath canning is to source high-quality tomatoes at their peak ripeness. The fresher the tomatoes, the better the flavor of the canned product.

Step 2: Prepare the Jars

Ensure your canning jars are clean and in good condition. Submerge them in simmering water to sterilize, along with their lids and bands. Keep them hot until ready for use.

Step 3: Blanch and Peel the Tomatoes

Score a shallow "X" on the bottom of each tomato. Blanch them by immersing them in boiling water for about 30 seconds, then transfer immediately to an ice bath. This will make the peeling process much easier. Peel off the skin and remove the cores.

Preserving Food **THE AMISH WAY**

Step 4: Prepare the Canning Liquid

In a large pot, mix two parts tomato juice or water with one part tomato paste to create a sauce or juice to preserve your tomatoes. You can also add herbs, spices, or garlic to enhance the flavor.

Step 5: Heat the Tomatoes

In a separate pot, heat the peeled tomatoes over medium heat. Stir occasionally to avoid burning. Once the mixture is heated through, it is ready to be packed into jars.

Step 6: Pack the Jars

Remove the sterilized jars from the simmering water and fill them with the heated tomato mixture. Leave a ½ inch (1.27 cm) headspace at the top and gently tap the jars to release any air bubbles.

Step 7: Secure the Lids

Wipe the jar rims, place the sterilized lids on top, and screw the bands securely. Be careful not to overtighten, as air needs to escape during the water bath process.

Step 8: Process in a Water Bath

Place the filled and sealed jars in a canner or large pot filled with enough simmering water to cover at least one inch (2.54 cm) above the jars. Bring the water to a boil and start the timer according to the recommended processing time specified in your recipe.

Step 9: Cool and Store

Once the processing time is complete, turn off the heat and carefully remove the jars using a jar lifter. Place them on a towel or cooling rack and allow them to cool completely. As they cool, you may hear the "ping" sound, indicating a proper seal. Store in a cool, dark place for up to a year.

Foods Suitable for Water Bath Canning

While tomatoes are a popular choice for water bath canning, there are many other vegetables that can be effectively preserved using this method.

Some examples of vegetables and recipes commonly water bath canned include:

- Cucumbers for dill pickles
- Green beans - they can be pressure canned too, but water bathing makes them crisper.
- Carrots
- Beets
- Peppers
- Squash (when pickled)
- Peaches
- Pears
- Applesauce
- Plums
- Radishes
- Zucchini
- Peppers (as salsa)
- Relish
- Cherries
- Berries
- Pie filling
- Fruit jams, jellies, preserves
- Apple butter
- Fruit and vegetable Juices
- Spaghetti sauce (meatless)
- Tomato sauce
- Ketchup

Different vegetables may require slight modifications in preparation methods or processing times - such as not all vegetables need to be blanched like tomatoes. Always consult trusted recipes or resources to ensure safe and successful preservation.

Pressure canning

Foods You Must Pressure Can	Foods That Cannot Be Preserved Using Home Canning Methods
• Soups	• Flour
• Stews	• Cream
• Stocks	• Corn starch
• Broth	• Paste
• Poultry	• Rice
• Beef	• Eggs
• Fish	
• Chili	
• Wild game	
• Baked beans	

Now, the USDA absolutely says that you cannot pressure can milk or butter at home because these food items will not safely prevent the growth of bacteria. But, the Amish and many rural folks have pressure canned these foods for generations.

Pressure Canning Meat

Below you will find the basic pressure canning meat instructions, using chicken as an example.

The traditional Amish method of pressure canning chicken offers a reliable way to preserve meat for the winter months. Culling flocks in the fall ensures that only the healthiest chickens are preserved, and pressure canning maintains the quality, taste, and safety of the meat. This method gives households the advantage of having a sustainable food supply throughout the winter when access to fresh poultry can be limited.

Pressure Canned Chicken

How It's Made

Step 1: Culling the Flocks (Fall)

✧ Select chickens that are healthy, free from disease, and optimal weight.

✧ Humane processes include either neck-breaking or using a sharp knife to sever the neck quickly.

✧ Properly dispose of the remains, adhering to local regulations.

Step 2: Preparing the Chicken

✧ Pluck feathers, ensuring the removal of all feathers.

✧ Cut off the head and feet, discarding appropriately.

✧ Carefully gut the chicken, removing all internal organs.

✧ Rinse the chicken with cold water to clean any remaining debris.

✧ Cut the chicken into desired pieces or leave it whole, based on personal preference.

Step 3: Sterilizing the Canning Equipment

✧ Clean all jars, lids, and rings with hot, soapy water.

✧ Rinse thoroughly, removing any soap residue.

✧ Place the jars, lids, and rings on a clean towel or in a heat-safe container.

✧ Sterilize jars by placing them upright in a large pot or canner, covering them with water, and bringing to a boil for 10 minutes.

✧ Boil lids separately for 5 minutes to soften the rubber seal.

✧ Keep the sterilized jars, lids, and rings hot until ready to use.

Preserving Food THE AMISH WAY

Step 4: Following Specific Canning Procedures

- Fill a pressure canner with the recommended amount of water, according to the appliance's instructions.
- Place the canning rack inside the pressure canner.
- Pack raw chicken pieces into hot, sterilized jars, leaving a 1-inch headspace.
- Add recommended amount of salt or desired seasonings (optional).
- Wipe the rims of the jars with a clean, damp cloth to remove any food particles.
- Place lids on the jars, ensuring they are centered and secured with rings fingertip tight (not too loose or too tight).
- Follow the specific canning procedures provided by the manufacturer of your canning equipment, adjusting pressure and processing time based on altitude and jar size.

Precautions and Safety Measures

- Always follow the latest guidelines from reputable sources such as the USDA or your local agricultural extension service.
- Use only equipment in excellent working condition and follow the manufacturer's instructions.
- Never substitute pressure canning with other preservation methods, as they may not ensure the same level of safety.
- Check jars for chips or cracks and discard any that are damaged.
- Use correct pressure and processing times to destroy bacteria and ensure safe storage.
- Allow the canner to fully depressurize before attempting to open it

Preserving Food **THE AMISH WAY**

PREPARING LARD LIKE THE AMISH

Rendering the fat into lard involves slowly melting it down to separate the pure fat from any impurities or residual meat. The Amish use large, heavy pots or kettles for this process, often cooking over an open fire or a wood-burning stove. The fat is cut into small pieces and heated gently, allowing it to melt without scorching. As it melts, the fat turns into a clear liquid, and any solid pieces, known as cracklings, rise to the surface and are skimmed off.

The liquid fat is then carefully strained through a fine cloth or sieve to remove any remaining impurities, resulting in a clean, pure lard. This lard is poured into jars or containers and left to cool and solidify. Properly rendered lard has a smooth, creamy texture and a neutral flavor, making it an excellent ingredient for baking, frying, and cooking.

Lard is a cherished ingredient in Amish kitchens, used in a wide variety of traditional recipes. It is valued not only for its culinary properties but also for its practicality and shelf-stability. Unlike many modern fats, lard does not require refrigeration, making it ideal for the Amish, who often live without electricity.

In addition to its use in cooking, lard has other practical applications. It can be used in making soap, as a lubricant, and even in traditional remedies and skincare products. The process of making lard is a communal activity, often involving multiple generations working together, reflecting the Amish emphasis on family, community, and self-reliance.

LARD RECIPE

Ingredients

11 lbs pig fat
A little chicken fat
Water

Equipment

Knife
Cutting board
A large pot
Potato masher (optional)

Instructions

Place the fat on a cutting board and cut it into small cubes.

After cutting it all up, grab a normal pot and, first, add a cup of water because this way the fat won't burn onto the pot.

Then, add the cubes of fat.

After placing everything inside, you can start melting the fat.

The cooking should take about 2 hours. When the fat cubes start to turn golden-brown and harden, take the pot off the fire. This is how it looked after the one-hour mark:

And the two-hour mark, when it was finished.

At this point, you will be left with two things:

1. The melted fat;
2. Greaves (which are a by-product of the melted fat).

Preserving Food THE AMISH WAY

Both can be served warm or cold, depending on your preferences.

Here are the chicken greaves, after separating them from the fat:

Using a potato masher, I was able to extract more fat from the greaves. Gently and slowly push the greaves down until most of the fat is being removed from the inside.

Do this while everything is still hot, this way you can remove the fat before it solidifies.

Now, remove the greaves from the potato masher. You can already see that they are way dryer than before.

After Finishing Up, I Was Left With:

1. 2.20 lbs. of greaves;
2. 3.5 liters of lard.

Drying Beef

The Amish have some great secrets for making dried beef. They start with high-quality, fresh cuts from their own livestock, like round or top round. They use simple, natural ingredients for curing, like coarse salt, brown sugar, and spices such as black pepper, garlic powder, and onion powder. The beef is coated in this mix and left to cure slowly in a cool, well-ventilated spot for one to three weeks, letting the flavors really sink in. Sometimes, they smoke the meat using hardwoods like hickory or applewood for extra flavor. After curing, the beef is air-dried for another one to two weeks in a clean, controlled environment, often a cellar or drying shed. They regularly check and turn the meat to ensure it dries evenly. Plus, many Amish families have their own special recipes and techniques passed down through generations, just like my own.

Dried Beef General Principles

Dried beef is a great long-lasting food option for a bunch of reasons. The drying process gets rid of moisture, which helps keep away bacteria and mold, so it doesn't spoil easily. It keeps a lot of its protein and important nutrients like iron and B vitamins. Plus, it's lightweight and doesn't need to be refrigerated, making it perfect for travel, emergencies, and easy storage. The flavor gets more intense, so it adds a lot to different dishes. People have been using this method for ages, so it's tried and true. If stored right, dried beef can last a really long time, which is super handy for emergencies or just having on hand. It also cuts down on food waste and can save you money because you can buy in bulk and store it for later. The curing process also makes it safer by killing off harmful germs. All in all, dried beef is practical, nutritious, and super reliable for long-term storage and cooking.

Amish Style Dried Beef

The technique I am about to describe works well for drying tit-bits, and long cuts of meat up to an inch or two thick.

Equipment

Knive
Cutting board
Container

Ingredients

Meat
Salt
Pepper
Sugar
Vinegar

Preparing the Meat

Step 1

Cut the meat into thin strips

Step 2

Spice the meat and gently work all the spices through

You will need around 20 grams of salt per pound of meat. The thicker the cut, the more salt you can add. I also add black pepper for taste.

You are welcome to add some chili, some Cajun pepper or even coriander to enhance the taste once it's dried. I also added a small amount of brown sugar, it's the way my grandparents did it, and it adds some taste.

Step 3

Place the spiced meat into the vinegar

> I prefer brown vinegar, but you can use other types of vinegar depending on your taste preference. What I do is mix the dry spice into the meat cuts, and then add it to a container with vinegar.

You want the vinegar to slightly cover the top of the meat. The way I do this is to add some vinegar to a bowl, and then lay my strips into the vinegar. I then add a small amount of vinegar every time the meat strips rise above the vinegar.

Step 4

Turn the container from time to time to assure all surfaces are marinated

Using a tight-fitting container or bowl for this will be your best option for not wasting too much vinegar. Once in the vinegar, I will move the pieces around every hour or so, using my hands or a large mixing spoon.

> Depending on the thickness of the cuts, you want to leave them in there for around 4 to 24 hours. 4 hours for titbits, 24 hours for two-inch cuts.

Drying the Meat

You can then hang the meat up or lay them on a grid to dry. Depending on the temperature, humidity and thickness of the cuts, this could take anything from 2 days to three weeks.

Do not attempt this if the humidity is too high, as the moisture content of the meat equalizes to the moisture content of the surrounding air.

If the humidity is too high your meat won't dry. Unless you expose it to dry air flow using commercial dryers or the dryer that you made with a server fan and a lightbulb.

Step 1

Place the meat on a grid or hang it out to dry.

I use a screen grid made from pine wood and 20% shade net.

Step 2

Cover the grid.

This is what the dried beef will look like over time.

Preserving Food **THE AMISH WAY**

Storage

Once the meat strips are fully dried, you can store them however you want. I pack them into pillowcases and hang them in my pantry. The pillowcases protect from bugs and rodents while allowing airflow.

They will eventually dry completely. If you want to retain a bit of moisture, you can store them in airtight containers or vacuum pack them. The Amish are known for also canning dried meat.

If you see mold growing on the meat, you can brush it with vinegar and hang it out to dry again. This rarely happens, but now you know how to deal with that.

Shelf Life

The dried beef has a long shelf life. Here it really depends on how well it is stored. If you keep it away from moisture and protected from light, it should last months if not years.

The fat on the meat will eventually dehydrate completely, and become almost like a powdery substance. The meat itself will turn brown, then yellowish, and eventually pale. By this time, thicker pieces will be as hard as wood.

You can continue eating, as the meat and fat don't spoil or become dangerous to consume. The issue is that the lipids in the fat degrade, and the amino acids in the meat also decay.

The problem with eating it after a few years is that it will have much less nutrition, so protein and energy are compromised. But it will not do your health in or cause food poisoning or other digestive issues.

The salt and minerals should stay more or less the same as with the fresh product.

Amish Dried Beef Gravy

Dried beef can be eaten on its own. You can also grate it finely, and serve it on a slice of bread with some butter.

The Amish dried beef gravy is the "uber" way of consuming dried beef and making it soft for eating. You can serve the gravy on rice or over potatoes. Grate some cheese over it to add something special.

Tools

Skillet
Wooden spoon
Measuring cup

Ingredients

¼ lb dried beef
2 tablespoons butter
3 tablespoons flour
3 cups milk
Black pepper, to taste

Instructions

Melt butter in a skillet.

Tear the dried beef into small pieces and stir into the melted butter. Cook meat until slightly browned.

Stir in the flour.

When the flour is dissolved, add milk, stirring constantly.

Cook over low heat until the mixture thickens. The longer it cooks, the softer the beef will become.

There you have it, folks. Dried beef – done. Different ways of eating dried beef – done!

> Though some Amish have adopted recent technologies, most still retain knowledge long forgotten by most modern folk. The Amish are food preservation experts.

Preserving Food THE AMISH WAY

How to make Forever Butter

The Importance and Uses of Ghee for the Amish Community

What Is Ghee?

Ghee is a form of clarified butter, made by simmering butter to remove water and milk solids, leaving behind pure butterfat. For the Amish, ghee is more than just a cooking ingredient; it is a cultural and nutritional staple.

Health and Nutrition

Ghee is rich in fat-soluble vitamins (A, D, E, K) and provides a valuable source of energy. The Amish, who prioritize natural and unprocessed foods, highly value ghee as a healthy fat source.

Longevity

Unlike butter, ghee has a much longer shelf life and does not spoil easily.

This makes ghee a preferred choice among the Amish, as it can be preserved and stored naturally for extended periods.

Medicinal Uses

In traditional medicinal practices, ghee is used to heal wounds and treat skin conditions. The Amish also use ghee for its anti-inflammatory and digestive properties.

Uses of Ghee

Ghee has a wide range of applications in Amish cooking and lifestyle:

Cooking

With its high smoke point, ghee is ideal for frying, sautéing, and baking. It is a common ingredient in Amish recipes, especially in meat dishes, vegetable preparations, and baked goods.

Bread Making

The Amish use ghee in traditional bread-making. It adds richness and softness to the bread, enhancing its flavor and texture.

Desserts

Ghee is frequently used in Amish desserts. Pies, cakes, and cookies made with ghee instead of butter are lighter and more flavorful.

Preserving

Ghee is used to preserve vegetables and spices. The Amish pour ghee over vegetables to keep them fresh for longer periods.

Medicinal and Cosmetic Uses

Ghee serves as a natural moisturizer for skin and hair care. Amish women use ghee in their skincare routines to nourish and soften their skin.

Traditional Preparation of Ghee

The Amish prepare ghee using traditional methods and old-fashioned equipment.

Heavy-bottomed copper or iron pots, wooden spoons, and natural ingredients ensure that the ghee is authentic and handmade.

Preserving Food **THE AMISH WAY**

Making Forever Butter

Ghee is a cherished ingredient in Amish kitchens, known for its rich flavor and numerous health benefits. Making ghee at home is straightforward and requires only a few ingredients and tools. Here's a detailed, step-by-step guide to help even beginners make perfect ghee:

Materials

Heavy-bottomed pot
Wooden spoon
Fine mesh strainer or cheesecloth
Glass jar (for storage)
Small metal ladle (for pouring)

Ingredients

500 grams of unsalted butter

Instructions

Step 1: Preparation

Ensure all your equipment is clean and dry to prevent contamination and ensure your ghee lasts longer. Sterilize your glass jars by boiling them in water for 10 minutes and let them dry completely.

Step 2: Melting the Butter

Place the unsalted butter in a heavy-bottomed pot. A thick-bottomed pot helps distribute heat evenly and prevents the butter from burning.

Set the stove to low heat and slowly melt the butter, stirring occasionally with a wooden spoon. Avoid high heat, which can cause the butter to burn.

Step 3: Foaming and Simmering

As the butter melts, it will start to foam. This foam consists of water and milk solids.

Keep the butter on low heat and let it continue to foam. Skim off the foam using a spoon and discard it. This helps in clarifying the butter.

Step 4: Clarification

Let the butter simmer for about 20-30 minutes. During this time, water will evaporate, and milk solids will settle at the bottom.

The butter will turn clear and golden, indicating that ghee is forming. You will also notice a nutty aroma, a sign that the milk solids are caramelizing.

Step 5: Finalizing the Ghee

Watch the butter closely as it simmers. When the bubbling slows and the butter becomes a deep golden color, remove it from the heat. Overcooking can burn the ghee, giving it a bitter taste.

Preserving Food THE AMISH WAY

Let the pot sit for a few minutes to allow the milk solids to settle at the bottom.

Step 6: Straining the Ghee

Place a fine mesh strainer or a piece of cheesecloth over a clean, dry bowl or another pot. Carefully pour the hot ghee through the strainer to remove the milk solids.

Be cautious while pouring, as the ghee will be very hot. Use a small metal ladle for better control if needed.

Step 7: Storing the Ghee

Pour the strained ghee into the sterilized glass jars and let it cool completely at room temperature before sealing with lids.

Store the ghee in a cool, dark place or in the refrigerator. Properly stored ghee can remain fresh for several months.

Tips

- **Handmade Look:** Using traditional copper or iron pots can give your ghee a more authentic, "handmade" appearance, emphasizing its natural and traditional preparation.
- **Flavoring:** Optionally, you can add a few leaves of fresh rosemary or thyme during the final stages of cooking to infuse your ghee with a subtle aroma.

Making ghee is a simple yet rewarding process that produces a healthy and delicious cooking fat. Inspired by the culinary traditions of the Amish, this golden liquid can enhance the flavors of your favorite dishes.

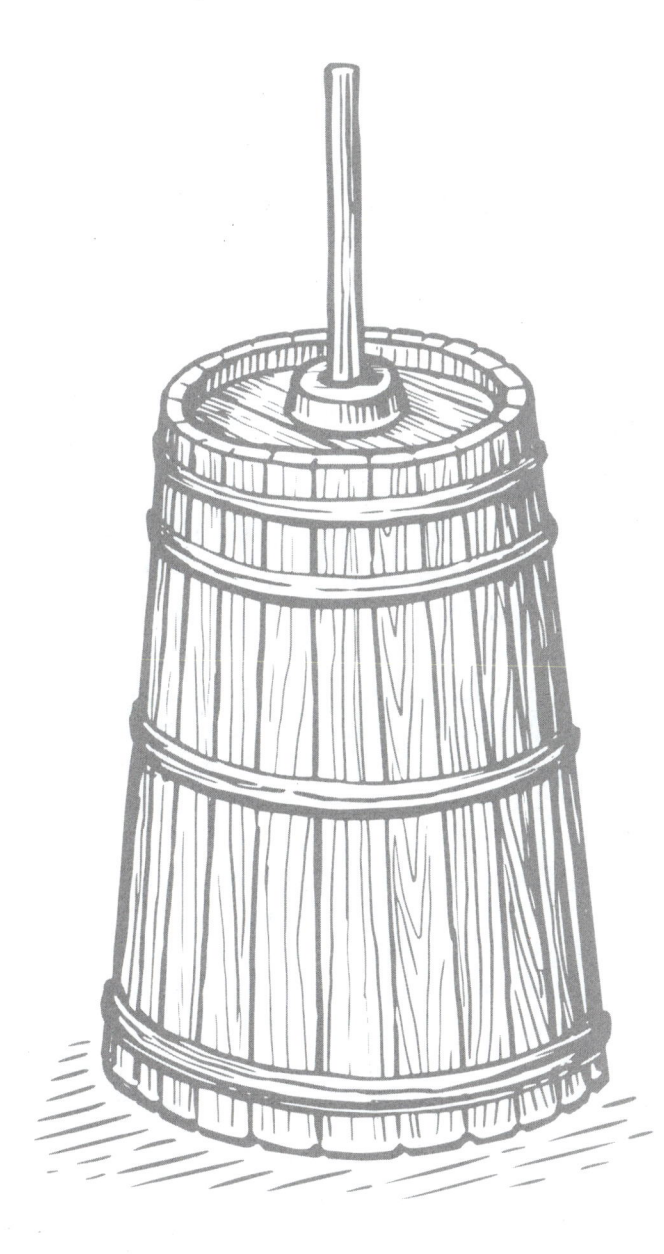

Long-Lasting Amish Recipes

By now you are very familiar with how the Amish live. Simply, close to the land, their faith, and their community. You may even have gathered that their lifestyle revolves around their farm animals and their crops. The same can be said about their eating habits. From my time on the farm, I remember a variety of meats, potatoes, noodles, loaves of bread, and an assortment of garden vegetables on that countryside supper table. And a well-stocked pantry at the back of the kitchen storing everything that's not in the cellar or freezer. Some of the things you might find in that pantry include various types of flour, cereals, whole grains, beans and legumes, dried pasta, sugar and honey, cooking oils, and various dried, dehydrated, and canned goods. In the root cellar, you would see potatoes growing in the ground that have been transplanted from the garden and you'll definitely spy mason jars lining wooden shelves that run floor to ceiling. I recall jars of all sizes and widths, their contents coming in an assortment of colors, textures, and combinations. In the freezer, I'd find some veggies but there was a big emphasis on meat. You must be thinking wait, the Amish don't use electricity, how do they have cold storage? We'll touch on this shortly!

We have a lot to learn from the way the Amish behave. One example of that is they eat-to-live. Many spend their days in manual labor, tending to large crops and farms, or preparing food using very physical means. Because of this, they tend to be unconcerned about the amount of fat or sugar in their diets. This whole concept might be very much opposed to the fad diets and consumerism so much of the world has become accustomed to. Fieldwork is grueling in the dead heat of the summer sun. I remember days of walking barefoot across hot stones in my hand-made dress just to deliver an ice-cold pitcher of peppermint tea to the man of the house, Mr. Eberly. I had the pleasure of watching the young family call together their community for a barn raising. One-hundred and seventy-five men scattered about the frame of a building hammering each nail by hand. Rest assured, there is no need for any extra physical activity to stay slim and trim in this community. They work hard for every single calorie consumed.

Think of it as a "work for your keep" society. Each person, young and old pulls their weight without the bat of an eye. Traditionally, the Amish view children as a gift from God so they tend to have large families who eat together during mealtimes. My dear friend Anne was only one of four and she knew that was rare. It's because the family provides a dense web of social support from cradle to grave. Typically you may see seven to ten children per family, and I'd bet they all are quiet, obedient, and responsible. You see, the Amish household functions like a team. The little ones are a huge support to the family farm and/or business. And when it comes to work, you'll notice there is a clear divide between the chores that the men and women are assigned. The men and the boys, once they reach a certain age of course, usually work on the farm and in the fields tending to crops and cattle. While the women and children do the washing, cleaning, cooking, gardening, and preserving.

People can be perplexed by the rhythms and rituals that the Amish live by, but these days those exact behaviors are gaining more popularity. Folks are now becoming more interested in ways to live off-grid by becoming more self-sufficient. Amish foods, therefore, have become popular as "survival foods" because they can be stored and relied upon in the event of long-term electrical failure or in hostile environments. If the Amish lifestyle speaks to you and you'd like to live in a way that is closer to sustainable, we have a treat for you!

Next, we'll take a look at some simple Amish rules to live by.

Grow Your Own Food

Nearly all Amish homes and farms have grape vines, fruit trees, massive gardens, and more than a few animals. Every season you will see these families harvest beets, potatoes, tomatoes, various beans and peas, corn, carrots, and sorghum from their gardens and fields. Highlighting one crop specifically, sweet sorghum is rated by some as the number one survival food due to its ability to grow in very harsh conditions, as opposed to traditional corn. It's also likely there will be a patch of fruit trees somewhere on the property where they will grow peaches, apples, cherries, and plums, too. I remember picnics with fresh melons and a sore palm from a full week of picking, prepping, and pitting cherries for jam. Let's not forget to mention, these households likely have chickens who are laying fresh eggs daily for use in baked goods. Cows who are producing full-fat milk that later may be sold, or churned into butter or cheese. And they may even be raising goats for milk and pigs for slaughter in the winter. You may be thinking, this is a ton of work and a ton of food. But do not worry, the families are professionals when it comes to using their seasonal harvest and all the children will have a hand in the picking, processing, and preserving of these foods. Talk about the original "Farm to Table" eating! This leads us to…

Eat What's in Season

We all know how terrible it is to bite into a fruit that's not close to ripe. The Amish don't tend to have this issue for a few reasons. With little ability or desire to visit the big chain grocery stores where those picked-too-soon imported fruits wait, the people in the Amish community will instead be picking what is ripe right off the vine, tree, or bush. Or maybe they are buying some from their neighbor's roadside produce stand! They are creative and resourceful people who are very conscious of seasons, best-growing conditions, and how to plan for an approximate yield. In fact, you'll even see notes about this in their recipe books. This is all generational knowledge that's been passed down through the years. In many of the traditional cookbooks or 'Doctor Books', you will find helpful tips on how to live! Like how much food to provide for a barn raising: 115 lemon pies, 16 chickens, 5 gallons of potatoes, 16 loaves of bread, etc. Or recipes for making natural laundry detergents and dish soaps with leftover meat scraps. Speaking of…

Use Everything

By everything, I mean plants, animals, and everything in between. As you might know, the growing season starts early, and indoors at that. The farm I grew up visiting had a mudroom, as so many practical farmhouses do. In that room, I can still see the little seedlings beginning to sprout in cadence with the planting season that was upon us. Those seeds may have been saved from last year's crop, I can't be certain. But I can assure you, every other bit of that crop was used, and then some. As another tip reads 'Boiled rice water makes an excellent starch for dainty collars, cuffs, and baby dresses.' The food scraps in our house were often composted or given to the cows after every meal. These conscious people are mindful of giving back to the planet that gives to them.

You will see this same rule of respect show up regarding animal products too. Not an ear, hoof, or tongue will go to waste, just check the local Pennsylvania Dutch butcher shop to see what I mean. One local favorite I must mention is scrapple or cornmeal mush. It is a mix of pork scraps and trimmings combined with cornmeal and wheat flour, often buckwheat flour, and some spices. It's then formed into a semi-solid loaf, sliced, and pan-fried before serving as savory or sweet. As you can see, the Amish will go to great lengths to avoid waste.

In our last rule, we mentioned that you won't see a weekly run to the local Walmart, but you might see a monthly trip to the 'bent-and-dent' store. (Still an upgrade from the olden days of a 150-mile horse and buggy ride to do a yearly stock-up.) These buildings are large no-frill bulk food stores where goods are discounted as they reach closer to their expiration date. These products might have minor imperfections and are shipped from commercial grocery stores and some small organic markets as they no longer adhere to the store standards. But the Amish are exceptionally savvy regarding the reuse, reduce and recycle policy. They will gladly snatch up these dented cans or bent boxes to make use of a perfectly good product. After all, the best-use-by date is often a suggestion. And what you can't use right away, you…

Preserve

Preservation comes in a ton of forms, the most widely known are canning, drying, smoking, and freezing. The Amish may not be connected to the electric grid, but surprisingly enough they still do have access to cooling devices like refrigerators, freezers, and ice chests. They are able to have these helpful appliances if they are gas powdered or run with a battery. The Amish fella running his grass-fed meat stand at Central Market shared that today, almost all of the meat is frozen and just a bit is canned. But we must not discount this widely associated form of preservation. It is still relied upon heavily for many other things. Taking a peek in a root cellar, you would see jars of chow-chow, bbq bacon green beans, red tomato sauce, salsa, pepper jelly, chicken corn soup, apple butter, and sauerkraut. As I was asked to grab a few jars from downstairs, I remember my job was to keep rotating the cans forward as we would use up the supply. Ensuring we are eating only the items that are nearing their shelf life while storing the freshly processed foods for later. As you can see, food is abundant and when you have abundance you…

Preserving Food THE AMISH WAY

Share with the Community

One day, take a stroll around a Central Pennsylvanian farmer's market to see what I mean. The Amish pretzel stand will be giving off a buttery aroma, while the man in a straw hat at the meat counter processes a chicken. The baked goods are looking extra sweet, to say the least, and the vegetable stand is gleaming with color. One of the many beautiful things about the Amish community is their natural urge to share with others. As a child, if we had extra eggs, it wouldn't be uncommon to visit our neighbors with them. Especially if we went over to help with quilting projects or newborn babies. The mothers and grandmothers of the family have long been considered the healers, like the medicine women of any good tribe. They know that in the instance of an illness or injury, a doctor will be a long buggy ride away so they better be ripe with knowledge of home remedies. These little reminders are scattered all through the recipe books. One note states the magnificent healing properties of spring onions, both medicinally and as a skin beautifier. And one thing that sure is beautiful about the Amish is their ability to…

Gather

In any Amish household, you will find a very large wooden expandable dinner table.

When fully assembled this table will make any kitchen (and living room) a proper gathering space. The Amish make a point to connect with one another and I had the luck of experiencing just that. The Eberlys had a reunion once during my visit. There must've been sixty women and children flowing in and out of the house busy like bees. When it was meal time, Ruth would step outside placing her fingers tightly together, and blow the loudest whistle my little ears had ever heard. 'The dinner call' meant supper was ready! And all the men and boys would come running. To eat was a treat, which brings us to our last rule…

Treat Yourself

These folks are certainly not the type of people to ward off sugar. In fact, sugar, eggs, butter, lard, flour, and salt are the main ingredients in most Amish dishes. This means their treats will definitely satisfy your sweet tooth. I can still see the homemade candies, cakes, breads, and cookies cooling on the table. Whoopie pies are a particularly famous treat. Which traditionally consists of two chocolate cake-like cookies, sandwiched together with sweet white icing. Today, you can find all sorts of variations on the original, like chocolate peanut butter, pumpkin cream cheese, and red velvet. But let's not let Whoopie pies take all the spotlight. The Amish are also known for their canned jams and jellies that make a great after-lunch sweet. Their thick fudge and spicy ginger cookies are sure to hit the spot. And the sticky shoefly pies and bread pudding will make you feel right at home.

Now that you've gotten a bird's eye view into the guiding principles that rule the Amish way of life, let's talk a bit about the tools they use to prepare those fabulous meals! We've already mentioned how practical and hands-on these people are. So you might guess that many of their tools are handmade or powered with good old-fashioned elbow grease. It is true, you will see sturdy wooden kitchen tools as well as some metal ones.

As you now know, dairy in all its forms is a large part of the Amish lifestyle. It is not uncommon for each person in the family to drink a glass of milk with every meal. The rest of that milk might be churned into butter, as it's an essential part of Amish homes. That means it's likely you'll find a hand-cranked butter churner tucked somewhere nearby. And to use all that butter, you'll need some bread from the hand-built bread box on the counter. If you'd like to fry those fresh chicken eggs for breakfast, it's likely you would use a cast-iron skillet to do so. If you prefer those eggs scrambled, you might fire up an old fashion hand-cracked egg beater to do just that.

Let's pretend we are serving a meal outside, we'd carry our dishes out on a hand-woven serving basket. We might even serve our food with a hand-carved wooden spoon. And it sure is possible we'd have freshly made bread or biscuits which were shaped by an old-timey metal biscuit cutter.

> The recipes included in this chapter are intended for canning right away. We've chosen hearty meals that will sustain your energy for a long time. Plus they are safe to eat right from the can! Though each meal would be much tastier when thoroughly heated. You will see the steps for canning in the section just after the recipes. Be mindful that the processing time for the vegetable soup is different than the rest. Enjoy!

Preserving Food THE AMISH WAY

Beef Stew with Vegetables

Yield: about 14 pints or 7 quarts

First up we have a hearty dish that combines chunks of beef with a variety of other ingredients, such as potatoes, vegetables, herbs, spices, and broth to create a savory one-pot meal. Beef stew is rich in flavor and is regularly served as the main dish. The cut of meat most often chosen for making this dish is chuck, which comes from meat extending from the foreleg to the shoulder of a steer. However, you can also choose from other meats suitable for slow cooking, such as beef, pork, venison, rabbit, lamb, poultry, sausages, and seafood. Get ready to get comfortable!

Materials

Large stock pot
Knives
Cutting board
Large wooden spoon
Ladle
Wide-mouthed funnel
Measuring spoons

Ingredients

4-5 lbs beef stew meat
1 tbsp vegetable oil
3 qts cubed potatoes (about 18 medium)
2 qts sliced carrots (about 15 small)
3 c chopped celery (about 6 stalks)
3 c chopped onions (about 4-5 medium)
1 ½ tsp salt
1 tsp thyme
½ tsp pepper
Boiling water

Instructions

Wash all your vegetables using cold water, then drain.

Peel potatoes and cut them into 1-inch cubes until you have 3 quarts cubed. Remove stems and peel carrots. Slice into ½-inch thick pieces until you have 2 quarts. Remove leafy tops and root from celery and cut into ½-inch thick pieces until you have 3 cups. Peel and chop onions; about 3 cups. Cut stew meat into 1 ½-inch thick cubes. Slice across the grain about 1 inch thick, then cut with the grain to make jar-sized pieces.

Bring a pot of water to a boil.

Heat the oil in a large saucepan or stew pot, brown meat cubes.

Stir in veggies and seasonings, then add enough boiling water to cover the mixture. Bring to a boil.

Using your wide-mouthed funnel, ladle hot stew into freshly cleaned and warmed jars, leaving 1-inch headspace.

Please check the canning instructions below...

A Few Tips

- Instead of water, you have the option of using beef stock and/or a bouillon cube for additional flavor. The Amish tend to use very plain seasonings like bay leaves and thyme.

- When they pull this dish out of the cellar, upon serving they may add some boiled egg noodles or pearled barley for a chewy nutritious grain. Lastly, they could decide to put the contents into a pie crust for a beef pot pie!

- Cornbread or biscuits would make a wonderful side to this dish.

Chicken Soup

Yield: about 8 pints or 4 quarts

For a nice poultry dish that is a staple 'rainy day' or 'sick day' comfort meal, we have a nourishing chicken soup. Typically this brothy soup is made from chunks of white and dark meat chicken simmered in water and layered with various other ingredients. The classic version often has carrots, celery, and a plethora of other root vegetables and a few seasonings. Commonly something starchy is added like noodles, dumplings, or grains such as rice and barley.

Materials

Large stock pot
Knives
Cutting board
Large wooden spoon
Ladle
Wide-mouthed funnel
Measuring spoons

Ingredients

4 qts chicken stock
3 c diced cooked chicken (about 1-3 lb chicken)**
1 ½ c chopped celery (about 3 stalks)
1 ½ c sliced carrots (about 3 medium)
1 c chopped onion (about 1 large)
Salt & pepper to taste
3 chicken bouillon cubes (optional)

Preserving Food THE AMISH WAY

Begin by washing all of your vegetables using cold water, then drain.

Remove leafy tops and roots from celery, then chop until you have 1 ½ cups. Remove stems and peel carrots. Slice them ¼ inch thick until you have 1 ½ cups. Peel and chop onion until you have 1 cup.

In a large saucepan or stock pot combine chicken stock, chicken, celery, carrots, and onion. Bring mixture to a boil.

Reduce heat to simmer for 30 minutes. Season to taste with salt and pepper and add bouillon if desired.

Using your wide-mouthed funnel, ladle hot soup into freshly cleaned and warmed jars leaving a 1-inch headspace.

Please check the canning instructions below...

A Few Notes

- Season your soup any way you desire. Amish are very fond of additions like parsley and garlic.
- Upon opening your preserved jars, boil them on the stove to heat.
- Add more broth if desired.
- If you would like to add some starches to make the dish even more soothing, when the soup is boiling, add in egg noodles, rice or even dumplings.

**This recipe is intended to start with cooked chicken. You could purchase pre-cooked chicken, pull it from a rotisserie or cook it yourself. If you plan to cook the chicken prior to your soup, simply rinse the breasts and pat them dry. Remove any extra fat or connective tissue, then cut into consistent chunks that will fit easily into your jars. Start by heating a bit of oil in a large stock pot on the stove. Once the pan is hot, add your chicken chunks. When it is cooked most of the way through, add your vegetables and chicken stock. From here, resume the above recipe.

Preserving Food **The Amish Way**

Beef Chili

Yield: about 6 pints or 3 quarts

Up next is a hearty dish with ground meat and tender vegetables. A true chili is a spicy stew containing chili peppers or chili powder, meat (usually beef), and often tomatoes and beans. The beans can vary but are usually pinto, black and/or kidney beans. Other seasonings may include garlic, onions, and cumin. This makes for a great gathering dish that is packed with energy and protein for sustainable energy.

Materials

Large stock pot
Knives
Cutting board
Large wooden spoon
Ladle
Wide-mouthed funnel
Measuring spoons

Ingredients

5 lbs ground beef
2 c chopped onions
1 clove garlic, minced
6 c diced tomatoes with juice (canned or fresh)**
½ c chili powder
1 ½ tbsp salt
1 hot green or red pepper, finely chopped
1 tsp cumin seed or powder

Instructions

Start by peeling and chopping the onions until you have 2 cups. Peel and mince the garlic. Rinse the pepper well and discard the stem. Finely chop.

Heat a large saucepan and brown the ground beef. Drain off the fat, then add garlic and onion. Cook until onions are tender.

Add remaining ingredients and simmer for 20 minutes. Remove from heat and skim off any excess fat.

Using your wide-mouthed funnel, ladle hot chili into freshly cleaned and warmed jars leaving a 1-inch headspace.

Please check the canning instructions below…

Tips

Be creative with how you serve your dish. The Amish might serve chili with a side of cornbread and a dollop of sourcream, or they could use it as a topping for baked potatoes. Always feel free to vary your recipe and adjust the ingredients to your tastes, try it with or without meat. Give it an edge by adding sweet corn or more spice with a few jalapenos.

**You can start this recipe with canned tomatoes or fresh from the garden. If you choose to begin with fresh, you will need to blanch your whole tomatoes in boiling water in order to peel, core, and dice them. To blanch: Heat boiling water on the stove. Once it is bubbling, gently drop them into boiling water for 30-60 seconds. Immediately transfer to cold water.

Preserving Food THE AMISH WAY

Amish Poor Man's Steak

Yield: 142 patties, or 28 meals-in-a-jar

This dish came about during times when money was tight, and every ingredient had to be counted. The Amish found a way to turn basic, affordable ingredients into a tasty and filling meal. The Poor Man's Steak became a beloved recipe, highlighting their knack for creating comfort food from simple beginnings. It's also a long-lasting dish, that can last for months. Its simple ingredients have a long shelf life, and it can be easily made in large batches.

Materials

A large pan
Knives
Cutting board
Large wooden spoon
Ladle
Whisk
Measuring spoons
Cookie sheets
Roasting pans

Ingredients

30 lbs ground beef
5 c chopped onions
5 c chopped celery
6 tubes (1 ½ lbs) crushed saltines
2 dozen whisked eggs
5 c milk
7 cans condensed mushroom soup
5 cans water
½ cup fat (strained from roasting pans)
½ c plain flour

Instructions

Start by chopping celery and onions.

Then crush the saltines.

Crack open and whisk 2 dozen eggs.

Measure 5 cups of milk.

All of these items should be placed in one container as they are measured.

Celery, onions, saltines, eggs, milk, salt and pepper should be mixed together now.

Then add the 30 pounds of ground beef.

Shove all the ingredients to one side of the container and place the patties on the other side using waxed paper to separate the stacks to prevent them from sticking.

I used the wide mouth rim and lid of the jar to form the patties. Using this method will ensure the patties will fit into the wide mouth canning jars.

THE AMISH WAYS

Preserving Food THE AMISH WAY

The Amish original recipe reads to bake on cookie sheets, but I want to drain as much fat as possible from them.

I baked in preheated 375 degree oven for 35 minutes and alternated the pans about half way through cooking time. It took me a little over 4 hours to cook them all. I piled up 2 huge roasting pan and covered them with tinfoil and placed them in the refrigerator as they came from the oven.

For the gravy, strain off some of the fat from the broiler and roasting pan and set aside to make the brown pan gravy.

Put ½ cup of the strained fat into a skillet and heated over medium heat until hot.

Next, add ½ cup of plain flour. The secret to making a good gravy base is to stir and don't cook it too fast. You can control this by lifting your pan on and off the eye of the stove. You want to brown the flour slowly without burning it.

Put 5 cans of the mushroom soup along with 5 cans of water in a pot to begin warming. I think this is almost 2 quarts. The recipe doesn't say how much gravy to make but you are going to need to make a lot.

Add some of the mushroom soup mixture to the browned flour. It gets angry during this procedure. Keep adding and stirring.

Then add the base from the skillet to the pot of mushroom soup, stir it well and simmer while reheating patties.

Put a patty in the jar, cover that with the gravy mixture and then another patty and more gravy until the ingredients are one inch from the top. Add 5 patties in a jar.

Vegetable Soup

Yield: about 6 pints or 3 quarts

This one-pot meal known for its healthy and comforting taste, is coziness in a bowl. Our vegetable soup is brimming with nutritious, vibrant veggies in a rich broth infused with herbs! This dish consists of mainly vegetables and a base of water or broth. It may include other ingredients, such as meat, noodles, rice, and legumes.

Materials

Large stock pot
Knives
Cutting board
Large wooden spoon
Ladle
Measuring cup
Strainer
Vegetable peeler

Ingredients

2 qts chopped tomatoes (about 12 medium)**
1 ½ qts cubed potatoes (about 9 medium)
1 ½ qts sliced carrots (about 12 medium)
1 qt lima beans
1 qt whole kernel corn, uncooked (about 8 medium ears)
2 c sliced celery (about 4 stalks)
2 c chopped onions (about 2 to 3 medium)
1 ½ qts water
Salt & pepper to taste

Instructions

Begin by washing the tomatoes, potatoes, carrots, lima beans, corn, and celery with cold water, then drain. To peel tomatoes, blanch them in boiling water for 30-60 seconds. ** Immediately transfer to cold water. Now you can remove the peel and core the tomatoes until you have 2 quarts.

Peel the potatoes and cut them into ½ - inch cubes until you have 1 ½ quarts.

Remove stems and peel the carrots. Slice carrots ¼ - inch thick until you have 1 ½ quarts.

Cut whole kernels of corn from the cob by starting at the narrow end and moving toward the stem.

Measure 1 quart of corn. Remove the leafy tops and root end of the celery and chop into 1-inch chunks until you have 2 cups. Peel and chop the onions until you have 2 cups.

Combine all ingredients in a large saucepan or stock pot, except for the salt, pepper, and other seasonings.

Bring mixture to a boil, then reduce the heat and allow to simmer for 15 minutes. Season soup with salt and pepper, to taste. Add any additional flavors such as thyme, parsley, garlic, or bay leaves.

Carefully using your wide-mouthed funnel and hot pad, ladle hot soup into freshly cleaned and warmed jars leaving a 1-inch headspace.

Please check the canning instructions below...

Preserving Food **THE AMISH WAY**

How to Serve

- Once you have retrieved your canned vegetable soup from the cellar, you can simply pop the top and eat it if needed. You can also heat and enjoy!
- In an Amish household, they might take it up a notch by adding in cooked noodles, meat, or rice. But we know it is definitely best served warm with butter bread.

** Blanching is the process by which foods (usually fruits and vegetables) are briefly submerged in boiling water and then immediately cooled to stop further cooking. The technique deactivates enzymes that can affect the flavor, color and texture of produce, allowing it to be stored in peak condition. Blanched foods are cooked so briefly that they are still considered raw.

Pork Sausage

Preserve in pints or quarts

In our next recipe, we are making pork sausage. Most people tend to recognize breakfast sausage as a familiar side, or they may have even had Famous Amos's Hot Sausage Sandwich from a local fair. Most sausage is recognized as "highly seasoned minced meat (such as pork) usually stuffed in casings of prepared animal intestine. I'll highlight for this recipe, you can also use loose meat that can be formed into patties.

Materials

Pork
Broth for canning meat (recipe on the next page)
Salt & pepper
Other herbs or spices (optional)

Ingredients

Saucepan
Tongs
Wide-mouth funnel
Measuring cup with a spout

Instructions

If beginning with fresh pork, grind pork with a manual food grinder, adding in desired spices. Note that sage does not can well and may become bitter. Shape into 3 - 4 inches links or patties and lightly brown the meat in a hot pan.

Drain. Bring broth to a boil, then reduce the heat to allow it to simmer. Keeping the broth hot, pack hot sausages into a freshly cleaned and warmed jar leaving 1-inch headspace.

Using your wide-mouthed funnel or spouted measuring cup, pour hot broth over the sausage still leaving a 1-inch space.

Please check the canning instructions below…

Preserving Food THE AMISH WAY

Hot Packing

Hot Packing is when whole or cut food is first cooked in a brine, syrup, fruit juice, or water and then placed in warmed ready jars. The food is then covered with hot brine, syrup, fruit juice, broth, or water. Note that you do not need to can with a broth or "hot pack" every food, but this method is preferred when the food to be canned is firm and handles well. This means nearly all vegetables, meats, poultry, seafood, and many fruits will best preserve when hot packed. You may see some recipes give instructions for both hot and raw packing options but keep in mind that mixed foods like soup, chili, and stews are always hot packed as well as is ground beef.

Below you will see instructions for making a meat-based broth. This recipe can be used for just about any meat that you plan to can. We used this broth to hot pack our sausages as we prepared them for canning.

Broth for Canning Meat

Begin by heating a large cooking pan on the stove. Using room temperature meat, you will start by browning it in the pan and then draining the juice, reserving the liquid. Allow the fat to separate and come to the surface. Skim the fat and measure. Then measure the juice. Combine 1 to 2 tablespoons of fat with 1 cup of juice in a large saucepan. Water or broth may be added as needed for the amount of meat you are canning. Bring broth to a boil for 2 to 3 minutes.

Canning Reminders

It's very important to use safe canning practices that will ensure the safety and quality of your home canned foods. The canning steps below are specifically for a pressure canner because the recipes above include low-acid foods.

Whether food should be processed in a pressure canner or boiling-water canner to control botulinum bacteria depends on the acidity of the food. Foods that have a pH value higher than 4.6 are considered low-acid foods. These include red meats, seafood, poultry, milk, and all fresh vegetables except for most tomatoes. This means these items possess very little acid that's needed to guard against bacteria and toxins. Even mixed high/low acid foods like soups, stews, and meat sauces will require a pressure canner.

Quality and safety go hand in hand.

Please note it is not recommended to home can the following products:

- Dairy as in butter, cheese, or milk;
- Oil and eggs;
- Starches such as pasta, rice, breads, and cakes;
- Really tender vegetables like eggplant, squash, and cooked cauliflower.

> Do not retighten lids after processing jars. As jars cool, the contents in the jar will contract, pulling the self-sealing lid firmly against the jar to form a high vacuum seal.

151

Preserving Food THE AMISH WAY

The Canning Process

- *For Beef Stew, Chili, Chicken Soup, and Pork Sausage recipes*

Materials

Freshly cleaned and warmed canning jars
New lids and rings.
Pressure canner with a canning rack
Can grabber
Wide-mouthed funnel
Air bubble tool
Oven mitt
A small clean kitchen cloth
A large towel

**For Vegetable Soup, all steps are the same except the processing time differs. Bring the canner to 10 lbs (psi) Process pints for 55 minutes and quarts for 85 minutes.

Once the time is up, turn off the heat and cool the canner down to 0 pressure. After 5 minutes, remove the lid and let the jars cool for 10 minutes. Using a jar grabber, remove from the canner and allow to cool on the counter for 12 - 24 hours. Check the seal by pressing the middle of the lid with a finger or thumb. If the lid springs up when you release your finger, the lid is unsealed.

Instructions

Pack hot food into warm sterile jars leaving 1-inch headspace. Remove air bubbles using the air bubble tool and wipe the jar rims with warm water or vinegar.

Center the lids and apply the rings by twisting them until they are finger-tight. Place the jars on the rack in the pressure canner containing 2 inches of simmering water (180 degrees).

Place the lid on the canner and turn to the locked position. Adjust to medium-high heat. Vent steam for 10 mins. Put weighted gauge on vent, bring pressure to 10lbs (psi). Process pints for 75 minutes and quarts for 90 minutes.

For the jars that are sealed, remove ring bands, wash the lid and jar to remove food residue without disturbing the sealed lid; then rinse and dry the jars. There may be food or syrup residues you might not notice with your eyes. Which can support the growth of molds outside the jar during storage. Wash and dry ring bands to protect them from corrosion for future use.

Label and date the jars and store them in a clean, cool, dark, dry place. For best quality, store between 50 and 70 °F for no more than 1-2 years. It is recommended that jars be stored without ring bands to keep them dry as well as to allow for easier detection of any broken vacuum seals. Be careful not to disturb vacuum seals if you choose to stack your jars. If jars must be stored where they may freeze, wrap them in newspapers, place them in heavy cartons, and cover them with more newspapers and blankets.

Amish Root Cellar

Building a root cellar using a wood barrel buried underground is a traditional method utilized by the Amish community to store food and other perishable products for extended periods of time. A root cellar built with wood barrels can significantly extend the shelf life of any item that is easily spoiled. The stable temperature, humidity, and darkness provided by the root cellar environment create ideal conditions for preserving fruits, vegetables, and even canned goods, reducing food waste and ensuring a constant supply of fresh produce throughout the year. The Amish community regularly enjoys delicious homegrown apples, potatoes, and other staples well into the winter months, thanks to their root cellars.

You will never, ever, come across a single Amish farm without a root cellar. Putting up food for future meals is a critical part of everyday chores for the women and girls in the Amish community - even if they run a woodworking or construction business and not a farm related business.

Building a more traditional root cellar cut into a hillside is simply not affordable for everyone, nor do we all have the space or proper terrain to accomplish such a task. Using this simple and inexpensive wood barrel root cellar that the Amish have surely perfected, not only you can quickly and cheaply preserve your everyday food, but these vital survival preps also remain portable in case you have to bug out from your planned place of residence during a disaster.

Preserving Food THE AMISH WAY

Building a Root Cellar

Materials

Wood barrel (food-grade quality) - 55-gallon capacity
Nails or screws
Metal strapping
Insulation material - straw or hay (optional)
Rocks or gravel for drainage

Tools

Shovel or backhoe for digging
Brace and bit or power drill
Claw hammer or ball ping hammer and a metal punch (rod)
Use a hand saw, limb saw, or a hole saw

Recommended Barrel Dimensions

The ideal barrel size for an Amish wood barrel root cellar is 55-gallons. This size provides sufficient space for storing a variety of produce and food. However, you can adjust the dimensions according to your needs. Wooden barrels offer excellent insulation, ensuring a stable temperature and humidity within the root cellar. The natural pores in the wood allow for proper airflow, preventing condensation and reducing the risk of mold or spoilage. The Amish have long recognized this advantage and have perfected their root cellar techniques based on generations of experience.

Step-by-Step Instructions

Step 1: Choose a Suitable Location

✦ Select a location that is relatively flat, away from any potential runoff, and receives minimal direct sunlight.

✦ Ensure the ground is not prone to flooding or heavy moisture accumulation.

✦ Use a scythe or sickle (or weed eater if you want to go all modern) to remove any vegetation from around the area where the hole will be dug.

Step 2: Dig the Hole

✦ Using a shovel, dig a hole deep enough to accommodate the wood barrel. If you are going to make multiple barrel root cellars, having access to a backhoe will vastly speed up the digging process.

✦ The hole should be deep enough to allow around two-thirds of the barrel to be buried underground.

Step 3: Prepare the Barrel

✦ Remove any plastic or metal lids from the barrel.

✦ Clean the barrel thoroughly using mild detergent and rinse it several times to eliminate any potential contaminants.

Preserving Food The Amish Way

- Allow the barrel to dry completely before proceeding.
- Use the hammer and punch to pound the metal straps on the barrel down to tighten them up - they loosen over time.

Step 4: Add Metal Strapping

- Use metal strapping approximately 1-inch wide to further tighter and secure the barrel both above and below where the door will be made into the barrel.

Step 5: Create Ventilation Holes

- Using a manual or power drill, create small ventilation holes at regular intervals on the sides and top of the barrel.
- These holes will help maintain proper airflow inside the root cellar.

Step 6: Door

- Cut a door into the barrel in between the strapping so that you can easily reach in and snag your food when needed.
- Use the brace and bit or a power drill to make a start hole for cutting out the door. 
- Use your hole saw to cut out the desired door size in the top and place another piece of metal strapping to serve as an additional stave to help preserve the airtight nature of the barrel. Repeat this step on the bottom of the door. Cutting the top straight line for the door and bottom straight line for the door up to the board space on each side will free the left and right sides of the doo without additional cutting or destruction of the wood you want to remain as tight as possible for the barrel root cellar. 
- Add door hinges and hardware with a screw driver as per the package instructions.

Step 7: Place the Barrel

- Lower the barrel into the hole, ensuring it is level and securely positioned.
- Leave a small space above the barrel for insulation material.

Step 8: Fill the Surroundings

- Backfill the hole, covering the frame and the sides of the barrel, leaving only the top exposed

Step 9: Insulate the Barrel - Optional

- Cover the barrel with a layer of straw, leaves or hay to insulate it from temperature fluctuations.
- Ensure the straw or hay is wrapped tightly without compressing the barrel

Step 10: Add Drainage Layer - Optimal

- Place a layer of rocks or gravel at the bottom of the hole to facilitate drainage.

What Foods Do the Amish Store in a Wood Barrel Root Cellar?

Root Vegetables

Root vegetables such as potatoes, carrots, turnips, and beets are excellent candidates for storage in a wood barrel root cellar. These crops require a cool temperature range of 32-40°F (0-4°C) with humidity levels between 90-95%. Carefully brush off excess soil, ensuring the vegetables remain unwashed to prevent moisture retention. Place them in layers within the barrel, separating each layer with a breathable material like straw or sawdust. Properly stored root vegetables can last up to several months, with potatoes often maintaining their quality for up to six months.

Apples and Pears

Apples and pears can be stored in a wood barrel root cellar as long as they are free from bruises or signs of rot. These fruits should ideally be stored at around 32-40°F (0-4°C) with humidity levels of 80-90%. Arrange the fruits in a single layer, ensuring they do not come into direct contact with each other. Regularly check for any signs of spoilage and promptly remove any affected fruits. When properly stored, apples and pears can last from three to six months.

Onions and Garlic

Onions and garlic thrive in conditions similar to those of root vegetables. These crops require temperatures within the range of 32-40°F (0-4°C) with humidity levels between 65-70%. Cure the bulbs by laying them in a single layer in a dry, well-ventilated area for a few days before storing. Once cured, move the onions and garlic into the wood barrel root cellar and arrange them in mesh bags or on racks to allow for proper airflow. Under suitable conditions, onions and garlic can be stored for up to six to eight months.

Preserving Food THE AMISH WAY

Winter Squash

Winter squash varieties, such as butternut, acorn, and hubbard squash, can withstand colder temperatures than other crops. Store them in a wood barrel root cellar at temperatures around 50-55°F (10-13°C) with a humidity level of 50-75%. Before storage, allow the squash to cure for a couple of weeks in a dry area with good airflow. Place the squash side by side, avoiding direct contact with each other, and rotate them periodically to ensure even ripening. When stored properly, winter squash can last up to six months or even longer.

Cabbage and Kale

Cabbage and kale require colder storage temperatures, between 32-40°F (0-4°C), with humidity levels of 85-95%. Remove any damaged or wilted leaves before storing. Place the cabbage heads or kale bundles on a shelf or hang them from the root cellar's ceiling, ensuring they do not touch the walls. Rotate the heads every few weeks to prevent moisture collection and inspect them regularly for any signs of decay. When stored correctly, cabbage can retain its quality for three to four months, while kale can last approximately two months.

A wood barrel root cellar allows us to prolong the shelf life of various food items by creating conditions that mimic nature's own storage methods. By adhering to proper temperature, humidity, and storage techniques for each food item, we can drastically reduce food waste and ensure our pantry remains stocked throughout the year.

Store Meat Like the Amish

It is entirely possible to store cured meats in a wood barrel root cellar. Wood barrels are known for their natural insulating properties. They provide reliable temperature and humidity control, crucial for proper meat preservation. The wood acts as a buffer against external temperature fluctuations, helping maintain a cool and consistent environment.

Storing cured meat in wood barrels can enhance flavor development. The wood imparts mild smoky or woody characteristics into the meat, adding complexity and depth to its taste. The texture and aroma of the meat may also benefit from the natural aging process that occurs inside the wood barrel.

Properly cured and stored meat in a wood barrel root cellar can significantly extend its shelf life. The controlled temperature and humidity levels inside the cellar delay the growth of spoilage bacteria. The salt, honey, or smoke used during the curing process also contribute to preservation, further elongating the meat's lifespan.

Scientific studies have shown that maintaining temperature and humidity levels below 50°F (10°C) and 85% relative humidity respectively can effectively preserve cured meat. Wood barrels have been observed to provide stable and appropriate conditions within these ranges. However, it is important to monitor and adjust these parameters regularly for optimal results.

The quality of the meat used, the curing process, and the cleanliness and sealing of the wood barrel all contribute to successful preservation.

Practical Tips and Recommendations for Storing Cured Meat in a Barrel Root Cellar

1. **Choose the Right Barrel:** Opt for a food-grade oak barrel or other suitable hardwood barrel. Ensure it is in good condition, free from leaks, and has been properly cleaned and conditioned.

2. **Prioritize Proper Curing Techniques:** Follow trusted recipes and guidelines for salt-curing, honey-curing, or smoking the meat before storing it in the wood barrel. This ensures the meat is safe and flavorful.

3. **Monitor and Regulate Temperature and Humidity:** Invest in a thermometer and hygrometer to regularly monitor the cellar's conditions. Make necessary adjustments such as ventilation or insulation to maintain optimal temperature and humidity levels.

4. **Regularly Clean and Seal the Barrel:** Thoroughly clean the barrel after each use, removing any residue, and allow it to dry completely. Before storing meat, seal the barrel to prevent oxygen exposure.

5. **Rotate the Meat:** Regularly rotate stored meat to ensure even exposure to the wood barrel's environment, helping to maintain consistent flavor and texture.

Preserving Food **THE AMISH WAY**

Storing salt-cured, honey-cured, or smoked meat in a wood barrel root cellar can be an effective method of preservation. The historical significance, flavors imbued by the wood, controlled temperature and humidity, and extended shelf life all contribute to the merits of this approach. However, it is crucial to follow proper curing techniques, maintain the cellar environment, and ensure regular quality checks for successful preservation.

Wood Barrel Root Cellar Food Storage and Shelf-Life Tips

- Maintain a temperature range between 32°F (0°C) and 40°F (4°C) for most vegetables and fruits.
- Keep humidity levels between 85-95% to prevent wilting and dehydration.
- Rotate produce regularly to ensure even exposure to temperature and humidity conditions.
- Store different types of produce separately to prevent spoilage.
- Regularly inspect stored items for signs of rot, mold, or decay.

Potential Challenges and Safety Precautions

1. **Deterioration:** Over time, wood barrels may deteriorate due to moisture exposure. Regularly inspect the barrel's condition and replace if necessary.
2. **Pest Control:** Take measures to prevent pests like rodents, insects, and critters from accessing the root cellar. Ensure the cover is secure and any ventilation holes are screened.
3. **Safety:** Exercise caution while digging the hole and using tools. Wear appropriate protective gear and use tools as directed during construction.
4. **Limited Space:** Wood barrels, being cylindrical in shape, may limit the available storage space compared to more streamlined alternatives such as modular shelving units or plastic containers. However, this disadvantage is often offset by the versatility and expandability of barrels, allowing for more efficient use of limited space.

Building an Amish wood barrel root cellar provides a traditional and efficient way to store produce and food items for extended periods. By following these, you can create a practical and reliable root cellar that helps maximize shelf life and minimize food wastage. Remember to maintain optimal storage conditions and regularly inspect and rotate stored items to ensure their freshness and quality.

In the event of power outages or extreme weather conditions, a root cellar allows families to sustain themselves without relying solely on perishable goods or refrigeration. The capacity to store non-perishable food items, such as canned goods or preserved produce, can prove invaluable during emergencies or natural disasters.

The Amish community's preference for using wood barrels in the construction of root cellars stems from a combination of practicality, cost-effectiveness, and centuries of experience. The advantages of wood barrels, including insulation, breathability, adaptability, and affordability, make them an attractive option for long-term food preservation and disaster preparedness. By embracing this traditional approach, you can incorporate sustainable and resourceful strategies into their lives while minimizing food waste and maximizing self-sufficiency.

Preserving Food THE AMISH WAY

AMISH PANTRIES 101

The Amish can go a whole year without restocking the food supplies in their pantry. And that is because they know exactly how to build and design a pantry.

In this chapter, we will take a look at the best place to locate a pantry, the ideal design, what foods you can preserve inside it and how. I will also share some secrets for transforming your pantry from a regular cupboard with doors filled with store canned goods, to a long-term food storage supply.

The Perfect Location for Building a Pantry

Finding the perfect location for a pantry requires surveying your home with a critical eye to see where the sun directly hits, so avoid conservatories or south-facing rooms. You need a shady, cooler area that will offer your preserved food better conditions. This could be a cupboard under the stairs, a special area where you make a new door and add shelves, or a shed or basement room where the sun rarely reaches.

The Amish often choose root cellars, designed to keep food cool in summer but also prevent it from freezing in cold winter months. A root cellar will be designed with shelves where canned preserves can be stored neatly, as well as fruit, nuts, potatoes, grain, and perhaps root vegetables sometimes stored in boxes of sand to ensure they do not rot or start to grow. You can often find dried squash and pumpkins here too, as these keep well until spring.

Your canned and dehydrated food needs a place out of direct sunlight, which can be as simple as a closed cupboard. It must not have a high temperature in summer, so a basement storage area is perfect. However, a lot depends on the quantity and type of food. Canned food and preserves with lids can be stacked on a shelf quite easily because pests will find these difficult to open.

To store potatoes (or grain) in a sack requires a cool place out of sunlight, but you will also have to bear in mind if insects, ants, and other pests can access your food. The perfect location involves knowing what local pests exist in your area and if they will try to raid your stores.

How often will you need to visit your storage room? If it is every day, make sure it is not down some rickety stairs or a long way from the house because you will feel reluctant in snowy or frosty weather.

159

Preserving Food **THE AMISH WAY**

How to Build a Pantry

After you decide where you are going to build the pantry, you'll need to gather a few basic materials and tools.

> **WARNING!**
>
> DO NOT build this pantry on drywall or any other kind of soft wall!
>
> Only build a pantry on a sturdy solid wall that is either made of brick or solid wood.

Materials

Hardwood boards (I highly recommend going for the thicker variety, anything past 2x4 in would do just fine. They also need to be around 92 in long)
Hardwood posts (In this example, we are going to use some 4x4 in timbers)
Wood screws (#8 ¾ self-tapping wood screws would work great for this project)
Heavy-duty wall plugs and screws
Heavy-duty metal washers
L-shaped corner braces

Tools

Saw
Impact drill
Screwdriver
Measuring tape
Level
Wire detector
Hammer

Instructions

Step 1: Planning the Layout of the Pantry

For this example, our pantry is going to be 6 ft tall and 15.3 ft wide. If we want to have 4 shelves in our pantry, that will give us a 1.5 ft shelf height, which is going to be just about right for any type of can or jar that you might want to store on it.

Using a level and a 2x4, draw a straight line on the wall along the length of the first shelf, at the 1.5 ft mark, starting from the floor. Keep in mind that the shelf is going to have the length of two boards. Using the level, mark 8 equally distanced dots on the wall, 2 in below each line, for the fixing points of the boards. These should be placed about 22.75 in apart. Repeat this process for all 4 shelves.

Step 2: Prepping the Boards

Do this for the remaining 3 shelves, keeping an even 1.5 ft distance between them. Now you should have 4 perfectly horizontal lines, evenly spaced at 1.5 ft.

Take a 2x4 and cut it into 4 equal parts. That should leave you with 4 lengths of board of 23 inches each. Take two long boards and mark them at the halfway point. This should be right about the 46 in mark. Mark 4 different points for where the mounting points are going to be placed, at about 22.75 in from each other and on the median line of the board (2 in from the top). Drill each hole using a wood drill bit, minding the diameter of the fixing screws that you chose. Repeat this process for all 4 shelves.

Step 3: Drilling the Holes and Installing the Plugs

The Amish didn't have to worry about drilling through any electrical lines in the walls, but you might want to double-check just to be sure. Using a wire detector, go over each marking to double-check if there are any cables behind each mark.

Using an impact drill, drill out each hole that you have previously marked on the wall. Depending on the plugs and screws you choose, make sure that you don't drill too deep or too shallow.

> **Pro tip:** Add some insulation tape on the drill bit at the length of the plug. That will give you a visual cue for when to stop drilling.

After you finish drilling all the holes, insert the plugs. Some of them might need a light tap with a hammer.

Step 4: Mounting the Boards to the Wall

Align the holes in the boards with the plugs in the wall and loosely insert 4 screws with some heavy-duty washers on them. Keep in mind that there are still some markings that you need to consider, so I strongly suggest orienting those towards you, not towards the wall. Tighten the screws using a screwdriver.

Step 5: Adding Horizontal Supports

Using the L-shaped corner braces, add a 23 in board that you have previously cut to each marking, as well as to every board joining place and the ends of the outer boards.

Pro tip: You should mount two braces to the sides of a 23 in board before lifting it up to the wall. This way it's going to be a lot easier to mount.

Step 6: Adding the Front Posts

Measure and cut 8 4x4 posts at a length of 6 ft. Place these posts vertically in front of the 23 in supports that correspond to the start and end points of each wall-mounted board and screw them in using a couple of #8 screws for each support.

Step 7: Adding the Shelving Boards

Now all that is left is adding the actual boards for the shelves. In order to do so, you are going to need 10 92 in long 2x4s for each shelf, adding them in 2 columns of 5 boards each. Fix the ends to the supports using 4 #8 screws for each board (2 on each side).

Now your pantry is done.

What to Store Inside Your Amish-Style Pantry

1. DRIED MEAT

Preserving meat for a long time, and keeping its nutritional value, is not a simple task. Besides the canned meat recipes shared throughout the book, which can be added to your pantry (see pages 143, 147, 150), I will also share a traditional Amish recipe for preparing jerky... deer jerky.

Commercial beef jerky usually lasts for 1 year, but if you are looking for a jerky that can last for much longer, I will let you in some tricks.

The Amish tend to use deer instead of beef for several reasons. One of them is the fact that deer meat is leaner than beef, which means it is higher in protein. Also, it is lower in fat, which means that the risk of meat spoiling and becoming rancid is reduced, so it is a better choice for long-term preservation.

Ingredients

Venison:	2 pounds of venison
Salt:	2 teaspoons
Black Pepper:	2 teaspoons, coarsely ground

Instructions

Start by trimming any fat from the venison. There should remain no fat at all on the meat, to make sure you prevent it from spoilage.

Then, slice the venison into thin strips, about 1/4 inch thick. My advice is to cut it against the grain, for a more tender jerky - cutting with the grain will most probably make it chewier.

In a large bowl, mix the strips with salt and pepper. Let it sit for about 30 minutes. This will allow the venison to get the seasoning flavors.

Preheat your oven to 160°F or set up your food dehydrator, in case you want to use one instead of an oven. However, in the community we rely on our Pioneer oven (see the *House and Water Heating* Chapter, page 183), thanks to the fact that it doesn't require any electricity and can be heated using any flammable resource available. Also, because of its slower process, the meat will dry out way better inside the oven and it will be preserved for longer.

Place the meat strips on the baking rack or dehydrator trays, making sure they do not overlap.

If you use an oven, keep the door slightly open to allow moisture to escape.

Dry the venison for 4-6 hours, or until it reaches a high leel of dryness. The drier the jerky, the better, as this will ensure the longer storage. I dry it so well sometimes, that I need to boil the jerky before eating it.

After the jerky is completely cooled off, store it in an airtight container. I highly recommend using glass containers, as they will keep the food safe and

2. CHEESE

The Amish, particularly in Ohio, make quantities of cheese using milk from their own cows so you can be confident that there are no added hormones or chemicals added to the animals' feed. They grow on grass from Amish farms only. The milk is pasteurized and then made into the cheese that Ohio Amish county is famous for, such as Amish Swiss, Amish Butter Cheese or Jack Cheese. Once cured, cheese can be stored for months in a root cellar. It will not last indefinitely, but certainly a lot longer than fresh milk.

Jack Cheese

Ingredients

2 gallons whole milk
1/4 tsp mesophilic starter culture – this ingredient can be purchased from an Amish store or market
1/4 tsp calcium chloride (if using pasteurized milk)
1/4 tsp liquid rennet
1 tbsp cheese salt
Cheese wax (optional)

Instructions

Heat the milk to 86°F (30°C).

Sprinkle the mesophilic starter culture on the milk, let it sit for 2 minutes, then stir.

Cover the pot and let it ripen for 45 minutes.

Stir in diluted calcium chloride and rennet.

Let the milk sit undisturbed for 45-60 minutes until a clean break forms.

Cut the curds into 1/4-inch cubes and let them rest for 5 minutes.

Slowly heat the curds to 102°F (39°C) over 30 minutes, stirring gently.

Let the curds settle and drain the whey until it's level with the curds.

Place the curds in a cheesecloth-lined colander for 15 minutes, then slice and stack them in the pot at 102°F (39°C) for 2 hours, turning every 15 minutes.

Cut the curds into 1/2-inch pieces and mix in cheese salt.

Press the curds in a mold at 10 lbs for 15 minutes, then at 20 lbs for 12 hours.

Air-dry the cheese on a mat for 1-2 days.

Optionally, wax the cheese and age it at 50-55°F (10-13°C) for 1-2 months.

3. CANNED GOODS

Meat

For canned meat recipes, you can check pages 143, 147, 150.

Eggs

A popular recipe which has been passed on for generations in the Amish community is Eggs Covered in Salt.

Eggs Covered in Salt

Ingredients

Eggs
Homemade vinegar
Salt
Sugar
Spices like cinnamon and cloves (which help extend the shelf life of stored food)
Aliced red beets

Instructions

Combine hard-boiled eggs with sliced red beets, giving the pickled eggs a bright red color. To prepare, hard boil the eggs, let them cool, and place four in a clean jar.

Add cooked beet slices, then fill the jar with equal parts vinegar, sugar, and water, leaving an inch of space at the top.

Seal the jar with a lid. The eggs will gradually turn pink or even purple as they absorb the beet color.

How to Check If the Eggs are Safe to Eat

When not sure whether an egg is still good to eat or not, fill a bowl with cold water and place the egg inside, gently, not to break its shell. If the egg floats, it is certainly spoiled and it should not be consumed. If the egg sinks and lies flat, it is very fresh.

Snacks and Sweets

When thinking about a long-term food storage, sweets and snacks are usually not something we consider. But the Amish are known for their several sweets recipes, especially baked ones. And they can 100% be canned in jars, for a long-term shelf life.

My personal favorite Amish sweet recipe is the classic:

Amish Friendship Bread Starter (for Canning)

Ingredients

1 cup all-purpose flour
1 cup sugar
1 cup milk
1 packet (2 ¼ tsp) active dry yeast
½ cup warm water (110°F)

Instructions

Activate the Yeast

In a small bowl, dissolve the yeast in warm water and let it sit for about 10 minutes until it becomes frothy.

Mix the Starter

In a large glass or plastic bowl, combine the flour and sugar. Mix well.

Add the milk and the yeast mixture to the bowl. Stir until the mixture is smooth and well combined.

Fermentation

Cover the bowl loosely with a cloth or plastic wrap and let it sit at room temperature.

Stir the mixture once a day for the next 4-5 days. By day 5, your starter will have developed a bubbly, yeasty aroma, indicating it's ready.

Can the Starter

Pour the starter into sterilized jars, leaving about 1 inch of headspace. Seal the jars with sterilized lids and rings.

Store the jars in the refrigerator. The starter can be stored for up to 6 months.

Amish Friendship Bread (Using the Starter)

Ingredients

1 cup *Amish Friendship Bread Starter*
2 cups all-purpose flour
1 cup sugar
1 ½ tsp baking powder
½ tsp baking soda
½ tsp salt
1 tsp cinnamon
3 large eggs
½ cup vegetable oil
½ cup milk
1 tsp vanilla extract
Optional: 1 cup nuts, raisins, or chocolate chips

Instructions

Preheat the Oven

Preheat your oven to 325°F (165°C).

Grease two loaf pans or line them with parchment paper.

Mix Dry Ingredients

In a medium bowl, whisk together the flour, sugar, baking powder, baking soda, salt, and cinnamon.

Mix Wet Ingredients

In a large bowl, beat the eggs, then add the starter, oil, milk, and vanilla extract. Mix until smooth.

Combine

Gradually add the dry ingredients to the wet ingredients, mixing just until combined. Do not overmix.

If desired, fold in nuts, raisins, or chocolate chips.

Bake

Pour the batter evenly into the prepared loaf pans.

Bake for 50-60 minutes, or until a toothpick inserted into the center comes out clean.

Allow the bread to cool in the pans for 10 minutes before transferring to a wire rack to cool completely.

4. HERBS

The Amish usually hand the herbs up on the rafters. They hang the onions and garlic there for better preservation, just as well as the medicinal or edible herbs harvested throughout the year. You can hand any of the herbs you prefer and find useful there, but I usually recommend hanging feverfew, which can be used for teas and for several other homemade quick remedies. For instance, you can quickly make the *Painkiller in a Jar* remedy using feverfew (see the recipe below). Also, I always have some Lamb's Ear in my pantry, to use as Band-Aid, whenever in need, and yarrow, for *Styptic Wound Powder* (see page 82).

Herbs can also be dried and stored in jars. Some of these herbs can be Lemon Verbena, Mint, Sage, Thyme, Oregano, Lavender or Rosemary. They can be used both culinary and medicinally, so there would be a big advantage to have them in your pantry.

Preserving Food THE AMISH WAY

PAINKILLER IN A JAR

Ingredients

- A small glass jar (4 ounces) with a lid
- A brown glass bottle with a dropper for tinctures
- Dried feverfew, at least 2 oz
- 80 proof alcohol, enough to fill the jar (e.g. vodka)
- Fine strainer or cheesecloth

Instructions

Step 1
Place your dried feverfew in the jar, packing it well to allow for more space.

Step 2
Once the jar is just over halfway full, pour your alcohol over it gently, all the way to the top of the jar.

Step 3
You can seal the lid and shake it or mix everything together with a spoon before sealing it.

Step 4
Put today's date on the jar so you know when you prepared it. Now place it in a cool dark place. Leave it here for the next 4-6 weeks. Your herbs cabinet is a perfect place for it.

Step 5
The tincture is ready after 4-6 weeks; all you need to do is strain it and pour it into a tincture bottle. Brown glass tincture jars protect the contents from sunlight, extending their effects significantly.

You can also store your homemade medicine inside the pantry, as it will be a good way to protect your natural remedies from direct sunlight. By increasing the temperature, the sunlight accelerates the breakdown of active ingredients and other compounds in homemade medicines, which will make them inactive or even dangerous if used both topically and by swallowing.

How to Organize the Pantry

It is recommended to store light, infrequently used items such as dry goods, herbs and spices on the top shelves. That is because, being less sturdy, they are better suited for items that are not too heavy.

On the eye-level shelves, it would be best to keep frequently used dried goods, like rice, cereals, or other cans that are used in the daily routine. Lower shelves should be reserved for heavy canned goods, jars, and other weighty items to ensure they are stored securely.

Building an Amish Buried Fridge

A buried barrel fridge, also known as an Amish fridge, is a sustainable, electricity-free food preservation solution. Ideal for off-grid living, camping, or emergency preparedness, it utilizes the earth's steady subterranean temperature (around 55-60 degrees Fahrenheit) and ice slabs from frozen waterways to keep perishable items cool and protected from predators.

Materials and Tools Needed

Before we look into the process of creating your own Amish buried fridge, we need to gather all the necessary tools and materials.

Here's what you'll need:

Materials

A hogshead or american standard barrel, preferably made of american white oak or similar wood
An aluminum band or heavy-duty strapping
Two larger strap hinges
1-inch wood screws
3-inch deck screws
Brass or aluminum door handle

Tools

Round digger shovel
Metal mallet
Chisel
Hand drill with a 1-inch wide drill bit
Folding saw
Ice Saw
Ice hook
A battery-powered drill or screwdriver

Where to Build Your Amish Buried Fridge

Selecting an appropriate site for your buried Amish fridge is a big step in ensuring its efficiency and longevity. Ideally, this project should be executed in winter. It is the optimum time of year as you can source the ice blocks from a nearby frozen body of water.

The location you choose should be sheltered from direct sunlight, even during the winter months. A spot on the northern side of a slope or hill can be excellent due to its naturally cooler environment. It is also crucial to ensure that your chosen site has good drainage to avoid water accumulation around the fridge, which can lead to inconsistent temperatures and potential damage.

The soil type at your chosen site is another factor. Loamy soil, a balanced mixture of sand, silt, and clay, is typically the best choice. It offers good drainage, preventing water buildup, while retaining enough moisture to help maintain a cool temperature within your buried barrel fridge. But don't worry too much about this like a lake or pond.

Preserving Food **THE AMISH WAY**

Building Your Amish Buried Fridge: A Step-by-Step Guide

Here's a complete, step-by-step guide to building your fridge using the equipment list provided.

Step 1: Excavate the Site

Using the round digger shovel, dig a hole approximately 30 inches wide and 40 inches deep for the barrel to fit in.

Step 2: Prepare the Barrel

The barrel typically has 4 hoops, two on each end. Using the metal mallet and chisel, loosen and remove the two hoops closest to the middle of the barrel. This will make room for the door you will cut later.

Step 3: Drill Guide Holes

Using the hand drill, drill a hole through the barrel where the removed hoop was, on both sides. The barrel should be lying on its side for this. The holes should be about 2 in below the bunghole of the barrel, forming a triangle if you connect a line between all three.

Step 4: Reinforce the Barrel

Using aluminum strapping, reinforce the barrel where the hoop was removed. The strap should be around 23-27in long and placed closer to the edge of the barrel where the remaining hoop is. Predrill the holes through the strapping and into the barrel using the metal screw. Apply the wood screws. Repeat this process on both ends of the barrel.

Step 5: Add Further Reinforcement

Apply a 20 cm piece of aluminum strapping over half the hole drilled earlier to reinforce the door. Ensure there's room left in the hole to fit the folding saw for door cutting. Predrill the holes for the wood screws. Repeat this process on both sides of the barrel.

Step 6: Install the Hinges

Position the large strap hinges halfway up the short piece of strapping, with the placement of the hinges on the inner side of the strapping, towards the barrel's middle. Fasten the strap part of the hinge with wood screws, and then use the 3-inch deck screws for securing the hinge itself.

Step 7: Cut Out the Door

Insert the folding saw in the half hole left exposed by the strapping. Cut downwards to the edge of the hinge, and repeat on the other side. Cut upwards from the hinge to the top of the short strapping piece. Cut across to connect the side cuts. When done the door should pop up a little as the hinges hold it to the barrel

Step 8: Install the Handle

Install a metal handle or door knocker over the bunghole using screws.

Step 9: Install the Latch

Install a catch and latch on the opposite side of the door to act as a stopper, ensuring the door stays closed.

Step 10: Cut Ice Slabs

Use the ice saw to cut several 12 cm thick slabs of ice from a frozen waterway. The thicker slabs will melt

THE AMISH WAYS

Preserving Food THE AMISH WAY

slowly, providing a cold for your fridge.

Step 11: Haul the Ice

Use the ice hook to haul the ice out of the water.

Step 12: Prepare the Insulation

Gather some dead marsh grasses. They will both insulate the refrigerator and keep the ice from directly touching your food.

Step 13: Install the Fridge

Lay a slab of ice on the floor of the dug hole. Lower the barrel into the hole with the door facing upward. Fill the barrel with an ice slab and other pieces so that the bottom is covered. Cover the ice with dried, dead grasses and reeds. Add a few chunks of ice on top of that.

Step 14: Store Your Food

You can now store your jarred food, meat, and other goods in your new Amish buried fridge.

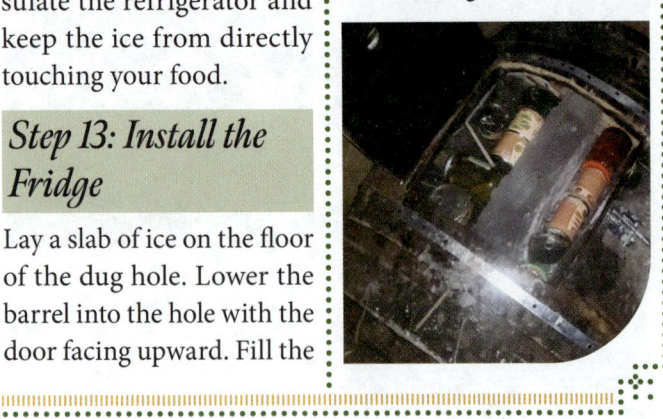

Additional Tips

While constructing your Amish buried fridge, here are some supplementary tips you may find beneficial:

1. **Insulate the Barrel:** After placing the barrel in the hole, fill in the surrounding space with grasses and dirt. This will provide an additional layer of insulation, helping to keep your food cold for longer.

2. **Shelter the Fridge:** Consider using a tarp to shelter the fridge from the rain. This will prevent the rainwater from seeping into the barrel, keeping your stored items dry.

3. **Alternative Barrel Material:** In the absence of a wooden barrel, a food-grade plastic barrel can be used as an alternative. While it may not provide the same aesthetic, it will serve the purpose effectively in a pinch.

The Amish buried fridge represents a clever and resourceful solution for preserving food in environments where conventional refrigeration is absent or impracticable.

During winter, the naturally low ¬temperatures act as an organic refrigerator, allowing the food stored in the barrel fridge to retain its freshness over extended periods. The sturdy barrel also acts as a robust protective barrier against wildlife, ensuring that your food remains uncontaminated and safe.

The combined effect of the insulation and shade can significantly delay the melting of the ice, extending the fridge's effectiveness into the warm summer months and even autumn

As the seasons transition into warmer periods, the Amish fridge still maintains its utility. While it is crucial to ensure that the area where you situate the barrel remains shaded and cool, the insulating properties of the earth can help keep the interior of the barrel cooler than the outside temperature.

Preserving Food THE AMISH WAY

AMISH SMOKEHOUSE

BUILDING AN AMISH SMOKEHOUSE

Materials

- Wooden posts (2x4 timbers)
- Side walls (1/4 in plywood)
- Screws (#8 3/8 self-tapping wood screws)
- Nails
- Furring strips
- Hinges for the entrance door
- Chicken wire for the spark arrester
- Heavy gauge wire

Tools

- Hammer
- Screwdriver
- Saw (for cutting wood and plywood)
- Angle grinder (for cutting chicken wire)
- Measuring tape
- Auger
- Wire cutters
- Shovel

Instructions

Step 1: Finding the Right Spot

Choose a semi-sheltered, flat area and clear it of brush and debris.

Step 2: Marking the Ground

Insert a twig in the ground to mark your starting point.

Step 3: Measuring the Base

Measure 4 ft. from the starting twig and place another stick in the ground. Repeat this step for the remaining sides to form a square, outlining your smokehouse's floor space.

Step 4: Digging the Holes

Dig holes at each stick marker, approximately 3 ft. deep, and remove loose dirt.

Step 5: Cleaning the Boards

Clean the 2x4 timber boards with the sharp end of a hammer to remove dirt.

Step 6: Measuring and Cutting the Timber

Mark your timber at 6 ft. using a tape measure, then cut it at a 45° angle on the wide side.

Step 7: Inserting the Posts in the Ground

Insert the cut timber into the holes you've dug. Repeat for the remaining three posts.

169

Preserving Food THE AMISH WAY

Step 8: Ensuring that the Posts are Vertical

Use a level to ensure the posts are vertically straight, then backfill the holes to secure them.

Step 9: Adding Median Supports

Measure the distance between two poles to ensure consistency and cut some 2x4 lumber to size.

Find the halfway point of the vertical posts and screw in the newly cut piece of wood between them for median support. Repeat this for all four sides.

Step 10: Adding Top Supports

Using the same length of boards as in the previous step, cut four more boards to size and add them between the poles, fastening them with #8 screws.

Use two screws on each side of the board to ensure it stays in place.

Step 11: Adding Bottom Supports

Using the same measurements as in the previous steps, cut down four additional boards.

Add them by fitting the support at an angle, then hammering it into position and screwing it into the posts.

Step 12: Making the Gable

To create the gable's outline, you will need a couple of furring strips for each side.

Screw them together at a 90-degree angle and secure them to the ends of the main posts on the front and rear sides of the smokehouse.

After they are secured in place, add a median support between the front and back sides of the gable, about halfway between them on both the left and right sides.

Step 13: Creating Walls for the Smokehouse

To create walls for this smokehouse, measure the lateral distance between two poles and the distance between the ground and the base of the gable.

Trim a piece of plywood to size and fix it to one side of the smokehouse using #8 screws. Repeat this step for three of the four sides of the smokehouse.

170

Step 14: Creating a Door for the Smokehouse

For the door, you will need another piece of plywood. Measure out another board using the same blueprint as for one of the walls.

After you trim the board to size, cut it in half. Use a level attached to a wooden board to mark a straight line at the center of the board.

Ensure the two halves are equal in size, then make the cut. Now you have two equally sized boards to use for the doors.

To make the door sturdier, create a frame for it. Measure the length and width of a board, then cut four furring strips to each of the two sizes.

Attach two lengths and two widths of furring strips to the sides of each panel. To finish the doors, screw in two hinges to each door.

Optionally, you can add an X-shaped bracing by cutting two lengths of furring boards diagonally on the door.

To fit it snugly with the frame, cut the ends at a 45° angle. To finish the structure, screw each door into place.

Position it on the smokehouse and add screws through the loose ends of the hinges.

Step 15: Finishing Up the Gable

Measure the lateral sides of the gable and cut two pieces of plywood to those dimensions.

Attach them to the sides of the gable using #8 screws. To finish, measure the front and rear triangular pieces.

Cut two pieces of plywood to match that exact shape and screw them to the back and front sides of the gable.

Step 16: Making a Rain Cover for the Firewood

This step is simple. Measure the width of the smokehouse, then cut down two furring strips to size.

Take two other furring strips that are about 6 ft. in length and create a rectangular frame. Measure the perimeter of the frame and cut an appropriate length of chicken wire to cover it.

Using some nails, attach the chicken wire to the frame. The only thing left is to screw this firewood-cover frame to the side of the smokehouse.

Rest it on the side of the smokehouse and attach it using two screws. Keep in mind that you will need to add the screws from inside the smokehouse.

You can cover this rack with a tarp to keep the firewood from getting wet.

Step 17: Digging the Fireplace Tunnel

Start by digging a 3 ft. deep hole inside the smokehouse that will cover most of the surface of its base.

Remove any dirt or debris from inside the smokehouse floor.

Then, dig another 3 ft. deep hole near the smokehouse, on the opposite side of the rain cover.

Connect the two holes, creating a tunnel.

Step 18: Creating a Spark Arrestor

Use an angle grinder to cut chicken wire for the spark arrestor top and sides. Tie the smaller sections inside the box with heavy gauge wire.

Place the wire box in the hole and dig a tunnel from the smokehouse to an adjacent fire pit.

Step 19: Creating the Racks

Screw in furring strips inside the smokehouse, spaced 2 in. apart, along the sidewalls. Add horizontal furring boards to create a rack for hanging meat.

Optionally, add chicken wire to the furring boards to create shelves for smoking meat.

Step 20: Lighting the Fire

Light a fire in the pit to direct smoke into the smokehouse through the underground tunnel.

Preserving Food **THE AMISH WAY**

Tips and Tricks

While the construction of this smokehouse is straightforward, there is always room for improvement. Here are some tips to help you shorten the time to build the smokehouse and even improve the final structure:

- **Measure twice, cut once:** This mantra is standard for all DIY projects, but still a good one to remember. Often, beginners will cut on the wrong side of the measurement, this is called a "deep sway". Double checking your markings and measurements is a good way to avoid these kinds of errors.

- **Use pre-made templates:** For repetitive shapes or structures like gables and the inside racks, create a template out of cardboard or scrap material. This will ensure consistency when you go to cut your pieces, speeding up the overall process.

- **Test fit before permanent fixing:** Before permanently securing elements like the door or roof pieces, do a test fit to ensure everything aligns correctly. This step can prevent potential issues that might require adjustments later on.

- **Cover your roof and sides with sheet metal:** If you are just using plywood as per the instructions above, covering it with aluminum siding or something similar can help protect the smokehouse from moisture damage and insect infestations.

- **Line the base of the smokehouse with chicken wire:** This will help keep rodents, small, and large animals from trying to get into the structure. Since you are cooking food in it, you will undoubtedly attract wildlife. If you can't use chicken wire, then a motion sensor LED light can help deter animals when you're not around.

Maintenance Advice for Your Wooden Smokehouse

To prolong the lifespan of your wooden smokehouse and safeguard against the risks of food spoilage or fire damage, here are some maintenance tips you can use:

- **Check the smokehouse often:** Routinely check for signs of wear and tear or damage such as loose boards or roof leaks. Early detection can prevent minor issues from becoming major problems.

- **Protect the wood surfaces:** Apply a sealant to the wood every year or two if you're not covering it in metal sheeting. This will protect against moisture, rot, and insect damage. Use a product that's safe for food contact surfaces if it will be applied inside the smokehouse.

- **Clean up any leftover food left in your smokehouse:** After each use, thoroughly clean the interior to prevent the buildup of grease and food particles, which could attract pests or become a fire hazard.

- **Be prepared for fire:** Have a fire extinguisher nearby, and regularly remove ash from the adjacent fire hole to prevent fire risks and root fires.

- **Covering the Smokehouse:** If the smokehouse is not in use for extended periods, consider covering it with a waterproof cover like a tarp to protect against the elements.

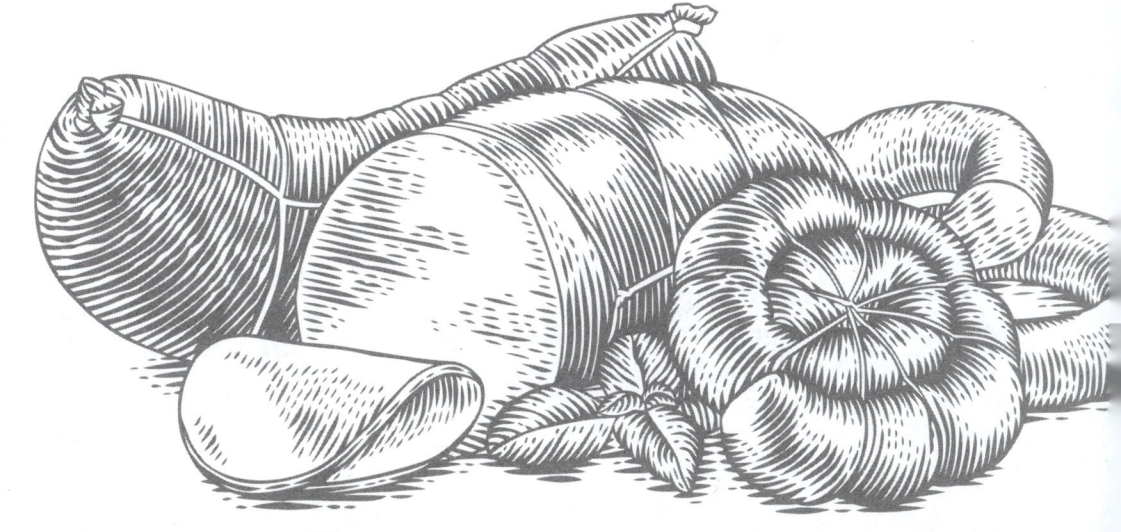

Be Aware of This When You Smoke Your Meat!

If your goal is long term preservation, you must cure your meats before smoking. Curing involves rubbing multiple layers of salts and sodium nitrite and sodium nitrate onto meats while allowing them to dehydrate.

Even after curing and smoking, make sure to store your food in dry, cool, and pest-free environments.

Food poisoning can originate from poor hygiene and contaminated animals or meat. Make sure that you only use cuts you can trust, and keep equipment and work surfaces sanitized. From slaughtering to eating, every step needs to be approached with diligence and the intent of maintaining food safety.

The Process

Hot Smoke

Hot smoking exposes meat to both heat and smoke. This should be done in a controlled environment where you can determine the heat and the amount of smoke.

Hot smoking is done at temperatures ranging from 52 to 80°C (126 to 176°F).

You can smoke food items from 1 to 24 hours.

If the smoker goes above 85°C (185°F), your food could become completely dehydrated and inedible.

Most foods can be cooked again after hot smoking, but in many cases, like smoked hams, this won't be necessary and you can immediately eat the foods.

Cold Smoke

Cold smoking is typically done at temperature ranges from 20 to 30 °C (68 to 86°F). It is important to fully cure meats before cold smoking. Could smoking is also ideal for imparting flavor to nuts and cheeses.

Ideally, you will cure your meat, like chicken, fish, or beef.

Then cold smoke for a while, and then do final cooking before eating.

Cold smoking is typically done for longer periods than hot smoking, and can sometimes go on for several days.

It's important to be aware that cold smoking is not a substitute for cooking. Also, be aware that meat that has not been exposed to sufficient heat may harbor diseases and parasites still active deep in the flesh.

Be sure to stick to health guidelines concerning the cooking of meat to eradicate flesh borne parasites or bacteria.

What Could Go Wrong

Curing

Too much curing can cause the meat to be too salty to enjoy. You could most likely still eat it in small amounts, but beware.

Too little curing will leave your meats susceptible to bacteria.

Many curing salts include sodium nitrate or sodium nitrite. These are important for preventing botulism, but should not be ingested above a certain threshold. Stick to health organizations' guidelines on the matter.

Burning

Hot smoking can burn or severely scald your meats. Rather smoke cooler and longer, than hotter and faster. Burnt meat loses its nutritional value and carbonized/blackened portions are bad for your health.

Balance

Just as too much heat can burn meat, too little heat can leave meat raw. The cooking process doesn't only change the nature of protein and fat but destroys bacteria and parasites.

Preserving Food **THE AMISH WAY**

What Wood to Use

A simple rule is to use clean and dry hardwoods of species you know that won't cause damage to your health or gut.

These can be used as smoldering logs or cut into shavings, moistened, and then placed onto coals to create smoke.

Hardwoods to use include Oak, Hickory, Maple, Pecan, Apple, Alder, Cherry, and Mesquite.

What Wood NOT to Use

Most softwoods like pine, or all needle producing trees, will give the meat a bitter taste.

Never use chemically treated or painted woods, including wood that is moldy or rotting. Chemicals present in paints or treatments will end up on your meat and could be severely detrimental to your health.

Some types of wood contain compounds that can lead to severe diarrhea and even death. If you are not sure about the wood you have access to, don't use it.

Species never to use include:

- Pine
- Redwood
- Fir
- Spruce
- Cypress
- Cedar

More comprehensive lists are available, and you would be well advised to familiarize yourself with them.

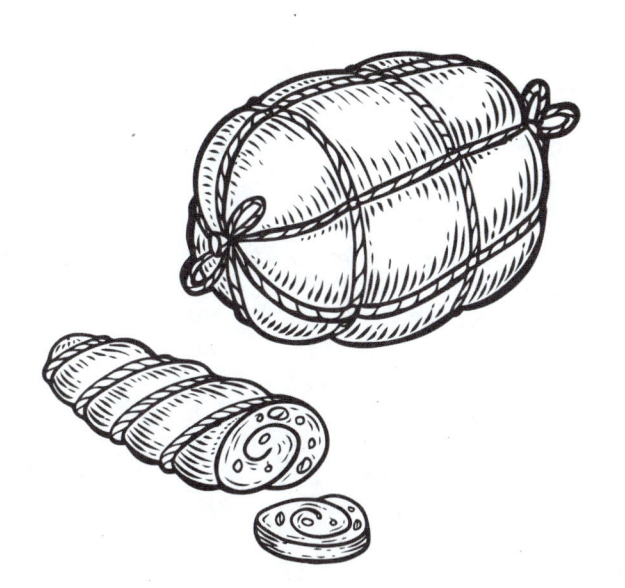

Remember

→ Smoking meat is not a technique for rescuing meat. Use only fresh cuts.

Meat from dead animals that may have been lying about for some time, or meat that may have started to spoil and have slimy layers of bad smells should not be smoked. In some cases, cold smoking may even make matters worse.

→ Before working with any meat, do a thorough inspection to make sure it's safe.

Look for any discoloration of flesh or fat, also look for signs of fluids leaking from the meat. Discolored water-like discharges or any slimy or viscous discharges could indicate unsuitability for human consumption.

Don't ignore any strange smells coming from the meat of blood. Spoiled meat will also sometimes feel slimy or grainy.

There are a whole host of diseases and parasites that can be contracted from both living and dead animals. Organisms such as bacteria, parasites, and even viruses can infect humans when handling meat or through exposure to animal blood or other fluids.

Bacteria such as *Salmonella*, *Escherichia coli* (*E. coli*), *Shigella*, and *Staphylococcus aureus* (to name but a few) can be present in raw meat and animal blood. Clean working environments and thorough cooking will limit the risk of contracting diseases.

Parasites such as Tapeworm can be ingested from raw or undercooked meat.

Other diseases, though rare, can also affect humans. The list includes anthrax, cryptosporidiosis, dermatophilosis, giardiasis, leptospirosis, listeriosis, pseudocowpox, Q fever, rabies, ringworm, tuberculosis. Not all exposure results in clinical disease, and it's also important to note that many diseases arise from exposure to milk, feces, or other bodily fluids.

→ You must follow hygiene protocols when working with meat to limit exposure and don't eat meat if there are doubts about its safety.

Self-Sufficiency
The Amish Way

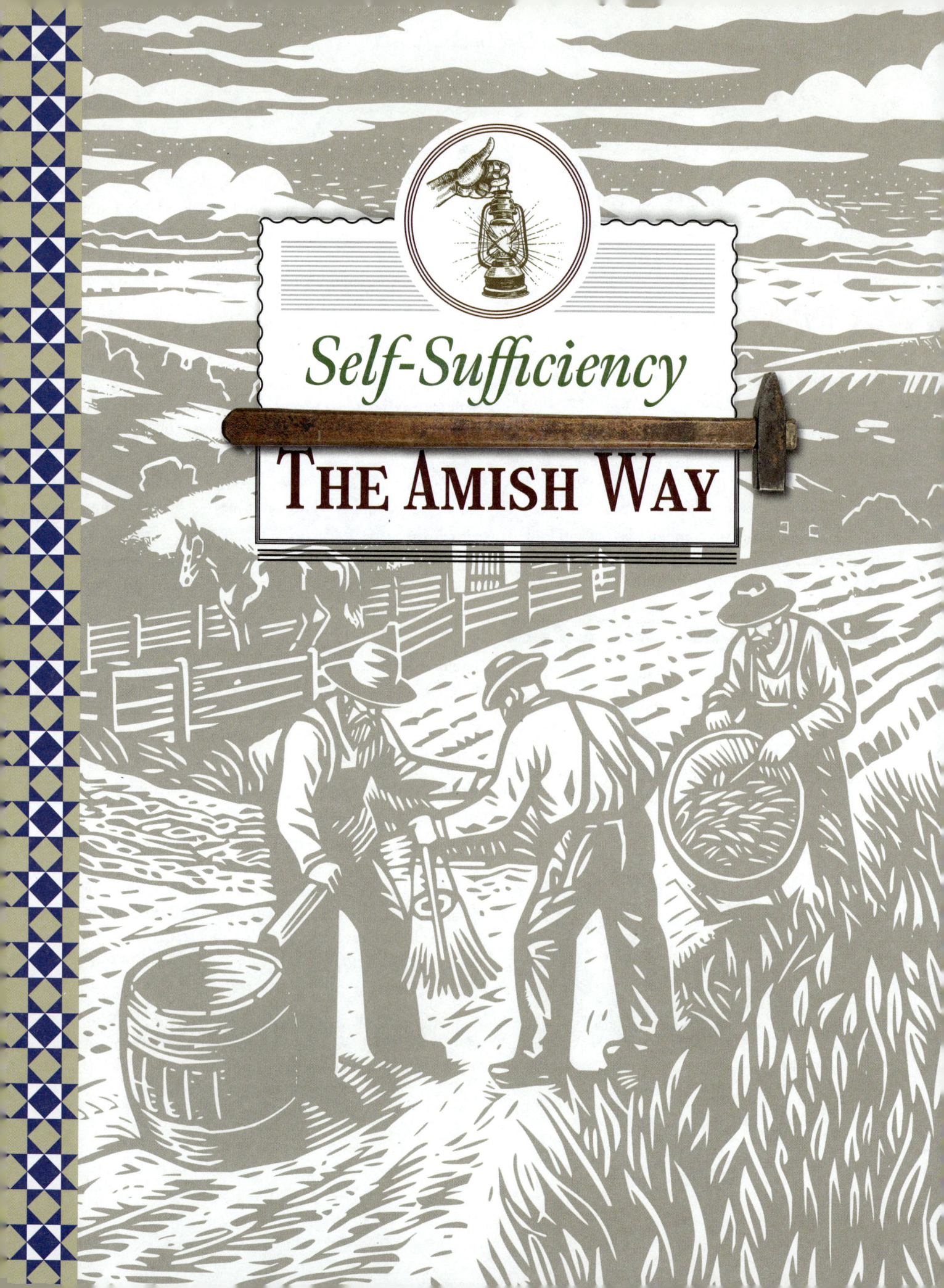

Amish Traditional Lighting Sources

While these methods may seem outdated for some, they are safe to use even during catastrophic situations, and you can make sure they won't be affected by blackouts or EMPs.

Kerosene Lamps

Not only do these lamps provide dependable lighting during power outages and in remote areas, but they also serve as an important cultural and aesthetic element within Amish homes.

One of the greatest advantages of kerosene lamps lies in their reliability. Unlike electric lighting, kerosene lamps are not dependent on an uninterrupted power supply. During severe weather events or unexpected power disruptions, the Amish remain unaffected, as their lighting source remains constant.

Kerosene, derived from crude oil, is a readily available and affordable energy source. Additionally, Amish households rarely require large amounts of kerosene, making it a sustainable choice for lighting.

Kerosene lamps offer a considerable amount of light. The intense flame emitted by these lamps can provide sufficient illumination for various activities, including reading, cooking and doing other household chores. The Amish have perfected the art of adjusting the lamps' wick to control the brightness of the light, providing versatility in their lighting needs.

Propane and Naphtha Fuel Lamps

These lamps have been utilized by the Amish community for generations. Amish homes tend to be well-insulated, and the heat emitted from propane or naphtha-fueled lamps can contribute to keeping these spaces warm during the colder months. Therefore, they these lamps have a dual functionality, which can be useful especially in regions with harsh winters, where the lamps serve both as a lighting source and as a heat provider. The cost of electricity, including installation and maintenance, can be substantial. However, propane and naphtha-fueled lamps are more affordable.

Hurricane Lamps

Hurricane lamps are portable, but they are most definitely not to be considered hardy. The heavy glass in the vase portion holds the lamp oil, typically giving it a good amount of weight to prevent easy tipping when placed on a table or when carried. But, the thinner glass flume at the top is more fragile and after heavy repeated use, the thin glass will eventually crack from the heat exposure. When you plan to use hurricane lamps as part of your grid down preps, first remember to always remove the protective lampshade covering before lighting, purchase multiple roles of wick tape, but an extra mantle, and flumes. Mantles are a ceramic mesh that encase the flame produced by the lantern. Also pictured are a wall mount candle sconce and a brass candle stand. These both hold taper candles and may be carried, but are more safely and typically used to provide light only where they are placed.

Candles

Candles, like kerosene lamps, remain unaffected by power outages. Almost every Amish family has a good supply of candles, which are often homemade. They require minimal resources to produce. Made primarily from beeswax or soy, both of them being renewable resources, they don't even produce waste.

Candles may offer a dimmer light compared to kerosene lamp. Candles are frequently used during religious services in the Amish community, but they can also be used in case of a disaster, when there is no other option available.

Solar Powered Lamps

In the last years, the community has adapted to, let's say, some modern alternative, such as solar powered lighting. Many Amish households across the United States already use them on a daily basis. In a study conducted in Lancaster County, Pennsylvania, it was found that nearly 80% of Amish households used solar-powered lamps for their lighting needs.

They use photovoltaic panels to convert sunlight into electrical energy. These panels have a long lifespan and require minimal maintenance, which is a great solution for going off the grid. They can operate for years without altering.

Although solar-powered lamps generally work perfectly, of course that certain conditions such as cloudy days or minimal sunlight can affect their performance. This means that, as a backup for a worst-case scenario, solar-powered lamps should not be the first choice. It's best to utilize backup lighting sources, such as the ones already mentioned above.

Self-Sufficiency THE AMISH WAY

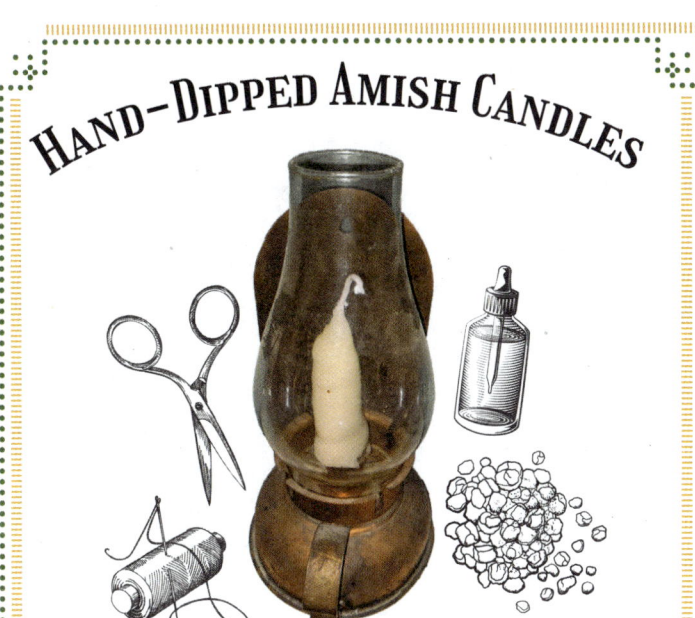

Hand-Dipped Amish Candles

Materials and Tools

Paraffin wax or beeswax
Candle wick
Candle dye or crayons (optional)
Fragrance oil (optional)
Double boiler or microwave-safe container
Thermometer
Metal skewer or chopstick
Candle molds or tall glasses
Clothespin or clip
Wax paper or newspaper
Paper towels or cloth rags
Safety goggles
Oven mitts or heat-resistant gloves

Before You Begin

- Choose a well-ventilated workspace and cover the area with wax paper or newspaper for easy clean-up.
- Wear safety goggles to protect your eyes from wax splatters.
- Ensure that all materials are within easy reach and prepare your molds by cleaning and greasing them with a thin layer of vegetable oil or releasing agent.

Instructions

Step 1: Melting the Wax

If using a double boiler:

a. Fill the bottom portion of the double boiler halfway with water and place it on the stove.

b. Add the wax to the top portion and set the heat to low or medium-low.

c. Stir occasionally with a metal skewer or chopstick until the wax completely melts (approx. 170°F, 77°C).

If using a microwave:

a. Cut the wax into small chunks and place them in a microwave-safe container.

b. Heat the wax in short intervals, stirring well each time, until completely melted.

Step 2 (Optional): Coloring the wax

Use candle dye or grated crayons to add color to the melted wax.

Start with a small amount and gradually add more until you achieve the desired shade.

Stir well to distribute the color evenly.

Step 3: Preparing the Wick

Cut the wick to the desired length, allowing extra for later trimming.

Attach a clothespin or clip to one end of the wick, leaving the other end free for dipping.

Step 4: Dipping the Candles

Dip the wick into the melted wax, ensuring it is fully immersed.

Lift it out and let any excess wax drip off before transferring it to a cooling rack or a newspaper-covered surface.

Allow the wax to harden fully before repeating the dipping process. Repeat until you achieve the desired thickness.

Step 5: Achieving Smooth Layers

For a smooth finish, make sure the wax is at the opti-

THE AMISH WAYS

179

mal temperature. If it cools too much, it may result in a bumpy texture. Reheat if necessary.

Avoid dipping too quickly or vigorously, as it may create uneven layers.

For an extra polished look, lightly rub the cooled candle with a paper towel or cloth rag to remove any imperfections.

Step 6: Trimming the Wick

Once the candles have completely cooled, trim the wick to approximately 1/4 inch (0.6 cm) above the wax surface.

Step 7: Choosing Candle Holders

Place your handmade taper candles in tall, sturdy candle holders or candlesticks.

Opt for holders with a snug fit to prevent any wobbling or tilting.

It is recommended to always work in a well-ventilated area to prevent inhaling excessive fumes. Never leave the melting wax unattended, and keep a fire extinguisher nearby in case of emergencies. Always use oven mitts or heat-resistant gloves when handling hot wax and molds. Be cautious not to overheat the wax, as it may catch fire or cause burns.

Molded Candles in Portable Containers

Mason jars and enamelware coffee mugs are both popular choices for candle making due to their durability and heat resistance.

Mason jars are available in various sizes, making them suitable for creating candles of different heights and burn times. The transparency of jars allows you to enjoy the candle's glow and monitor the wax level.

Enamelware coffee mugs offer a rustic and vintage charm, perfect for creating a cozy atmosphere.

Both are portable, making them versatile for use in different settings like outdoor gatherings, camping trips, or as decorative elements in your home.

Materials and Tools

Wax (such as soy wax or beeswax)
Candle wicks
Fragrance oils or essential oils (if desired)
Candle dye or coloring chips (if desired)
Mason jars or enamelware coffee mugs (clean and dry)
Double boiler or a heat-resistant container and a saucepan
Thermometer
Stirring utensil (preferably heat-resistant)
Adhesive (such as hot glue or candle adhesive)
Pencil, chopstick, or clothespin (to center the wick)
Scissors
Optional: label or decor for the candles

Instructions

Step 1
Prepare your workspace by covering it with newspaper or a disposable tablecloth to catch any spills.

Step 2
Ensure the Mason jars or enamelware coffee mugs are clean and dry.

Step 3
Attach a candle wick to the bottom center of each jar or mug by using a small dab of adhesive. Let it dry completely.

Step 4
To center the wick, wrap it around a pencil, chopstick, or clothespin, and rest it

across the top of the jar or mug, allowing the wick to hang freely.

Step 5

Fill a double boiler with water and place it on the stove. If you don't have a double boiler, use a heat-resistant container placed in a saucepan with a few inches of water.

Step 6

Cut the wax into small pieces for easier melting and place them in the top of the double boiler or heat-resistant container. Heat the water on medium-low heat until the wax melts, stirring occasionally with a heat-resistant utensil.

Step 7

Check the temperature of the melted wax using a thermometer. The optimal temperature varies depending on the type of wax you're using, but it is typically between 120°F and 180°F (49°C–82°C).

Step 8

If desired, add fragrance oil or essential oil to the melted wax according to the manufacturer's recommended amount or to your preference. Stir well to ensure even distribution.

Step 9

You can also add candle dye or coloring chips at this stage to achieve your desired color. Follow the manufacturer's instructions for the preferred amount and mixing instructions.

Step 10

Carefully pour the melted wax into the prepared Mason jars or enamelware coffee mugs, leaving about a 1/2-inch space from the top.

Step 11

Let the candles cool and solidify for at least 24 hours or until completely set. Avoid any movement or disturbance during this period.

Step 12

Once the candles have completely cooled and cured, trim the wick to about 1/4 inch using scissors.

Step 13

Optionally, decorate your Mason jar candles with labels, ribbons, or other decorative elements to personalize them.

Step 14

Place the lids on the Mason jars to preserve the fragrance and protect the candles, or cover the enamelware coffee mugs with a saucer or coaster when not in use.

Homemade Lamp Oil
for Emergency Lighting

Recipe 1: Crisco and Vegetable Oil Blend

Materials

1 part vegetable oil
1 part crisco shortening
Cotton wick

Instructions

Step 1
Clean and dry a suitable container for storing the lamp oil.

Step 2
In the container, mix an equal ratio of vegetable oil and Crisco shortening. Adjust the quantity depending on the container size.

Step 3
Stir the mixture thoroughly to ensure proper blending.

Step 4
Close the container tightly to prevent leaks or spills.

Step 5
Soak a cotton wick in the homemade lamp oil for a few minutes until it is fully saturated.

Self-Sufficiency THE AMISH WAY

Step 6
Place the soaked wick into a lamp or lantern suitable for use with oil. Position the wick carefully and trim any excess.

Step 7
Light the wick and adjust its height as required for a steady flame. Your homemade lamp oil is now ready for emergency lighting.

Recipe 2: Olive Oil and Vegetable Oil Blend

Materials

1 part olive oil
3 parts vegetable oil
A small amount of alcohol (optional)
Cotton wick

Instructions

Step 1
Clean and dry a suitable container for storing the lamp oil. A glass jar or bottle with a secure lid is recommended.

Step 2
In the container, mix 1 part olive oil with 3 parts vegetable oil. Use a ratio of 1:3, depending on the size of your container.

Step 3
If available, add a small amount (about 5%) of alcohol to the oil blend. This helps improve the lamp oil's combustion and efficiency. However, only use alcohol if you are confident in handling flammable substances.

Step 4
Securely close the container to prevent any leaks or spills during transportation and usage.

Step 5
Soak a cotton wick in the homemade lamp oil for a few minutes until it is fully saturated.

Step 6
Place the soaked wick into a lamp or lantern designed for use with oil. Ensure the wick is properly positioned and trim any excess.

Step 7
Light the wick and adjust its height, if necessary, to achieve a steady flame. Enjoy your homemade lamp oil for emergency lighting purposes.

Amish Techniques Used for House and Water Heating

Growing up as a little Amish boy, I never knew there were such things as electric, propane, or gas heat. I had also never heard of a water heater. My goal in this chapter is to show you how to heat your house, take a hot shower, and still enjoy your cup of hot coffee and your favorite meal without all the modern technology we have today.

Growing up, part of my twin brother's and my chores was filling the wood boxes every morning when we got up and every night before we went to bed. We had one stove to heat the living room and a cookstove to heat the kitchen. This stove was also used to heat water for washing dishes and for heating coffee, and of course this stove is where all the yummy meals were prepared and all the baked goods came from. Filling the boxes in the morning ensured mom would not have to carry wood during the day, and she could keep the house nice and cozy while also preparing delicious meals for us. Filling the boxes at night ensured we would be able to stay warm in the mornings if we had a lot of snow overnight and it might take us a while to shovel a path to the woodshed. In the summertime, we only had to fill one wood box, the kitchen box. The cook stove that was already being used to prepare meals and heat water easily generated enough heat during the summer and most of the spring and fall to keep the house cozy.

Self-Sufficiency **The Amish Way**

House Heating

We will start with how to heat your house, and after we figure that out, we can talk about how to heat your water.

I have always preferred wood stoves that load the wood from the top instead of the front. Wood stoves that load the wood from the top have much less risk for ashes or hot coals spilling out on the floor and potentially causing a fire or ruining your flooring over time. If you plan on getting a stove that loads the wood in the front, I would recommend you have tile installed in the area where the stove will be; this will help prevent a potential fire. Wood flooring underneath the stove is also acceptable. Carpet underneath wood stoves is never acceptable; this is a huge risk for a potential fire.

If you get a standard wood burning stove for your living room, like the one in the picture (my Amish parents' stove), it should heat between 2,000 and 4,000 square feet comfortably depending on the climate you live in and how well your house is insulated. You can see the draft hole on the top left side of the stove; this controls the heat. For example, in the winter mornings, when it's cold outside and we have been sleeping all night, we might wake up to a house that's 55 degrees Fahrenheit instead of 75 degrees. This is because the wood has burned down to a pile of hot coals. In order to get the house back to 75 degrees, we fill the stove with wood and open the draft hole all the way. This will give the fire the draft it needs to burn fast and bring the overall temperature of the house back to 75. Once the house is back to the normal temperature, we close the draft hole to between 70 and 90 percent shut, depending on the outside climate; this will keep the temperature steady while also slowing down the burn rate of the fire. If we leave the draft hole all the way open, our house will get too warm, and the wood will burn up too quickly.

When we go to bed, we always fill the stove up with wood (preferably big, solid pieces) and turn the draft hole 90 percent shut. This will allow the wood to slowly burn all night, and there will likely only be a pile of hot coals in the bottom of the stove in the morning when we get up. This is when we open the draft hole and take the smallest pieces of wood we have to get the fire going again. Once the fire is burning nicely again, we use larger pieces to fill the stove and regulate the draft hole accordingly. Whenever we leave the house to go somewhere, we make sure the draft holes are at least 80 percent shut.

We like to burn only hardwoods in the woodstoves. Some of the best firewood is white oak, red oak, elm, ash, and hard maple. These kinds of wood burn hot and slow, not leaving much ash behind in the stove. On the other hand, all the softwoods, like basswood, cottonwood, and soft maple, burn very fast and leave a lot of ashes in the stove.

You may be wondering how much firewood costs. Well, on the farm I grew up on, we never had to pay for firewood. As I mentioned earlier, we had 60 acres, and about 10 of those acres were wooded. There were always dead trees in the woods that we cut up for firewood. My dad also had a sawmill business. From my dad's sawmill, we always had an abundance of firewood, to the point where we sold firewood to neighbors. The average cost per year for our neighbors who had to buy their firwood was between $300 and $600.

As for the kitchen stove (cookstove), the Pioneer Princess is an Amish favorite. Chances are, if you walk into an Amish house, they will have a Pioneer Princess cookstove. This stove operates similarly to the living room stove. It weighs 700 pounds and heats approximately 2,000 square feet. Every time my twin brother and I filled the wood boxes, we put the smaller wood in the kitchen box. With the smaller pieces of wood, we could regulate the oven better. When the stove is filled with smaller pieces of wood, we can open

Self-Sufficiency THE AMISH WAY

the draft hole to increase the oven temperature and close the draft hole to decrease the temperature.

The kitchen stove also has a 15-gallon reservoir on the back and a warming shelf on the top. The 15-gallon reservoir gets filled with water. This water does not get boiling hot, but it does get nice and warm. We use it for washing dishes. The front of this stovetop gets very hot, and this is where all the cooking is done. Every morning, my mother makes breakfast on the front of the stove. Whether it's oatmeal, eggs and bacon, French toast, fresh sausage, or biscuits and gravy, it can all be done on the Pioneer Princess. We can lift the lid on the front of the stove and make some of the best homemade toast over the open fire.

Water Heating

So how do the Amish heat their water without any electricity, a generator, or a water heater? As I mentioned earlier, hot water for stuff like washing dishes, cooking, and baking is heated up on the cookstove. Generally, the water for the dishes is heated up in the reservoir, and water for coffee and tea is heated up in a tea kettle on top of the woodstove.

Heating water for things such as taking a shower or a bath and doing laundry is different because it's a much larger amount of water that has to be heated up. For this, we use what we call a big kettle. As shown in the picture, you can see it's basically a large round, barrel with a box on the bottom for the wood fire. We have this kettle set up upstairs by the washing machine. Every Monday morning, we fill the kettle with water and start the fire underneath in the box. By the time the family is done eating breakfast, the water is hot and ready to do the laundry. As for the shower, like I said, the kettle is set up upstairs. This is the only way to have a shower without having a pump or electricity; it has to be gravity fed. The kettle is upstairs, and the shower is downstairs. As shown in the picture, the kettle has a faucet on the side where we can attach a garden hose and run it down to the basement and attach it to a two-way hose connector fitting. The other hose coming into the connector is cold water. The hose going away from the connector goes to the showerhead.

To take a shower, we make sure there's enough water in the kettle, start a fire underneath in the box when the water is hot enough, turn on the hot valve, and check the temperature of the water. If it's too hot, we turn the cold valve on just enough to add cold water until the water is the perfect temperature for a shower.

As for our water supply, we have spring-fed water. We have never had to pump water since my dad bought the farm in the 1980s. The spring is on a hillside at a higher elevation than the house; therefore all the water is gravity run to the house and the barn. Of course, we are in a northern climate, so we had to bury the pipes that carry the water deep enough into the ground to prevent them from freezing in the wintertime. This spring has supplied us with water for the family and all the cows, horses, chickens, pigs, dogs, and cats for many years. Not to mention the quality of the spring water—even in the hot summer, we can open the faucet, let the water run for 10 to 20 seconds, and have some of the best cold, refreshing spring water. If you have fresh spring water, you do not need a filtering system. So I guess the only expense we ever really had for the water was digging in the piping to carry the water to the house and the barn. If we hadn't had access to the spring water, we would have drilled a well and pumped the water out of the well with a large windmill or a gas engine. This is a common method the Amish use for a water supply.

I hope this helps you out on your journey, whether you're trying to completely live off the grid or you are just trying to be more self-sufficient and resourceful and not rely on all the modern technologies that could easily be taken away from you at any time.

> One of the things that always comforts me and that I'm so thankful for is that I grew up Amish. I know if there is a big world event, whether it's a pandemic or any kind of black swan event, I will be just fine because of the skills I have learned. Becoming self-sufficient isn't just about saving money; it's about having peace of mind.

Self-Sufficiency **The Amish Way**

Amish Air-Powered Tools that Make You Self-Sufficient

Amish Alternatives to Electricity

Electricity provides a lot of benefits and most of us couldn't imagine living without it. For some, it lies at the very heart of what they do for a living. From an outsider's perspective, many might say the same for the kind of work that many Amish communities perform to make a living.

As masters of various trades, such as agriculture, sewing, and carpentry, the Amish are put to the test to provide high quality work, with a high level of safety. With other businesses outside of their communities utilizing all of the new technologies they can get their hands on, the competition can be fierce. This has led to an accepted level of adaptation to the way their businesses are run.

Gas Power

Many communities have come to rely on gas power as their alternative to being connected to the main electrical grid. Sometimes this looks like a diesel generator that provides the necessary electricity at the moment while some modern appliances have been retrofitted to run from a propane tank.

Later we will look at how gas power comes into play by providing the necessary power to compress air and store it for future use in pneumatic tools.

Off-Grid Solar

With separation from the wider world being the main goal of most Amish communities, a completely off-grid solar system has been considered to be appropriate for some. While it isn't completely accepted, this system of car batteries and solar panels allows for Amish businesses to stay up to date by using more modern tools.

This method trends the closest to the modern world and isn't accepted by many of the Old Order. A lot of communities draw a line and say that even this form of electricity is too much. Others will utilize it as they are still disconnected from the larger world, which is one of the many interpretations of their theology.

Another fascinating way that the Amish use the sun is through a setup that brings the light of the sun in through a skylight and into a series of tubes with highly reflective materials lining them. This can transform a dark warehouse into a much brighter space without a single lightbulb needed.

In looking for other solutions to modern-day problems, the Amish began to work with the wind and air around them.

Wind and Air Power

With all of the restrictions on ways of living, the Amish people have become masters of creative solutions to modern day problems. From wind power to reflective light tubing, their ability to keep up with the ever-advancing tech world is impressive to say the least.

Harnessing the air and the wind to power some of the same tools that rely on electricity is one of the most innovative adaptations that many Amish communities have made. Wind power by itself has been utilized by humans since 200 BC, if not earlier. The wind is still harnessed by sails to make global sea travel possible for small crafts. The Chinese powered water pumps while many in the Middle East were using the wind to grind grain around the same time.

Self-Sufficiency The Amish Way

In 1888 the first wind turbine was set in motion to produce electricity in Scotland, setting the stage for us to implement this system on a large scale and begin to power parts of entire countries.

A simple setup will utilize a large wheel, in the past made of cloth and today with massive carbon fiber propellor-like blades, that capture the wind and take the wind's kinetic energy and turn it into circular motion. These blades connect back to an electric generator which then can be stored in a battery system or sent out to where it will then be directly used.

Naturally, the Amish have taken a massive lesson from the histories of civilization and modified wind technology, blending old with new, in order to push themselves into a more modern age of living. However, they don't always rely on just collecting more electricity and then using it to power normal battery-operated tools. They've gotten even more creative with it to power all of their tools.

The various adaptations of wind and air power are so impressive that it's worth taking a much closer look at to understand a bit better.

Collecting and Compressing Air

The first stage of setting up this system that the Amish have put together for wind power is to collect air. Many systems achieve this in one of two ways. The first, more modern, is to use a diesel generator that simply powers an air compressor with the electricity produced. The second is to utilize a wind turbine that creates the same effect.

The electricity that is normally produced by a gas generator is replaced by the wind turbine through some genius engineering. Wind-driven air compressors use the movement of a wind turbine to power the compressor's pump shaft, something normally done by electricity. A lot of systems still have a gas generator on hand for the days where the wind isn't moving, or the demand on air is much higher.

Once the tanks that are connected to the air compressor are full, the wind turbine will stop turning and signal that the tanks are fully ready for use.

Storage

All of that air being compressed needs somewhere to go, and the more storage that the system has, the more space that can be powered. A larger multi-tank system that is set up around a business in different buildings can easily give enough power to run tools for the day.

Many communities will repurpose old propane containers that once powered others' ovens or heating systems. These serve as the perfect place to stash all of the air they need to bring a different type of power.

Self-Sufficiency THE AMISH WAY

Piping System

From the storage containers, a single line runs into a central hub, often located inside the building. From here, the flow of air can be regulated and dispersed out to the different lines that power various tools or fans.

At the central hub there are filters that take out the moisture from the compressed air. This stage can be incredibly important as it delivers dry air to all of the machinery, where moisture can quickly deteriorate and destroy a tool.

On the contrary to the seemingly chaotic mess that these lines present as, this is a well-thought-out system that can be easily adapted, swapped, and manipulated to power countless tools.

Pneumatic Tools That Use Air Instead of Electricity

The number of tools that can be powered by compressed air is incredible and puts to rest any hesitations one may have about being fully reliant on an air power system.

The genius way that many convert electric tools into air-power is much simpler than one may think. By removing the electric motors and replacing them with similarly sized pneumatic motors, the conversion is done. Which type of tool you want to use will determine the motor necessary for the proper conversion to air power.

There are two different types of pneumatic motors, linear and rotary. A linear motor utilized compressed air to push a piston forward. When the air is released, the piston moves back into place. Repeat at a high frequency and you can power tools like a jackhammer.

A rotary motor relies on utilizing the compressed air to spin blades inside the motor and produce the circular motion necessary for tools like a power drill or even a large table saw.

Almost anything that utilizes circular or reciprocal motion to complete a task can be converted to use pneumatic power rather than being fully reliant on battery power.

Today, the Amish and all others looking to use a different system have found a way to convert:

- Kitchen appliances like blenders
- Circular, jig and table saws
- Power drills and impact wrenches
- Sewing machines
- Ceiling fans
- Jackhammers
- Riveting guns
- Nail guns
- Different grinders

All of these tools will operate in the exact same way when the right system is put into place.

One of the greatest adaptations of pneumatic power is running a line of compressed air into a motor that powers a ceiling fan.

Self-Sufficiency THE AMISH WAY

Ceiling Fans as an Alternative to AC

By running lines along the ceiling and installing plenty of ceiling fans, it can be easy to trick yourself into thinking that you have a fully set-up air conditioning system.

Ceiling fans are often used as an alternative to AC, but with the air-powered system they are even cleaner and more accessible than before. Many Amish businesses build warehouses that have a cool concrete floor and plenty of ceiling fans, creating a space that is just as cool as a similar space with electric or gas-powered air conditioning units.

The Amish people aren't quick to adopt new ways of living. They see advances in technology and explore the question, "Will this be beneficial or harmful to the Amish way of living?" This tactic has led to creative modifications that bring the modern world a bit closer to home while staying in line with their core beliefs.

There is a lot to learn from their intricate and highly-effective air-powered system. Maybe pick up an air-powered tool and explore self-sufficiency before blindly accepting what others may say is best.

How to Preserve Water the Amish Way

This was my experience with our water supply growing up. We had a natural spring that we got our water from. My parents moved from Ohio to Minnesota in the 1980s. They settled on 60 acres of land. There was no house or barn on these 60 acres; they had to build everything from scratch, but they did discover a natural spring on the side of a hill. A constant stream of fresh water was coming through the rocks from the side of the hill. This is one of the best resources for water, as spring water did not have to be filtered. Also, the spring was at a high enough elevation that gravity ran the water to the house and the barn.

So basically, once we dug piping from the spring to the house and the barn, we had water for all the needs in the house and all the animals in the barn. To this day, they still have fresh spring water. When my twin brother and his wife bought their little farm, they did not have a spring on their property. Instead, there was a well on the property. They built a tall, 12-foot-wide, and 16-foot-long insulated ice house. This building is heavily insulated and is used for storing ice that is harvested in the wintertime. The ice house is then used in the summertime to store refrigerated foods. But they also installed a large stainless-steel tank on the very top of the building. They put a pump in the well that they run with a small gasoline engine. They use the pump to fill the stainless-steel tank; this will last them upwards of a week, and the water is cool and fresh because it is being stored in the ice house. Side note: A couple of years ago, my wife and I were exploring Alaska. During our time there, we did a lot of hiking. One Sunday, we were on a hike, and it turned out to be much longer than we originally thought. It was a warm afternoon; we drank all the water we had and still had a long way to go, and there was nobody else on the trail. Luckily, we found a spring along the way and were able to fill our water bottles.

But if you cannot rely on a spring, these techniques below will teach you what you can do instead.

Underground Cisterns

Cisterns are large enough to provide a secure solution for storing huge amounts of water, and it can be reliable even in times of drought or water scarcity.

In the rural Amish community of Lancaster County, Pennsylvania, water cisterns can be found everywhere. Many families rely on these structures for everyday tasks such as cooking, cleaning, and watering livestock.

Here's How to Do It:

1. You have to choose an area on your property that is easily accessible and also protected from potential contaminants, such as animal waste or chemicals.
2. Use machinery or manual labor to create a hole of appropriate dimensions. Consider factors such as necessary depth, width, and length, which depend on your water storage needs and available space.
3. Use appropriate materials, such as poured concrete or bricks, to build the walls of the cistern.
4. Apply a waterproof sealant or membrane to the interior walls and floor of the cistern to prevent leakage and seepage.
5. Install a suitable pipe with a screened opening to allow water to enter the cistern. This pipe should be positioned to capture rainwater from surfaces such as rooftops or gutters.
6. Attach another pipe at the base of the cistern as an outlet for withdrawing water. This pipe should be fitted with a valve or faucet for easy access.

Self-Sufficiency **The Amish Way**

Above-Ground Storage Tanks

For those who do not have the means or space for underground cisterns, above-ground tanks are a good alternative. These tanks come in various sizes, materials, and shapes, allowing flexibility in installation and capacity.

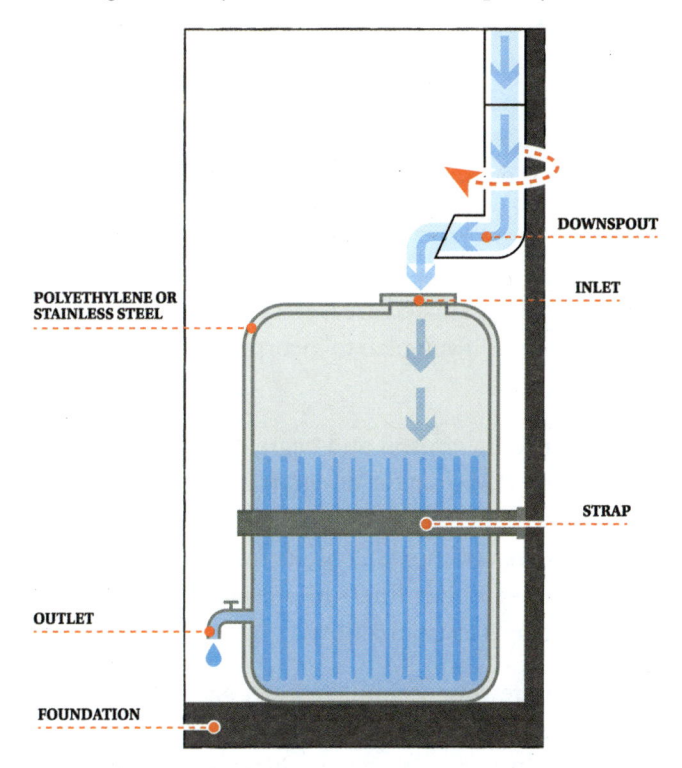

Here's How to Do It:

1. You have to know exactly the available space you have, the budget, and desired storage capacity for your needs. Tanks made of durable materials such as polyethylene or stainless steel are recommended for longevity and resistance to corrosion.

2. Ensure the chosen location provides a stable, level foundation for the tank's weight.

3. Place the tank on the foundation and secure it using appropriate straps or mounts to withstand potential weather events.

4. Direct the downspout or gutters from your rooftop into the tank's inlet to capture rainwater effectively.

5. Install an outlet on the tank's bottom, allowing water withdrawal at a convenient height. Use a valve or faucet for control and ease of use.

Rooftop Rainwater Harvesting

Even though this is not particularly an Amish water harvesting system, many people in the community choose to use it, as it is very simple to build.

Step 1

Divert downspouts: Position downspouts to redirect rainwater from your rooftop towards a storage container or directly into your cistern/tank.

Step 2

Install screens and filters: Attach screens and filters at the entrance of gutters or downspouts to prevent debris, leaves, and insects from entering. These screens ensure the water collected is cleaner and easier to store.

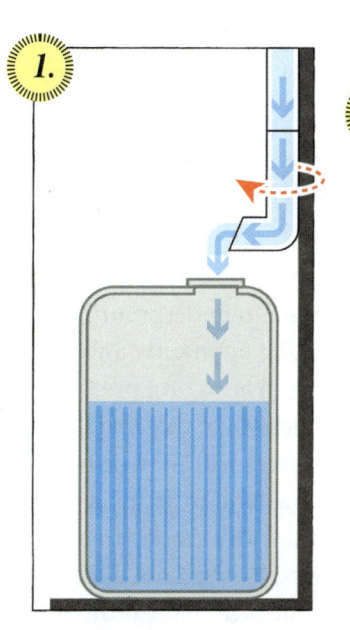

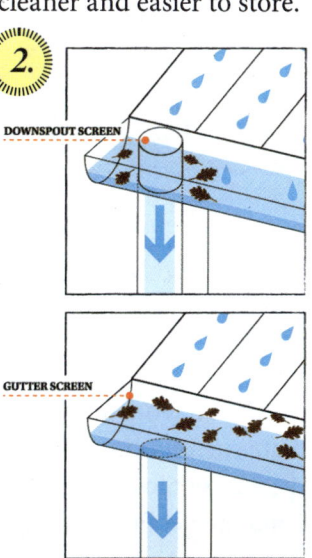

Step 3

Connect the storage: Connect the storage container to your downspout, ensuring a secure, leak-proof connection.

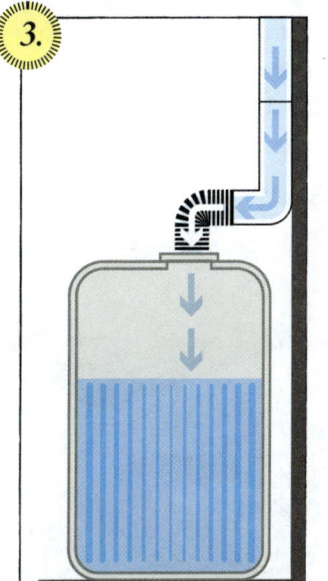

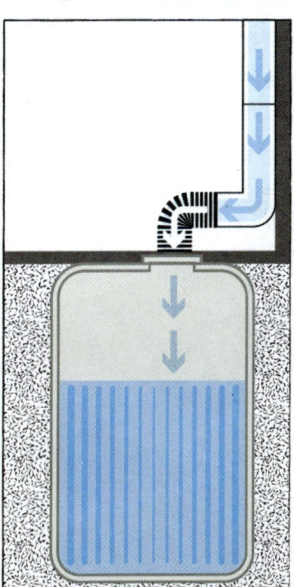

Self-Sufficiency THE AMISH WAY

Recycling Greywater

1. Determine the water sources on your property that can be recycled, such as sinks, showers, and washing machines.

2. Install a separation system: Set up a diverter that separates greywater from blackwater (toilet waste).

3. Use appropriate filters, such as sand and gravel, to remove debris and sediment from the greywater. Additional treatment methods, such as UV disinfection or biological systems, can be employed to ensure water quality.

4. Once treated, direct the greywater to non-potable uses, such as irrigation, toilet flushing, or cleaning.

Secondary Water Sources

Because the Amish live exclusively in rural areas, they nearly always get their water from an underground well, whenever possible. But, depending upon only a well for water is not something either the Amish or a prepper, is likely to do. The self-sufficient lifestyle of the Amish emphasizes relying on natural resources within their immediate surroundings. When buying land to set up a farm, the Amish most usually seek land with a creek, stream, or pond - preferably a spring fed pond that will not likely run dry during times of drought. If the right land at the right price does not include a pond, the Amish review the terrain well for at least one spot likely to sustain a pond they will put in after purchasing the property.

Having a secondary water source is a safety net during any unexpected crisis that may affect the primary water supply. Depending on a single water source is pretty risky, especially for a community like the Amish that relies heavily on agriculture and other water-intensive activities.

Digging a Pond

Before starting to dig, it is important to verify the soil composition of your property. Clay soils are ideal for pond digging, because they retain water better than sandy or loamy soils. Conduct a soil test or consult local experts to determine if your soil is suitable for pond construction.

1. Start by mapping out the desired size and shape of your pond. Account for its functionality (e.g., irrigation needs) and aesthetics. Seek advice from local experts or consult with experienced pond owners from an Amish community.

2. Clear the area of any vegetation or debris. Excavate the designated area, creating shelves or varying depths if you plan to incorporate fish or aquatic plants.

3. Remove the topsoil and begin digging, ensuring you are following the design you planned. Aim for a consistent depth throughout the pond to avoid excessive variations. Consider lining the pond with clay or synthetic liners to prevent water seepage, ensuring its sustainability.

4. Integrate your secondary water source by diverting water from an existing stream or using drainage systems to direct rainwater into the pond. Explore various options that suit your property's specific needs.

5. You can add natural elements like rocks or pebbles around the edges. Additionally, you can plant native aquatic vegetation, which provides additional filtration benefits and aids in maintaining water quality.

6. It is important to regularly remove excess sediment and debris. Also testing water quality, and inspecting the pond for leaks or cracks is something you want to do, to make sure your water will be safe to use. A small solar-powered pump and filter system should run less than $200 … and the peace of mind it will provide would be priceless.

Warning

Consuming contaminated water can lead to serious health problems, such as gastrointestinal illnesses, skin infections, and even long-term health effects.

Self-Sufficiency **THE AMISH WAY**

Methods and Techniques to Test Water Quality

Having a kit for water testing is probably the easiest and fastest way to verify it. However, you can do that without having to use a kit, just like the Amish already do. Below we will take a look at some of these ways, and also at some natural water purification methods.

Bleach Water Purification

Bleach works by killing harmful microorganisms such as bacteria, viruses, and protozoans that may cause waterborne diseases.

1. Make sure you use the proper bleach: only unscented bleach containing 5.25-8.25% sodium hypochlorite, without any additional additives like dyes.

2. Depending on the water's clarity, the dosage of bleach will differ:

   a. For clear water: Add 8 drops (about 1/8 teaspoon) of bleach per gallon (3.8 liters) of water.

   b. For cloudy or turbid water: Double the dosage to 16 drops (about 1/4 teaspoon) of bleach per gallon (3.8 liters).

3. Stir the mixture well and let it sit for at least 30 minutes. If the water temperature is less than 20°C (68°F), extend the waiting time to 60 minutes.

4. After the waiting period, the water should have a faint chlorine odor. If it doesn't, repeat the treatment process and wait again.

5. If the water is still cloudy after waiting, you can remove sediment or particles by carefully pouring it through a clean cloth or coffee filter.

Note: Bleach can be stored for a limited time; therefore, it is advisable to rotate your stock periodically, ensuring its effectiveness.

Boiling Water

Boiling is a straightforward and reliable water purification method, as heat kills most microorganisms present, including bacteria, viruses, and parasites. Proper boiling techniques are essential to ensure its effectiveness:

1. Collect the water: Gather water from a reliable source, such as a stream, well, or rainwater collection system, aiming to filter out large debris or sediment.

2. Heat the water: Place a pot on a heat source and bring water to a rolling boil. Maintain a boil for at least one minute.

3. Cool and store: After boiling, let the water cool naturally or by using a heat-resistant lid. Once cooled, transfer it into clean and sanitized containers for storage.

Amish Wells

Introduction

There are three types of wells we use, to have quick and easy access to water in our house, on our farms, and at our businesses. Each well type possesses its own technical features that impact its construction and water availability. Construction materials, depth, and water flow differ from one type to the other.

Types of Wells

Hand Dug Wells

Hand dug wells are the oldest wells used by the community. Amish farmers would manually excavate wells using shovels, picks, and other hand tools. They are typically filled with stones or bricks. The water table, depth, and flow capabilities vary depending on the geographical location.

Driven Wells

Driven wells are constructed by sinking a long pipe, such as galvanized iron or PVC, into the ground.

Spring Fed Wells

When natural springs are discovered on an Amish farm, they are tapped into using simple techniques. These springs often produce a reliable and clean water source. Spring wells can be carved into the side of a hill or incorporated into a small catchment area.

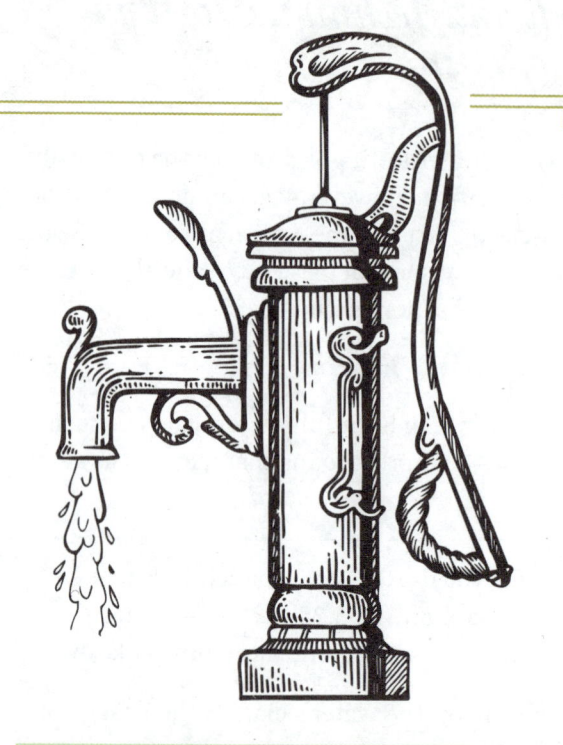

Water Flow

Hand-dug wells are often dependent on the water table level and may experience inconsistent flow. Driven wells, on the other hand, usually provide a more reliable water flow. Spring wells generally offer consistent and clean water throughout the year.

When Building a Well on Your Property, Don't Forget This

- **Potential Contamination:** Wells are vulnerable to contamination from nearby sources, which means that a lot of precaution needs to be taken before using the water.

- **Intensive Work:** Building wells might not be the easiest (or often) the cheapest option to get potable water without depending on the Grid, especially when it comes to hand-dug wells.

- **Technical Expertise:** Driven and spring wells may require specialized equipment to be built efficiently.

How to Dig a Hand Dug Well

Materials

Well Casing: A metal or PVC well casing will help prevent the sides from collapsing.

Gravel and Sand: These materials will be utilized to provide filtration and support.

Tools

Shovels: A durable round-point shovel and a narrow trenching shovel are necessary tools for excavation.

A Well-Boring Auger: A handheld, four-foot auger is required to remove soil and debris from the well.

Step 1: Locating the Water Table

Water Prospecting

- Observe/ask local residents about nearby sources of water such as streams, wetlands, or natural springs.
- Conduct a groundwater survey to identify potential underground water sources.

Water Table Determination

- Dig test holes using a post hole digger or hand auger in the anticipated well site until water is visible.
- Water levels in these test holes will help you determine the approximate depth of your well.

Step 2: Excavation

Digging the Well

- Start digging with the round-point shovel and excavate the topsoil.
- Switch to the narrow trenching shovel for deeper excavation.
- Remove soil and debris using the well-boring auger.

Well Support

- As you dig deeper, install the well casing to prevent the sides from collapsing.
- The casing should be longer than the anticipated well depth, to accommodate potential variations.

Proper Support and Filtration

- Add gravel around the bottom of the well casing to provide support and filter sediments.
- Place a layer of sand on top of the gravel for additional filtration.

Removing Water

- Use a bucket or a well bucket with a rope to remove excess water during excavation.
- Consider using a manual water pump to remove water more efficiently.

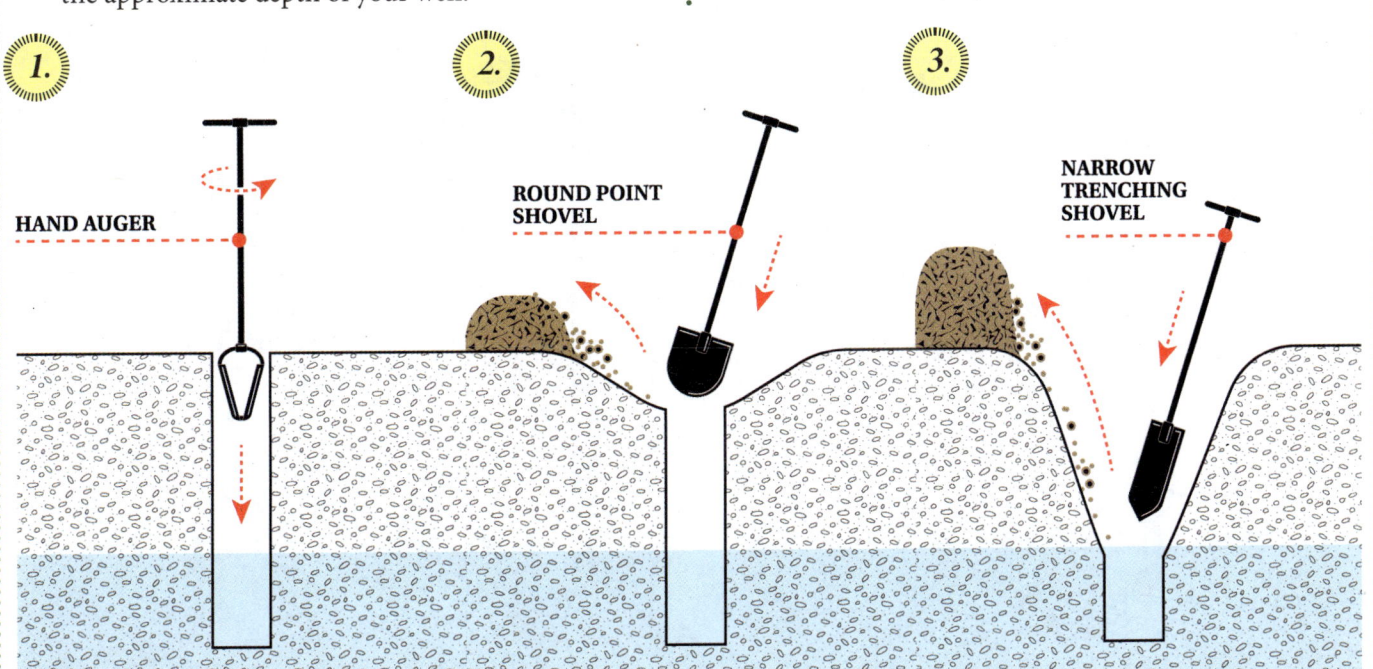

1. HAND AUGER
2. ROUND POINT SHOVEL
3. NARROW TRENCHING SHOVEL

Self-Sufficiency THE AMISH WAY

Step 3: Ensuring Suitable Flow Capabilities

Jetting Method (if needed)

- In regions with a high-water table, you may need to use the jetting method.
- Fit a PVC pipe onto a high-pressure water source and insert it into the well casing.
- The water jet will create a cavity, allowing water to flow from the surrounding aquifer.

Well Depth and Flow Rate

- Research official standards, consult local experts, or well drillers to determine an ideal well depth for your region.
- Observe the flow rate of water during testing periods to ensure an adequate water supply.

Building a hand-dug well requires diligence, hard work, and careful planning. By following these step-by-step instructions, you can create your own well, tapping into a traditional and reliable water source. Remember to prioritize safety during excavation, consult relevant local guidelines, and seek expert advice when necessary.

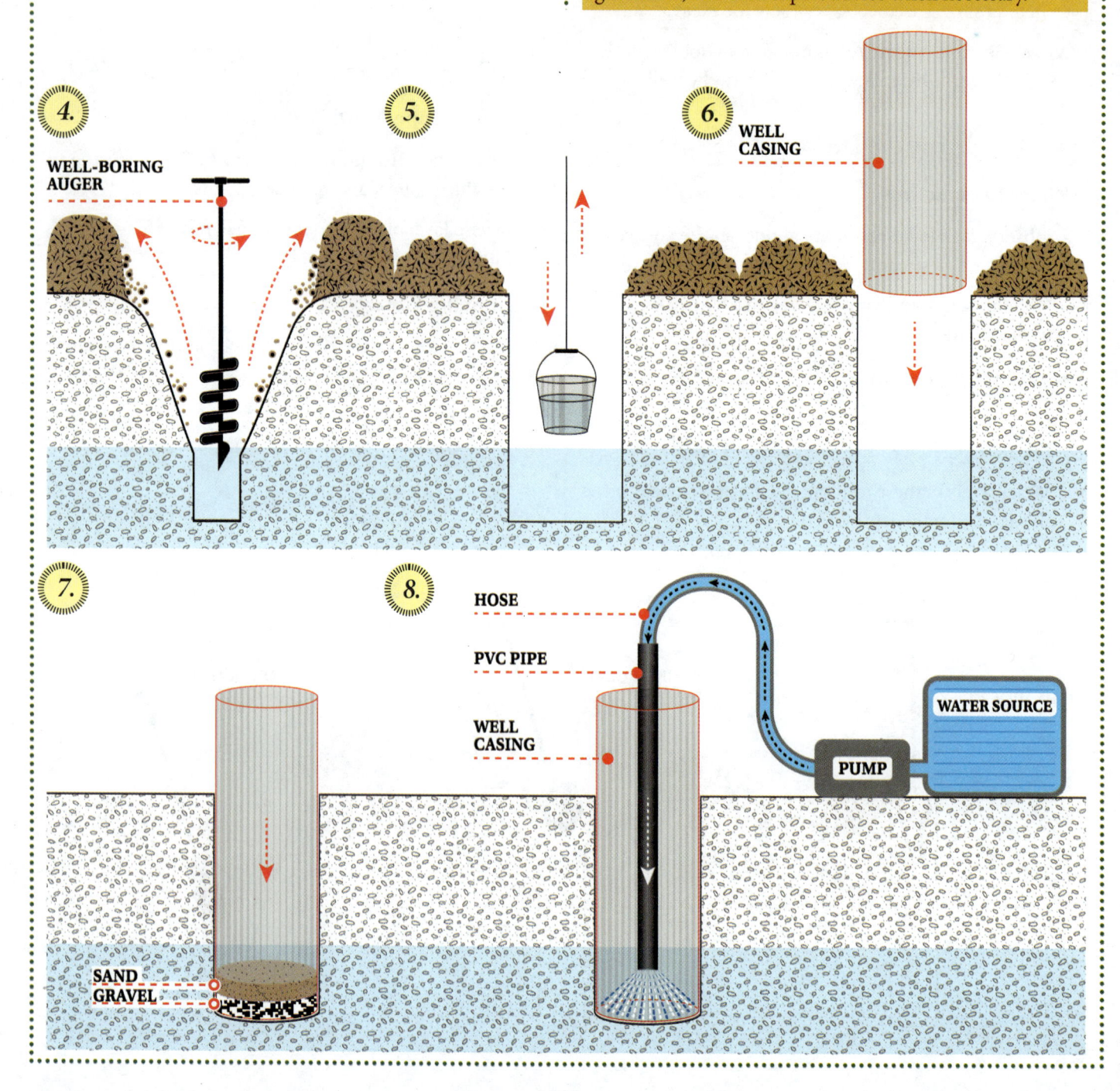

4. WELL-BORING AUGER

5.

6. WELL CASING

7. SAND / GRAVEL

8. HOSE / PVC PIPE / WELL CASING / PUMP / WATER SOURCE

Self-Sufficiency THE AMISH WAY

How to Install a Driven Well

Materials

Galvanized iron or PVC pipe: Choose a pipe with a diameter of at least 6 inches and a length suitable for your desired well depth.

Filters, screens, or gravel: To prevent debris from entering the well.

Rope or cable: For lifting and lowering the pipe.

Water source or hose: For flushing the well during installation.

Tools

Shovel or post-hole digger: For digging the well hole.

Sledgehammer or maul: For driving the pipe into the ground.

Wooden or rubber mallet: For sealing connections and reducing noise during installation.

Step 1: Choosing the Appropriate Depth

1. **Research your location:** Understand the soil and rock formations in your area. Digging a test hole can provide valuable information.
2. **Determine the water table depth:** Consult local experts or use a water divining method to estimate the depth needed to reach the water table.
3. **Add an extra 2-3 feet to the estimated water table depth:** This will ensure a reliable water supply during droughts.

Step 2: Preparing the Well Hole

1. **Select a suitable location:** Choose an area free of potential contaminants such as septic tanks, chemical storage, or livestock waste.
2. **Start digging the well hole:** Use a shovel or post-hole digger to dig a hole slightly wider than the diameter of the pipe. Begin with a depth of a few feet.

Step 3: Installing the Driven Pip

1. **Connect the pipe sections:** If using galvanized iron pipe, thread the sections together with appropriate couplings. If using PVC pipe, apply PVC primer and cement to join the sections.
2. **Install a well screen or filter:** Attach a screen or filter to the bottom of the pipe to prevent debris from entering the well while allowing water to flow freely.
3. **Attach a cap or seal to the first pipe section:** This will prevent soil or debris from entering the pipe during installation.
   Begin driving the pipe: Slowly insert the pipe into the well hole, using the sledgehammer or maul to drive it into the ground. Alternate between striking the pipe clockwise and counterclockwise to prevent binding.
4. **Continue driving until reaching the desired depth:** Use a wooden or rubber mallet to seal connections between pipe sections, reducing noise and vibrations.
5. **Flush the well:** Use a water source or hose to flush the well while driving the pipe to remove excess sediment and ensure a clean well.

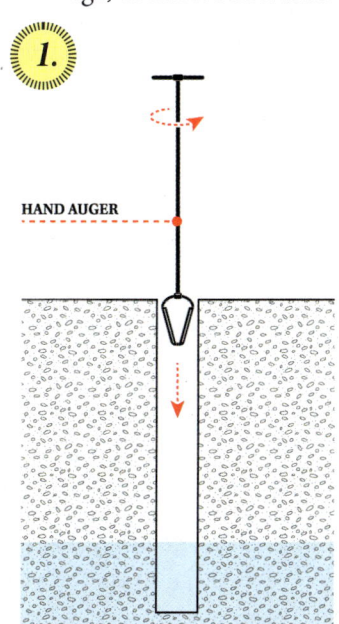

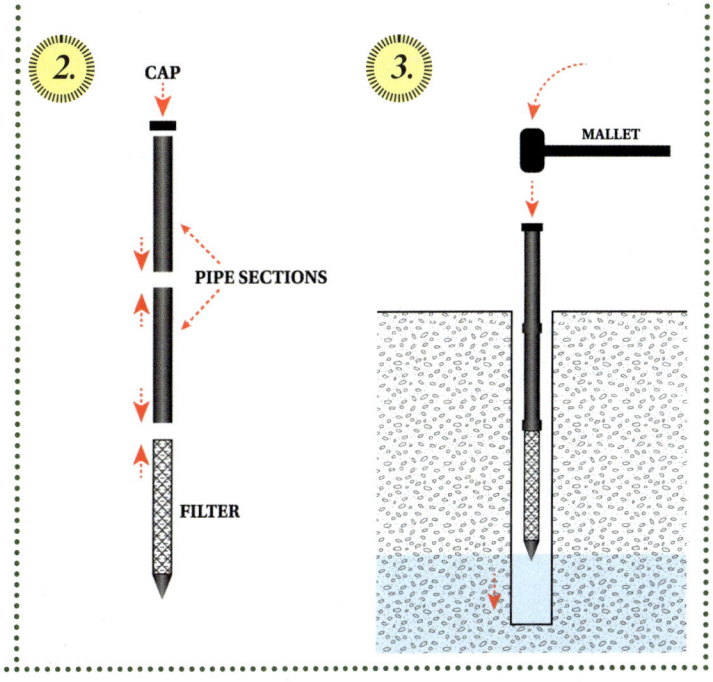

197

Step 4: Completing the Driven Dug Well

1. **Fill the well hole:** Use gravel or stone to backfill the well hole, ensuring proper drainage and stability.

2. **Install a pump or hand-operated mechanism:** Depending on your needs, install a pump or a manual pump handle to extract water from the well.

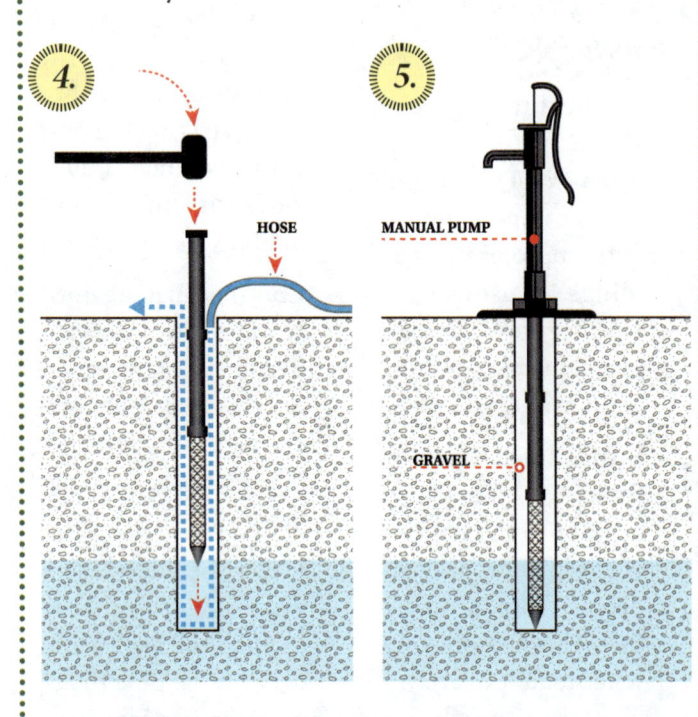

Potential Challenges and Considerations

1. Rocky or hard soil conditions might require additional efforts or specialized tools to effectively drive the pipe.
2. Unstable soil or high-water tables may necessitate the inclusion of well casing or a well liner for added stability.
3. Ensure proper sealing of pipe connections to avoid leaks or contamination.
4. Regular maintenance is essential to keep the well clean, ensuring a continuous water supply and preventing clogging.

Efficiency and Benefits of Driven Wells

1. Provide a consistent water supply, even during power outages or during periods of low rainfall.
2. Minimal equipment and maintenance required compared to other well types.
3. No reliance on electricity or fuel for pumping, making them sustainable and cost-effective.
4. Driven wells can be installed in rural or remote areas where other water supply options are limited.

Constructing a driven dug well enables you to have a reliable and continuous water supply. By following this comprehensive guide and considering the necessary materials, depth selection based on soil and rock formation, and effective sinking methods, you will be able to successfully build your own driven dug well similar to those used by the Amish community. Keep in mind the challenges and considerations, and enjoy the benefits of a dependable water source for years to come.

How to Install a Spring Fed Well

A spring fed well is arguably the best type of well to have from a self-reliance and sustainability perspective. Even when your pond gets low or your creek runs dry, a spring fed well will almost assuredly still bring forth this most crucial survival essential.

This type of well will only be an option if you have chosen your land wisely with this natural resource in mind. If you are still browsing for the right plot of land to create your sustainable homestead, farm, or household, make this attribute high on your list of priorities and be willing to pay extra for the land, if necessary.

Step 1: Identifying a Natural Spring

1. **Study the topography:** Look for signs of water seepage, such as damp spots or lush vegetation in otherwise dry areas, which could indicate a hidden spring.
2. **Observe landscape features:** Natural springs are commonly found at the feet of hills or mountains, along valleys, or near natural depressions.
3. **Consult geological surveys:** Local geological maps or records can provide valuable information about the presence of natural springs in your area.

Self-Sufficiency The Amish Way

Step 2: Carving a Well into the Side of a Hill

1. **Select an appropriate location:** Choose a spot on the hillside where the spring emerges, ensuring it is easily accessible.
2. **Excavate the site:** Use shovels and other digging tools to carve out the well, keeping the dimensions wide enough for comfortable access during maintenance.
3. **Dig deep enough:** The well should be dug deep enough to reach the water source, ensuring a constant flow and protecting against dry spells.

Step 3: Creating a Small Catchment Area

1. **Construct a smaller depression:** Alongside the well, create a catchment area to collect the spring water.
2. **Line the catchment area:** To prevent contamination, line the catchment area with gravel or rocks, allowing water to seep in while filtering out possible contaminants.
3. **Construct a drainage system:** Avoid stagnation by creating a proper drainage system that allows excess water to escape, preventing flooding or bacterial growth.

Step 4: Precautions to Prevent Contamination

1. **Ensure proper well casing:** Use high-quality materials such as concrete, stone, or metal to construct the well casing, preventing surface water and contaminants from infiltrating the water source.
2. **Install a sanitary seal:** Create a tight seal between the well casing and the surrounding soil to prevent any potential contamination from above-ground sources.
3. **Regular well maintenance:** Periodic inspections, cleaning, and disinfection will help preserve water purity. Check for signs of pollution, such as discoloration or bad odor, and take corrective actions if necessary.

Step 5: Additional Tips for Longevity and Efficiency

1. **Use a screen or grill:** Install a screen or grille at the spring source to prevent debris, organic matter, or larger organisms from entering the well.
2. **Install a pump system:** Depending on your needs, consider installing a pump to ensure the water reaches your desired location reliably and efficiently.
3. **Test water quality periodically:** Regularly test the water quality for contaminants and ensure that it meets safety standards. Seek professional advice on water testing and treatment if needed.

Constructing a spring-fed well provides a reliable and clean water source, similar to the ones used by the Amish community. By identifying natural springs, carving wells into hillsides, creating catchment areas, and taking necessary precautions, you can ensure a consistent supply of pure water for your household. Regular maintenance and periodic water quality testing will help preserve and optimize the longevity and efficiency of your spring-fed well.

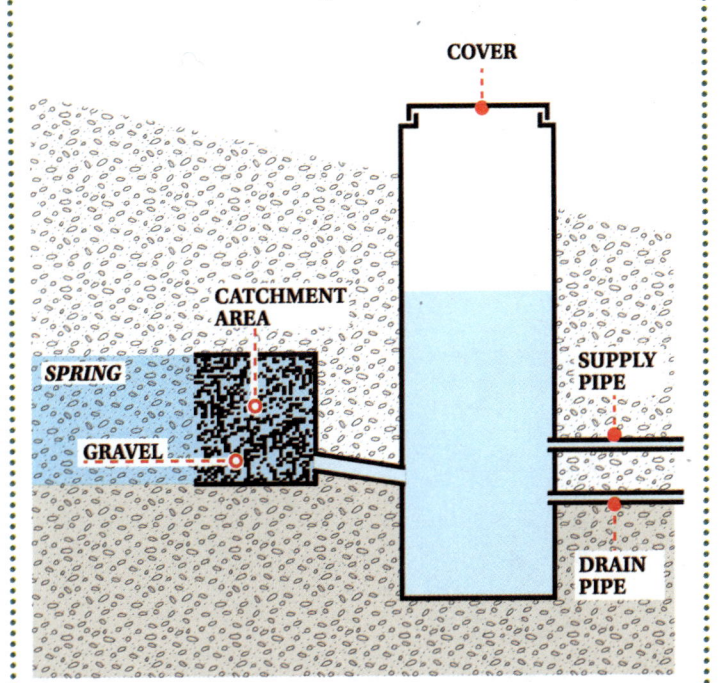

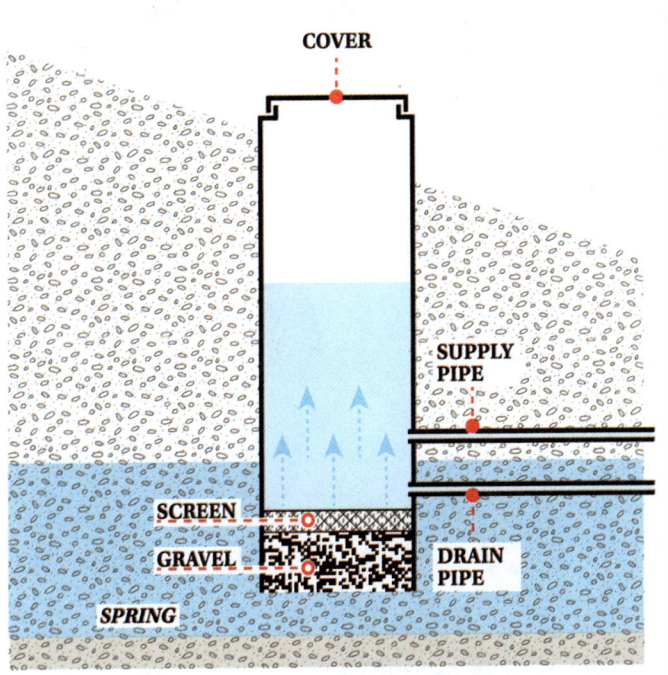

DIY Amish Water Filter

Introduction:

The community I grew up in never had a water filter system. We relied on a natural spring as our water source, which did not require filtration. None of our neighbors had a water filter system either. Most of them used well water, which also remained unfiltered. It is very typical for us to open the faucet and let the water run for 30 to 40 seconds before filling our drinking cup. Doing this, the water will be much fresher.

However, I know of other Amish communities that use an off-grid water filtration system, which is an incredibly inexpensive project. This filtration system is designed to purify water by removing suspended particles, sediment, and other potentially harmful substances from it.

Materials

Two 5-gallon food-grade plastic buckets with lids
One 5-gallon food-grade plastic bucket without a lid
Food-grade silicone sealant
Rubber washer or gasket
Activated carbon (charcoal)
Clean medium-sized rocks or pebbles
Fine gravel
Fine sand
Cheesecloth or cotton fabric
Plastic or rubber tubing

Tools

Drill with a hole saw drill bit
Scissors

You Will Also Need

Water source (well, river, or rainwater collection system)

Self-Sufficiency THE AMISH WAY

Instructions

Step 1: Prepare the buckets

1. Drill a hole near the bottom of one lidless 5-gallon bucket using the hole saw drill bit*.

*We typically use hand or manual-powered tools much like our pioneering ancestors did, to accomplish tasks that we would use battery or gas-powered tools to tackle. But, for Amish living in communities that utilize solar energy, using a power drill like shown in the photos is entirely likely. The old-world Amish still exclusively use manually powered tools, like the one shown in the photo. They work just like an egg beater. You simply choose the required bit (slide it up into the reservoir and twist to lock) and then turn the wheel on the side to force the bit inside of the material being drilled. You must push steadily and consistently as you turn the wheel so there is enough muscle power to create the whole.

2. Insert the rubber washer or gasket into the drilled hole to create a water-tight seal.

Step 2: Filter Layer Assembly

1. Place the lidless bucket (now with the rubber washer) onto the second bucket, which has a lid.
2. Fill the bottom of the lidless bucket with fine gravel, making sure they cover about one-fourth of the bucket's depth. 
3. Add a layer of clean rocks or pebbles on top of the gravel.
4. Follow with a layer of fine sand. 
5. Cut a square of cheesecloth or cotton fabric slightly larger than the width of the bucket.
6. Place the fabric on top of the sand layer.

Step 3: Activated Carbon Layer

1. Pour about one inch of activated carbon on top of the fabric.
2. Spread it evenly using a spoon or your hand (wearing gloves).

Step 4: Finalize the Filter

1. Carefully place the remaining (third) bucket, without a lid, on top of the filter layers, aligning the holes in the bucket's bottom and the lidless bucket.
2. Secure the connection between the buckets using food-grade silicone sealant, ensuring no leaks.

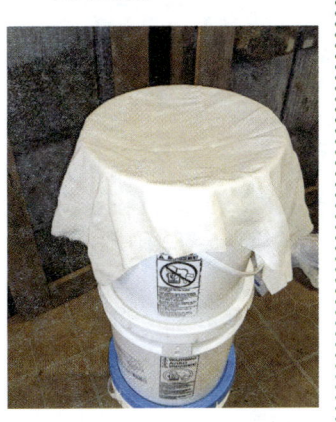

Maintenance Tips and Troubleshooting

- Regularly inspect the filter system for any signs of damage or leaks.
- Replace the activated carbon when it becomes saturated and unable to remove impurities effectively.
- Clean the rocks, gravel, and sand periodically to maintain optimal water flow.
- If water flow becomes slow, check for clogs and remove any debris from the layers.
- In case of a malfunctioning filter, inspect the components, repair any leaks, and reassemble if necessary.

Please note, while the Amish style of water filtration works quite well, it still may be advisable to boil the filtrated water if there is any possibility of unusual harmful bacteria or chemicals may be gotten into the water source, such as: livestock feces, human feces from flood waters, or chemicals caused by a man-made disaster.

Amish Livestock

The Amish rely on horses for both transport and agriculture, cows and goats for milk, and meat from bulls, pigs, and sheep, which can be seen grazing on Amish grassland. Depending on the climate where the Amish farm is located, chickens and poultry are part of the drive towards self-sufficiency. The Amish try to feed and care for all the livestock without the use of chemicals and most Amish farms have only enough animals to support self-sufficiency, say up to 50 animals per farm. Animals are part of the household and fed with crops produced on the farm or grassland.

Photo by Tina Lawlor Mottram

Animals You May Find in Amish Farms

Horses

Horses are a typical farm animal for the Amish because they do not drive vehicles filled with gasoline, so horses can pull carts and plows. They are used in any situation where power is needed, such as for furrowing agricultural land, transport, and even irrigation at times. Several horses can be attached to one plow, and then they set off making even rows for crops to be sown. Having horses means the Amish can travel short distances by horse and cart, and agriculture is easier than without them. An advantage of using horses (or mules) to plow the land is that, unlike heavy modern farm tractors and equipment, these animals do not cause soil compaction, which is a common problem for modern farmers who use modern methods. The weight of a high-tech combine harvester or a large tractor causes damage to the soil, and the Amish believe that nature is to be respected and treated with care and attention.

Mules

Mules are used as animals for plowing and also moving supplies from one location to another, with heavy weights placed in panniers or baskets on their backs.

Cows

Cows for milking may be Jersey, Guernsey, Holstein, (Brown) Swiss, and Ayrshire breeds, which originated in Europe. Sometimes milking is still done by hand, and the milk is stored in containers supplying Amish households with full-fat, unpasteurized milk for personal use.

Bulls, cows, goats, mules, and sheep are all grass eaters, so in warmer months, you will spot them munching on pasture land on Amish farms or maybe at work if they are horses or mules. In summer months, the animals live outdoors in fields, close to the home of the Amish family or community.

Self-Sufficiency THE AMISH WAY

Photo by Tina Lawlor Mottram

An excellent by-product from pasture-fed animals like these is that they drop large amounts of manure, which is collected and composted and then spread as a natural fertilizer for crops the following year (check page 9). So the Amish do not spend large amounts on chemical fertilizers; they substitute animal manure instead. In the colder winter months, depending on the state where the Amish farm is located, animals are moved into barns or sheds and fed harvested and stored straw, hay, and sometimes maize or cornmeal.

These sheds and barns are constructed by large communities of the Amish, who gather at the farm on weekends to make the barn collectively or build new houses for newly married couples. The construction will be done by the men while the women will prepare food for the workers. These occasions are famous inside and outside the Amish community, with questions like "Can the Amish really build a barn in a weekend?" The answer is yes, if enough members of the community are there, and the fellowship of the Amish is world-famous. The building work means no direct expenses are involved apart from materials, and wood is freely available on the farms as the Amish are famous for building furniture too. This means construction is cheaper and also that income can be earned by selling furniture to the wider community outside of the Amish.

All these animals provide meat and milk for the Amish farmer, providing them with valuable protein in their diets. Amish meats are salted and cured, and you can buy Amish sausages and meat pies in Amish stores too. Cows and goats offer the farmer milk which is drunk fresh but is also used in cheese-making, which is then used in various dishes in the Amish kitchen and sold in Amish stores if there is excess produced.

A Note About Amish Farm Milk

Amish don't pasteurize milk, so they drink it raw. This means it does not go through any heat treatment or chemicals to reduce any nasties. Modern advice is that drinking "raw" milk may contain germs or pathogens. However, raw milk contains bad and good bacteria, and the Amish have been drinking unpasteurized milk for centuries and have developed ways to curdle milk safely to make cheese, for example. The Amish call this "Clabber" milk. The process involves allowing the raw milk to turn sour by placing it in a container with a cover under controlled conditions and temperature, and it can only be made with unpasteurized milk. This curdling process divides the milk into more solid curds, which become cheese, and whey, a liquid leftover of the process which is strained away through cheesecloth and then fed to pigs or animals.

We place milk in the refrigerator, but the Amish may not use electricity as a rule, so in warm weather, the milk needs to be kept cool. The Amish have developed cold storage rooms called milk rooms, using cool baths with running water and thick walls for insulation to keep the milk at an even temperature.

The Amish secret to safely preserve milk is excellent hygiene, using clean hands to milk the animals that go straight into a bucket, then transferred into milk churns, which are those old-fashioned large metal containers you can see from history books.

So raw milk for immediate use is stored in cool places, the cream is separated, and the extra milk is processed into cheese, which makes the milk viable for longer. The lactic acid in the milk increases as the cheese-making process starts, so it stores better than fresh milk. Natural yogurt and cream are other Amish products that you can find in stores or on the Amish meal table.

Pets

Dogs are common animals on an Amish farm as an aid to moving animals but also for breeding puppies for sale. Pets are not really an Amish thing. Each animal has its place in the system, and although puppies are sold by Amish breeders, they are not usually kept as pets but for their working role on the farm.

Poultry

On most Amish farms, you will see many varieties of birds including chickens, geese, and ducks, which provide both eggs and meat for the Amish diet, and you may notice them running around in open fields or ducks near ponds on Amish farms when you visit. Most poultry will be housed close to the Amish kitchen where Amish housewives can keep an eye out for signs of distress or predators. Commercial chicken feed contains a mix of grains, cereals, and maize. If the farmer is growing sorghum, for example, it may find its way into the poultry feed, and the same goes for barley, wheat, rye, or corn.

Chickens often have a scavenging area close to the Amish farmhouse, where food can range from kitchen scraps to grass and weeds on pasture land. They are very fond of nettles, dandelions, and any fresh greenery they can peck, and they enjoy insects in their diet too. Poultry are usually contained behind fences, though. Otherwise, the birds might eat all the produce growing in the extremely productive Amish kitchen gardens where salads, herbs, beans, soft fruit, carrots, beets, and leeks are often on view depending on the season.

Amish auctions sell a range of birds, and some farmers raise chicks especially to sell to homesteaders and other farmers. You could spot any size and variety of birds, from small chicks to fully grown birds, with a wide variety from Orpingtons to some rarer types of poultry including quails and Guinea fowl. You may even see rabbits, puppies, and parakeets on sale at these auctions, where you can browse for canned food, fresh fruit, and vegetables while you buy some new birds for your homestead. It is a wonderful sight and well worth a visit.

Amish farms produce eggs for personal use in the Amish kitchen of the household, but extras are sold in Amish stores. Amish pickled eggs are on sale, and a range of other canned home-grown vegetables and fruit. Fresh eggs enable the Amish to reach their goal of self-sufficiency, and eggs are also used in cooking. Hens, geese, and ducks destined for the table are also bred in large numbers, particularly chickens, which is a main ingredient in many typical Amish recipes.

Some farms allow their poultry to run around in the open as free-range birds, but many farms have large barns where chicks and birds run around freely inside. Inside here, they are fed, have access to water, and lay their eggs, which are then collected for sale or use by the farmer. Most birds are usually locked up at night to stop predators.

What Do the Amish Feed Their Livestock?

The Amish aim to be self-sufficient, so grass grown on fields is the major food for large grazing animals. Amish-grown maize is an early cash crop in Amish food stores, and it is often the first available sweetcorn anywhere. Maize grown later is supplied as a winter food when the animals may live indoors in colder climates. Pigs eat any leftover scraps when Amish housewives are canning fruit and vegetables, and they may also get some leftovers from time to time. Geese and ducks tend to survive on food found near the ponds where they live, but sometimes supplemental feed may be supplied. For example, if there is a glut in the kitchen garden, the poultry might find some extra greens in their food! Pigs love whey, which is a by-product of making cheese, and the Amish ladies will empty whey into troughs for the pigs, who lap this up. Sheep may need a mineral salt added to their food now and then to keep their insides happy.

Photo by Tina Lawlor Mottram

Chickens are traditionally fed on scraps from the kitchen, but they also scavenge in the fields where they spend their days outdoors eating grubs, insects, weeds, nettles, and anything they can find. Sometimes as a treat, maize grown on Amish farms is added to winter feed or to fatten the birds for special occasions such as Thanksgiving or a wedding.

Hunting

The Amish will know their local area, and if deer or wild fowl are present, the men of the family may hunt during the season to provide meat for winter storage.

How the Amish Keep Livestock Healthy

Some traditional Amish families do not take prescribed medicine themselves, nor do they feed chemicals to their livestock, particularly if they are bred to be eaten eventually. Prevention is better than cure, as the old saying goes. Providing animals with enough space with no overcrowding is a given. Good hygiene in barns or coops is a must, with waste being swept regularly and composted to make fertilizer. Plentiful access to water for birds and animals is essential, and you can see troughs in fields for larger livestock and where chickens are outdoors in summer. In winter, there are water containers inside barns, but in summer, cows might be drinking from streams or ponds on Amish farms, and ducks and geese enjoy the outdoor life too.

The Amish community has a designated person to treat cuts, injuries, and minor skin irritations because some Amish families only visit doctors for themselves or their families when the condition is so serious they need urgent emergency care. To keep their livestock healthy, they also have some simple methods for keeping diseases at bay, but they will call in a professional vet if the injury or condition is very serious.

Vets do visit Amish farms for checks on pregnant livestock, to check on newborns, and for other problems. The difficulty for the Amish farmer is often getting a message to the vet in times of need because most Amish do not use cell phones or telephones, so somebody may need to visit a neighbor with a phone or visit the vet directly. Many Amish communities schedule regular visits with the vet to assess the health of livestock and poultry.

Common pests for livestock can include lice, fleas, and flies, including the ordinary house fly, the horn fly, and the heel fly. Other common pests include mosquitoes depending on local conditions. Removing still water is a preventative measure for mosquitoes, but one that is difficult for farmers with water containers in fields. If cattle can drink at a stream, the problem is minimized. Cows use their tails to wave at flies, who are often attracted by the dung lying on the field.

Horn flies can be very costly to the Amish farmer, as they bite the livestock and extract blood, which needs to be controlled. Dust bags filled with insecticide are the modern farmer's response, and cows walk under the bags when they leave the milking parlor, for example. The Amish may substitute an aromatic oil instead of the insecticide, as some are known to repel insects naturally. However, this can be costly and needs frequent application, for example, at milking time. Mosquito bites can bring other diseases too, and modern agricultural methods include chemicals to control the spread of disease, but Amish farmers prefer to use barrier methods, like ear blocks.

The heel fly lays eggs on the animals' fur, and when these hatch, they dig into the animal's flesh, which badly affects the muscles and the hide, but also the meat. Amish farmers examine hooves and feet regularly and examine hides for eggs.

The common louse can rapidly spread right through a herd and needs to be controlled, so grooming the animals is a necessity when an outbreak occurs, much like humans when children come home from school with head lice! Combing is laborious, but it does keep the animal healthy. The animals feel "lousy" as is often noticed when an infestation occurs. In addition, the Amish farmer carefully examines the animals' feet and hooves regularly and removes any obvious pests.

Good nutrition is thought to help to keep pests at bay, and crops are home-grown to feed animals or poultry over the colder months, such as maize and grass dried as hay or straw. Keeping a careful eye on individual animals or birds for problems is part of the routine for Amish farmers, who keep a close eye on their animals at milking time or regular checks if other local farmers report a pest invasion. This helps the farmer to spot any signs and deal with the issue promptly. If it is an infectious or transferable disease, an animal or bird may need to be isolated from the rest of the group to prevent it from spreading. Young chicks may vomit or get diarrhea, and a good farmer is watching for the signs and will remove any sickly animal or bird to a location where it can be bathed or bottle-fed separately if necessary. Chickens may become "hen-pecked," which means the dominant bird attacks other hens lower down the hierarchy, and the farmer may notice scratches or blood on the body of this bird. Removing it until it heals is one option or feeding it separately may be another option while the dominant bird is not looking. The Amish farmer, like any farmer, keeps a close eye, but they will call a vet if their own treatment is not successful.

Self-Sufficiency **THE AMISH WAY**

DIY Amish Chicken Coop

Building a chicken coop guarantees a safe and comfortable space for growing your hens and roasters. On the other hand, a well-built coop using the correct materials should protect your chickens from bad weather and predators, giving them a nice place to lay their eggs.

Before building a chicken coop, consider the chickens you want to keep. This will determine the size and design of the coop. Usually, each chicken needs about 3 to 4 square feet of space inside the coop and about 8 to 10 square feet in the run area.

Here is a comprehensive guide to help you build your chicken coop from scratch.

Materials

2x4s and 4x4s pressure-treated lumber for coop frame and walls
4x4 pressure-treated lumber for corner posts and support beams
8x1 timber
Plywood sheets (½ inch thick)
Chicken wire for run enclosure
Roofing material (corrugated metal or OSB board)
Galvanized nails, including roofing nails and screws (various lengths)
Hinges and latches and small metal corner brace joint fastener (optional)
DIY nest boxes

Tools

Measuring tape
Circular saw, power saw, or hand saw
Drill and drill bits
Hammer
Staple gun (optional)
Screwdriver and marker
Spirit level
Square (speed square)
Wire cutters
Safety glasses and gloves
Lader

Laying the Foundation and Building the Coop Frame

Measure and construct the coop's floor frame using 4x4 pressure-treated lumber.

Lay the lumber pieces on the ground to form a rectangle, and use a speed square to ensure the frame edges are flush. Also, use a square to check they are at 90-degree angles.

Use at least 5-inch galvanized nails to secure the corners, and drive them through the ends of the shorter pieces into the longer pieces.

Self-Sufficiency THE AMISH WAY

Step 1

Using a wood saw, cut both pieces of wood to the correct dimensions to create a dovetail joint:

Step 2

Remove the waste wood between the wood and fit the shorter wood (width), assembling the two pieces with sturdy nails.

They should fit snugly as seen here:

Continue building a rectangular frame for the foundation as you can see here:

Constructing the Coop Frame

Next, construct the coop frame by cutting and attaching 2x4 lumber vertically to the floor frame. I used a level to ensure the vertical lumber was straight and a hammer to insert at least two nails per joint.

I also used metal brackets (corner braces) to reinforce the joints.

Constructing the Roost

Raise the wall sections with 2x4 lumber and secure them to the floor frame with nails. These frames will also support the entire roosting area.

Ensure corners are square using a level and secure the wall sections with additional 2x4 lumber along the top and bottom for stability. Remember to level and square all the vertical sections.

Erect the other walls and attach them to the floor frame using screws securely. It should look like the pictures below:

Self-Sufficiency THE AMISH WAY

Constructing the Roof

Building a roof can be challenging if you do not have an idea of how to go about it.

So, choose a sloped roof design for efficient rain runoff.

But before you continue, measure the roof's length and construct roof trusses using 2x4s, depending on your chosen roof pitch.

For the roof's peak framing joint, I used an obtuse angle butt joint craft. This technique is one of the simplest ways to join two rafters at the peak.

Here is a picture of how the roof peak joints should look like.

After the joint is complete, support the roofing frame with the vertical frames of the chicken coop using nails and screws

Next, space the trusses evenly to the top of the coop walls.

Cover the trusses with plywood and secure them with screws.

Continue cutting and securing the OSB with screws until the roof is complete.

Using a power saw to cut accurate cross sections:

Self-Sufficiency **THE AMISH WAY**

Here's what the final outcome should look like:

Installing Fixtures and Fittings

It's time to install fixtures and fittings after the frame is complete.

We will begin with the door:

Step 1

Measure a doorway opening in one of the coop walls large enough to fit you.

Step 2

Frame the doorway using 2x4s and 6x1 lumber, and attach a pre-hung door with heavy-duty hinges.

Building the Ladder

After the door is complete, proceed to the ladder:

Step 1

Determine the ladder's length based on the height of the coop entrance and the angle of incline (a gentle slope is best).

Step 2:

Cut two pieces of 6x1 lumber to the desired length and multiple pieces of 1x2 or 1x3 lumber to the width of the ladder.

Step 3

Attach the rungs perpendicular to the sides, spacing them 4-6 inches apart, using wood screws. Ensure the rungs are evenly spaced and secure.

Ladder Installation

Position the top of the ladder at the entrance of the coop, ensuring a stable connection. You can secure it with screws or brackets. Also, ensure the bottom of the ladder rests securely on the ground within the run area.

Building the Nesting Boxes

It's time to focus on the interior after the roof is complete. The first step is Installing nesting boxes at a height chickens can reach easily.

My nesting box was about 12x12 inches and 12 inches high. Also, I used 6x1 timber for the back, sides, bottom, and front of each box.

I attached the sides to the back piece using screws, securing the bottom to the sides and back. Here is a picture to illustrate more:

Building the Chicken Run

Cover the frame for the chicken run attached to the coop using 6x1 wood, 2x4 lumber, and wood screws. This is what will support the chicken run.

Note: The chicken run should stretch a few feet outside the roost.

Here is a picture of the construction process:

Bring the chicken wire on site.

Carefully unroll the wire along the frame:

Secure the wire mesh along the chicken run frame with nails as you can see here:

Note: While installing, always ensure all wire edges are smooth to prevent injuries and check the entire run for gaps and weaknesses.

Cover the sides and top of the run entirely with 6x1 wood. This will provide your chickens with a safe outdoor space to roam and forage while protecting them from predators.

Five Pro Tips for Building a Chicken Coop

1. **Ventilation and Airflow:** Chickens are at risk of respiratory problems due to ammonia build-up from droppings. So, install vents on the walls, away from roosting areas
2. **Access and Maintenance:** Build large doors for easy access to the coop's interior for cleaning and egg collection.
3. **Hygiene:** Use dropping boards under the roost to catch waste.
4. **Roosting Space:** Construct adequate roosting space, ensuring roosts are higher than the nesting boxes to discourage chickens from sleeping in them.
5. **Location:** Choose a well-drained location that receives at least 6 hours of sunlight daily. Avoid low-lying areas prone to flooding.

Self-Sufficiency THE AMISH WAY

Essential Items the Amish Always Keep on Hand

Firewood

Firewood is one of the most important items for the Amish to stockpile to survive the winter. Without firewood, there is no heat in the house and no baking or cooking. Having the woodshed full of firewood by the end of October or the middle of November is one of the most satisfying feelings. We always have a fun time cutting firewood in the fall. It's when all the Amish neighbors gather and help each other cut firewood and brag about who will bag the largest deer in a couple weeks.

Lake Ice

Equally as important as firewood is lake ice. Whenever someone tells me they think they could live without electricity, my first question is always, "Do you know how to preserve food without your refrigerator?" Most people my age (their twenties) have never thought about how to preserve food without electricity. Having ice is vital to be able to keep milk, butter, cream, and other refrigerated items from going bad on hot summer days. We always fill the ice box in the winter with 12" by 12" ice blocks that are cut from a nearby lake or pond. The ice box is heavily insulated with three layers of 2" ISO boardstock insulation. A 10' wide by 10' deep by 8' tall ice box will easily last a family through the summer months. It's important to install a drain on the bottom of the ice box for any ice that melts to be able to drain away.

Canned Meat

The Amish stock meat every winter; typically, this is done in December. The reason we prefer to do it in December is because winter is starting to set in, and we have cold temperatures. Also, this is during hunting season. It's impossible to stock the meat in the summertime because of the warm temperatures. To process a deer, hog, or heifer, the temperature has to be below 30 degrees Fahrenheit. It takes four to five days to process the meat into bologna or sausages, and without electricity to cool stuff, the meat can be ruined if temperatures do not stay below 30 degrees Fahrenheit during the process. After the meat is ground, seasoned, and smoked, it's ready to eat. To preserve the meat until next December, everything is cut up and canned. To can the meat, you just put it in mason jars, tighten the lid, and pressure cook it until it seals. Once the lid is sealed, it will preserve the meat for two to four years.

Canned Vegetables and Fruits

Vegetables are always canned during the summer months. Vegetables are considered sides to go with the main meal. The canned fruits are usually what's for dessert. Vegetables and fruits are canned throughout the summer as the garden produces them. One of my favorite things to smell growing up was whenever Mom was canning fresh sweet corn or peas. Vegetables and fruits are canned the same way the meat is canned. The goal is always to can enough vegetables and fruit to last one calendar year, until the garden is producing fresh produce again.

Gardening Tools

Gardening is an important part of off-grid living. If you ever go to an Amish house in the summertime, you will most certainly notice their large garden. The Amish take gardening very seriously. Late in the fall, before the ground freezes over but after all the vegetables have been harvested, we plow the garden. But before the garden is plowed, we spread a layer of animal manure over the entire garden; the manure will serve as fertilizer. We avoid any toxic and harsh chemicals. One of the most important parts of the garden's success is keeping all the weeds pulled early on. We usually take the cultivator through the garden once or twice a week, depending on how fast the weeds are growing. We keep the plant rows far enough apart to be able to get the cultivator between the rows. If the weeds start to outgrow your plants, it will take the sun off the plants and start taking all the nutrients out of the soil, leaving the plants little to no chance to survive.

Chickens

Chickens are an important part of the Amish lifestyle. When most people think about chickens, they think about eggs to eat for breakfast. However, eggs are used in almost every baking recipe and so many other cooking recipes the Amish use. Of course, we do eat a lot of eggs for breakfast as well.

We have a chicken coop with between thirty and thirty-five hens. Every year we get and keep thirty-five new baby chicks to replace the older hens. We then take the older hens and process them and can the meat for the next year.

Kerosene

Kerosene is essential to our Amish community, both in the summer and in the winter. In the summer, it is mostly used for the kerosene burner to heat and cook the meals, but the kerosene burner is often also used to heat the pressure cooker for canning purposes during the summertime. The reason we don't want to use the stove for canning in the summer is because of all the heat the stove creates. Again, we don't have electricity, therefore there really is no way to cool down the house. It is also used to start a fire in the kettle to heat water to take a bath. In the wintertime, kerosene is mostly used for lighting. These are lamps that burn on kerosene. Typically, we have one or two lamps in each room, depending on the size of the room. We always store a 55-gallon barrel of kerosene.

Corn, Hay, and Oats

If you don't have animals, then this does not apply to you, but in the Amish community, we have animals like horses, cows, hogs, and hens; these are all essential to the Amish lifestyle. Without horses we cannot go anywhere; we can't plow the fields or the garden. Without cows, we have no milk, and we have no calves to replace the old cows. Without hogs, we don't have our year's supply of sausage. Without chickens, we would not have eggs and chicken meat. We always fill the upper barn full of hay during the summer to last the animals all winter. Same with the oats box and the corn crib.

Home Remedies

Most Amish don't rely on modern medicine. In our family, a lot of preventive measures are taken to strengthen our immune systems, and we consume Vitamin A and Vitamin C regularly. We also consume strong peppermint tea on a regular basis. We also took baths regularly, adding Epsom salts and dry mustard to the hot water. These are some of the things that we keep stocked up on in case of an illness:

- **Essential oils:** Mom would take a kettle with water, add essential oils, and boil it on the stove. This will get through the whole house and help everyone as you're breathing in that air.
- **Raw onions:** Raw onions are often used for a cold. We simply cut up the onion, heat it up, take a towel, place the hot onion on one side, fold the towel as to not spill the onion, lay down and place the warm towel with the raw onion on your chest, and take a nap for an hour.
- **Burdock leaves:** We gather these during the summer months and lay them out in the attic to dry. Burdock leaves work well on burns and open cuts or wounds.

Games

I know what you are thinking: Games? Why are games important to the Amish way of life? Think about your own life for a moment. What if you could never log into the Internet or social media ever again? What if you could never watch another movie or have a TV again? What would you do during that time instead? Now imagine if you had ten kids? How do you keep all those kids entertained? My mom and dad had ten children; I have an identical twin brother, and we were the youngest. I have six brothers and three sisters. My mother has forty grandchildren. Even though we did not have technology growing up, we had plenty of fun on the farm, everything from playing baseball in the hay-

Self-Sufficiency THE AMISH WAY

field and swimming in the creek to all the chores that we had to do daily. Summertime always has less time to play because it is a busy season for planting and harvesting, and the daylight hours are long. However, in the wintertime, we have a lot of free time as the silo is full of silage and the barn is full of hay, oats, corn, and straw. Also, this is the time of year when the daylight hours are very short. While we did go downhill skiing quite a bit on Sundays and sometimes on full moon nights, most of our entertainment was spent indoors playing all kinds of board games. Some of the most popular games in the Amish community are Dutch Blitz (card game), Life on the Farm (board game), and Checkers.

Firearms

Every Amish household has multiple or at least one firearm. The most common type of firearm used in our communities is an 870 shotgun. We use firearms primarily for hunting. Venison is a large part of our meat supply. We always stock up on ammunition in the fall.

Insulated Ice Chests

Every Amish family has an insulated ice chest. This is where we store refrigerated items like milk, butter, etc. The ice chest is large enough to fit a 12" by 12" block of ice plus the refrigerated items. During the warmest summer days, we have to add one 12" by 12" block of ice every day.

Flashlights

Flashlights are a must when living without electricity. We always have four or five flashlights in the house. While they may not be as important in the summertime because of the long daylight hours, they are essential in the wintertime when the daylight hours are much shorter. You never know what part of the day or night you may have to step outside for some firewood or to use the outhouse. It's always a good idea to stock up on batteries in the fall to last all winter.

Amish Off-Grid Laundry

How do the Amish do their laundry without electricity? We have a washing machine that is powered with a little gas engine. To dry the laundry, we always hang it outside. Yes, even in the wintertime, we hang the laundry out on the line. It is ideal to do laundry on a breezy or slightly windy day. In the summertime, this will dry the cloth quickly, and in the winter, it will at least take some of the water out of the wet cloth before it freezes. Once the cloth freezes, we take them and hang them next to the stove. After a couple hours spent hanging next to the stove, the cloth will be dry and ready to be folded.

I'm incredibly thankful that I grew up in the Amish family and community that I did. I think it has helped me realize what is really important to me. Sure, it was always very competitive and a little chaotic at times as everyone wanted to win the game SOOO bad, but looking back, I realize what was important was all that time I was spending with my siblings and parents. I have seen a lot of kids outside of the Amish community miss out on important time spent together with their families. I have seen children outside of the Amish community almost panic if they are not able to watch their favorite show or play their favorite video game. It begs the question: What would you do if you had no access to power or the Internet tomorrow? Do you know how to survive without all these modern conveniences that many have gotten used to?

I hope this chapter helps you prepare with some of the basic necessities that you will need to keep yourself and your family safe in the event that something bad happens. Many countries are extremely reliant on the electrical grid, and if the electrical grid goes down, many lives will be lost because of the lack of preparation.

DIY Off-Grid Washing Machine

Introduction

When the grid goes down, we will still need to do our laundry. The problem is that in today's society, almost nobody will wash their clothing by hand. The Amish often wash their clothes by hand, but they also learned how to build their own washing machine, when in need.

Building a washing machine is a great option to make clothes washing easier. There are dozens of off-grid washing machine plans available online, but what I will detail here is accessible enough for anyone to build and use.

How Does the Off-Grid Washing Machine Work?

This design of an off-grid washing machine essentially consists of two five-gallon buckets nested inside each other. The inner bucket has holes drilled into it to allow water to move through it. The outer bucket holds the water to soak the clothes inside the inner bucket. To agitate the clothes, soap, and water, a plunger is used to push down on the clothes and churn up the water, making it soapy.

The handle of the plunger comes up through a hole in the lid of the inner bucket. This lets you operate the washing machine without splashing soap and water everywhere.

What Detergent to Use?

You will not have the luxury of the sewer system to take all the grey water away after you do your laundry. When you are done washing, you'll probably be disposing of the dirty water by tossing it out the back door.

You could also dispose of greywater in the storm sewer system.

This water will end up working its way into the local waterways, which means you need to ensure that the detergent you use is as natural and eco-friendly as possible.

Many commercially available options are available on the market, but you can also make your own detergent.

Many recipes exist online, most of which use similar ingredients. Castile soap, borax, washing soda, baking soda, and vinegar are all common ingredients in these DIY laundry soaps.

Whichever you choose, you should always avoid dumping your wastewater directly into any waterway. It is better to let the ground filter out many of the soap particles before they reach the water.

Self-Sufficiency **The Amish Way**

Building the DIY Off-Grid Washing Machine

Putting this washing machine together requires only a few tools and supplies readily available at your local hardware store. Everything needed is also easily scavenged in a post-disaster environment.

Materials

Two 5-gallon buckets
One 5-gallon bucket lid
One toilet plunger

Tools Required

Drill with drill bits

Instructions

Step 1

Pick one bucket to serve as the inner bucket in the washing machine. Layout and drill a series of holes throughout the sides and bottom of the bucket. I used a ½" drill and spaced my holes about 3 – 4 inches apart.

Step 2

Measure the diameter of the handle on your plunger.

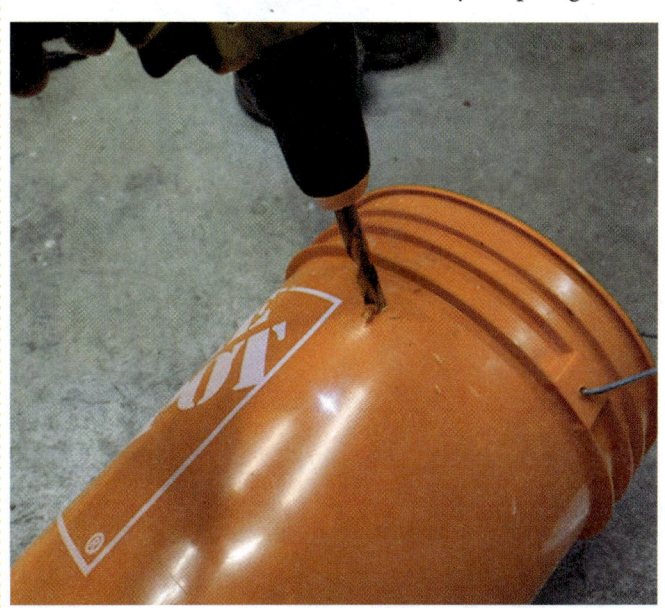

Step 3

Drill a hole in the centre of the lid, which is slightly larger than the diameter of the plunger handle.

215

Self-Sufficiency THE AMISH WAY

Step 4
Drill two holes in the plunger head.

Step 5
Place the inner bucket inside of the outer bucket

Step 6
The plunger goes inside the buckets.

Step 7
The lid is secured so that the plunger handle sticks out of the lid.

Operation of the DIY Washing Machine

To operate the DIY washing machine, you simply have to follow this simple procedure.

1. Fill the inner bucket with clothes about halfway full.
2. Add water until the clothes are covered.
3. Place the plunger into the bucket.
4. Add detergent and secure the lid.
5. Agitate the water by plunging the plunger up and down.
6. Allow the clothes to soak in the soapy water.
7. Plunge again.
8. Replace the water with clean water.
9. Plunge again.
10. Repeat until the soap is rinsed from the clothes.
11. Remove the inner bucket and spin it back and forth to help remove water from the clothes.
12. Wring and hang the clothes to dry.

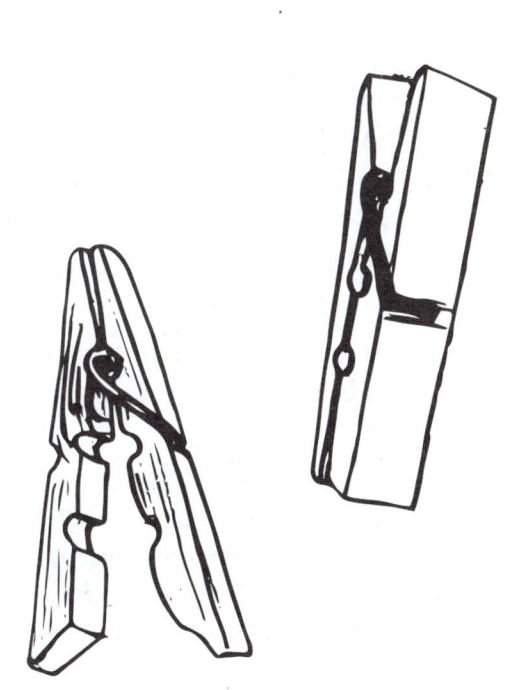

Where to Get the Water for the DIY Washing Machine

The last thing that any of us want to do is use our clean, potable water for washing clothes. The better option is to use water from a local creek or river which runs clear. You can boil this water over a fire to sterilize it or use a homemade filter system to clean the water.

Filtering and sterilizing the water is important. There is little point in cleaning clothes with water which is contaminated.

You can also use rainwater, but you might want to avoid it because it is better to collect rainwater in the garden rather than for drinking or washing clothes.

Drying the Clothes

Spinning the inner bucket around will not get the clothes very dry. You will still have to wring them out and hang them to dry in the sun. If you do not have outdoor space to do this, hanging them above your bathtub is another option.

Modifications You Might Consider

If you have access to pressurized water, you could consider attaching a garden hose to the side of the outer bucket. This would allow you to feed fresh water into the bucket while plunging the soap out of the clothes.

Adding a drain with a plug to the bottom of the outer bucket is another modification that may also prove helpful.

Final Thoughts

Staying clean is essential to our health, especially in a SHTF scenario. Dirty clothes will lead to bacterial growth, which could result in many types of skin infections. Being able to construct a simple but effective washing machine will not only keep you and your family smelling good but also protect you from disease and illness.

Self-Sufficiency THE AMISH WAY

Why The Amish Paint Their Barns Red

Have you ever wondered why barns are typically painted red? In Amish communities especially, red barns can be found in almost every household. And this isn't just a random aesthetic decision.

As we'll soon see, painting your barn red might be a smart choice if you haven't already. And it could be worth considering for your outdoor storage shed, other structures, and even your home as well.

The tradition of painting barns has its roots during the 18th and 19th centuries in Europe and America. Initially, barns were left unpainted, which exposed the wooden structures to harsh elements. This lack of protection meant that barns would rapidly deteriorate due to weather, moisture, and pests. Farmers quickly realized they needed a way to safeguard their barns and extend their life spans as much as possible.

Back in the day, store-bought paint wasn't something you could just pick up at the local market like you can now. Instead, farmers had to get creative and make their own protective mixtures. And one of the most popular recipes included linseed oil, which comes from flax plants and acts as a natural preservative. Farms would mix the linseed oil with milk, lime, and iron oxide.

The iron oxide, basically rust, wasn't just for show. Rather, it helped to kill fungi and mosses that would commonly grow on barns and cause further decay. Plus, it gave the mixture that distinctive red hue. This homemade recipe created a durable coating that had the capability to protect the wood from rot and weather damage. It proved to be a real game changer when it came to farm maintenance.

Later, as time went on, commercial paints started to become available to the general public in the 19th century. Red paint emerged as one of the most affordable options.

Why Red?

Again, it all comes down to the iron oxide. This pigment was widely available and cheaper than other colors, which made it one of the most economical choices for large structures like barns. Painting a barn is no small job, and using red paint allowed farmers to cover these big buildings without breaking the bank.

As more and more farmers painted their barns red, the sight became a staple in rural landscapes all over Europe and America. Red barns started to symbolize the farming lifestyle, and they still do today.

As mentioned above, red paint provides excellent protection against the elements. The mixture of linseed oil, milk, lime, and iron oxide creates a tough coating that helps to prevent rot and decay and extend the lifespans of barns for as long as possible:

- Linseed oil is derived from flax seeds and is an important ingredient due to its ability to deeply penetrate wood. This is what provides the protective layer that helps to prevent moisture from seeping into the wood and therefore prevents rot.

- Milk is used to create a milk paint, which is biodegradable and non-toxic. It's a safe option for any livestock housed in the barns.

- Lime is included in the mixture for its antibacterial properties, which help in keeping the wood free from mold and mildew.

- The iron oxide gives the paint its distinctive red color. Historically, iron oxide was readily available and inexpensive, which is why it was a cost-effective choice. Iron oxide also adds an extra layer of protection against the elements, as it primarily helps to prevent fungal growth.

Each of these ingredients are commonly available for the average person. Linseed oil is available at various online retailers as well as most hardware and home improvement stores. You can get milk and lime at grocery stores and supermarkets, and iron oxide at most art supply stores or online retailers as well.

The Amish are very dependent on their barns as they rely on them daily for housing their livestock, equipment, and harvested crops. This is why by painting their barns red, the Amish can maintain their barns without incurring high expenses.

For those living off the grid, using a durable and protective red paint can reduce maintenance needs. This is particularly important when access to repair materials and services may be limited. A well-maintained structure is crucial for ensuring that you can withstand long periods without outside support, which makes red paint a very smart choice for long-term preparedness. And when you consider the fact that it could take the country that you're living in (or the world for that matter) months if not years to recover, making sure that your structures can last over the long term with minimal maintenance on your part becomes even more important.

On top of that, it's possible to make your own out of mixing together nothing more than linseed oil, milk, lime, and iron oxide. In other words, making your own paint means that you don't have to be dependent on commercial supplies, which will surely be scarce in an extended emergency scenario.

Another benefit of the color red can also have is in regards to energy efficiency. Dark colors absorb more heat, which can be beneficial in colder climates by helping to keep buildings warmer. For preppers and homesteaders who are looking to maximize their energy efficiency, painting their barns and homes red means they may need less dependence on an external heating source.

Using Money
The Amish Way

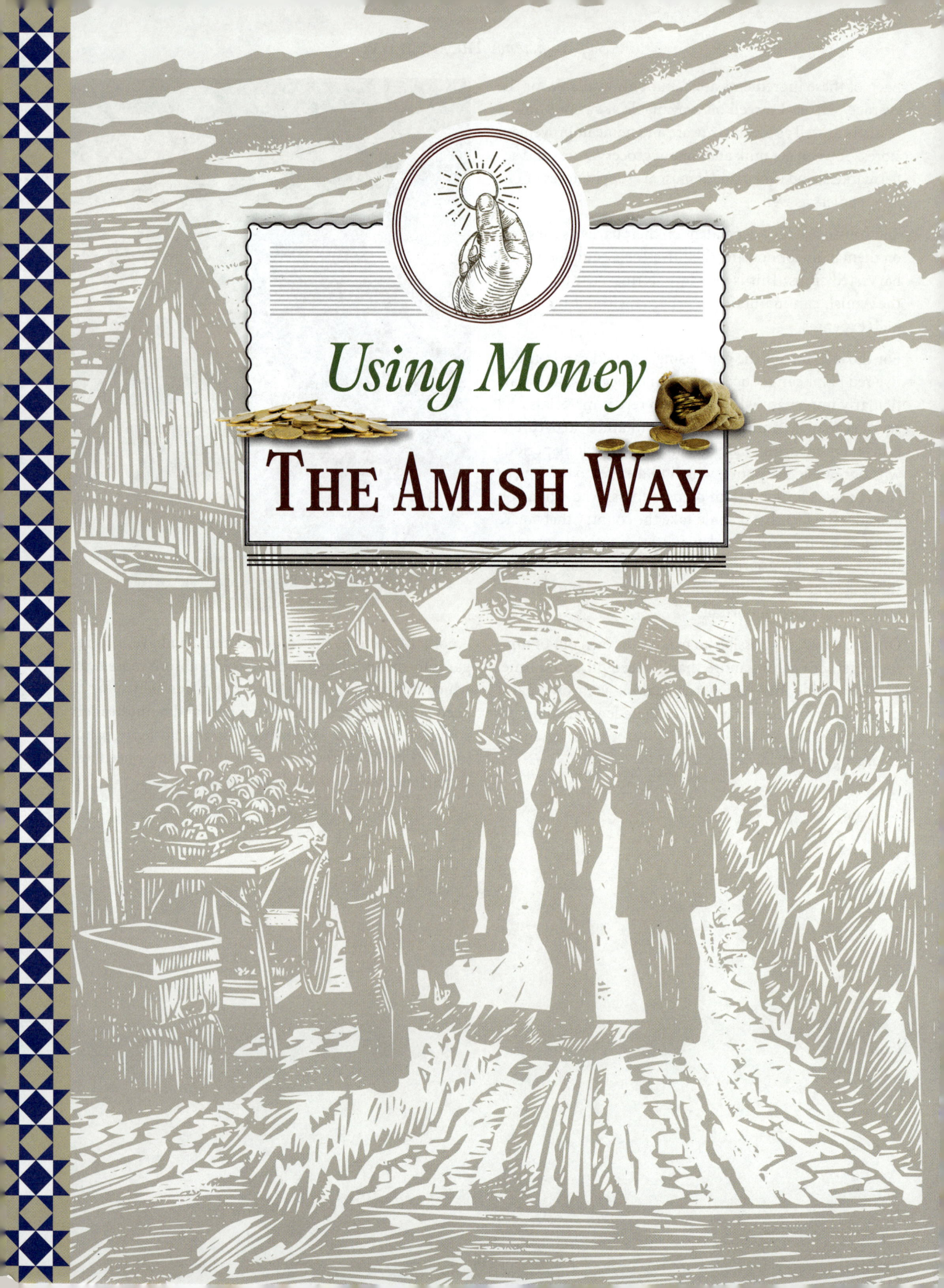

Handling Money Like the Amish

We scrape the bottom of the barrel more than most, Bishop Eli, a member of the Amish community, once said, and this might highlight the money mindset the Amish live by.

Not only that but *Waste not, want not*, the Pioneers' old saying, is another principle you can add to your day-to-day practices, when trying to follow the Amish example in handling finances.

Apart from these beliefs the Amish always swear by, when it comes to the practicability of handling money like them, it's important to know how they approach business, in general. Many Amish are surprisingly good business people – they're usually able to avoid IRS problems and other pitfalls by setting up their businesses correctly, despite a lack of some of the modern technologies that make this easier.

Many Amish are practically business-minded, and also wise in the ways of mechanical engineering. They favor a warehouse of physical goods over a slick digital interface, and a nicely working machine over something intangible.

Crafts and Trades

Many in the Amish community are adept at various trades that are helpful in business – electrical work, roofing, and plumbing, just to name a few. This knowledge comes in handy, not just in service businesses, where so many of them thrive, but in a certain kind of business innovation that you can see when you visit an Amish shop. Having this sort of interest in mechanical systems doesn't just benefit the Amish, either – it's a good way to prepare for any future contingencies as a do-it-yourself kind of person who wants to be less reliant on the system and the grid.

Circular Economy

In addition to being able to start and maintain businesses, the Amish also tend to embrace the 'circular economy.' That's the economy of local cooperation – some would call it 'bartering' or 'neighbor commerce.' It's the idea that in some forms of commerce, there's no corporate middleman involved. People trade with each other personally, and not through high-profile franchise storefronts. You could call it the "anti-Walmart" model – or just contrast it to the kind of selling done in your local mini-mall. Again, those who are trying to disentangle from the commercial and corporate world can take a page from their playbook.

What this means is that many Amish farms and businesses have learned to bypass a lot of the distribution problems faced by retailers. The trend of selling off of the farm or at local markets allows for strong cash sales that are not funneled through complex accounting software, or managed by top-heavy business teams in an expensive office somewhere. This doesn't mean that the income isn't reported – it just means that the overhead is low. For example, when goods are sold off of the farm, there's no shipping cost, because the buyer visits the local farm to purchase the items. There's typically no advertising, except for some signs along the road.

Using Money THE AMISH WAY

Cash Only

Another important thing to know about Amish commerce is that the community promotes purchasing things like real estate with cash, as opposed to financing. The idea of making large purchases without financing gives the buyer a lot of economic firepower – the costs are not just marginally, but substantially lower, over time. Equity doesn't have to build slowly, and the asset owner can start out making money on day one. If you're in big debt to a lender, it's hard to be self-reliant, so think about adopting this kind of long-term strategy.

This strategy is often more accessible to the Amish, because they have community and family support – because money is pooled together, and those who have already gained equity in property can help others to avoid the enormous amounts of money that the average real estate buyer pays in interest. When you skip the mortgage process and buy a property for cash, someone is saving hundreds of thousands of dollars. In the Amish community, that someone is the buyer as well as those who lend the money.

So again, the Amish promote local cash business in a way that is simple and direct.

Decentralization

Another key principle of Amish culture goes along with this – it's the value of natural products. This is why you will see a small garden next to most Amish farms. It's why you will see livestock, particularly avian livestock like ducks and chickens, running in the open on Amish farms, or kept in simple open-air coops. Many survivalists and preppers already do this, as well, at some extent for some similar, yet different reasons. One of the most important reasons is that when you have your own food, you are not as dependent on big ag and all of its (perhaps weak) infrastructure for your daily living!

One of the main values of these processes involved decentralization. Increasingly, the Amish are not bringing products to massive big agribusiness warehouses and distribution centers. They're selling in the community and saving money, and decreasing their carbon footprint as well. But this model also works with their way of life – their means of transport, and the time and money they save by foregoing some of the modern amenities we enjoy. Anyone who's not part of the Amish can use this strategy for living as well – getting outside, doing physical work, and innovating local systems, instead of just passively ingesting streaming media from far away. This will not only help you on the short-term, but it will also prepare you for the worst.

Sustainable Business Practices

So, in handling money like the Amish, convert some capital into cash. Injected in the local economy through small local cash purchases. Build business incrementally in a stable way that involves making transactions with individual people one at a time. As you scale and grow, you can build more of a business infrastructure, but it's always based on what you can support yourself rather than hiring a lot of third parties, paying a lot of consultants, and paying for a wide spectrum of third-party services. This can apply to non-Amish businesses, as well – trust yourself to do more, and rely on others for less. You can change as you scale, but having that initial self-reliance will almost always come in handy.

Havesting the Wind

The windmill is actually a great symbol of the Amish economy – it's something simple that is self-built, and collects power from a natural source – the wind. You can see these principles at work on Amish farms everywhere.

Using What You Aready Have on Hand

Last but not least, don't forget to reuse and fix every item in your household. At least, this is what the Plain people always did. This way, they not only save a lot of money, but also learn how to make the most out of everything, a skill that can be used when the worst is already there!

Using Money THE AMISH WAY

> That's a little bit about how the Amish economy works and how it's been so successful. Thinking like the Amish, in some ways, means using your money in a different way, making different priorities, and building community where you are, rather than buying from somewhere half a world away.

Growing up Amish and always being around my family, I realize the Amish handle money much differently than most people. I think money and resources were valued more. I remember growing up, Mom and Dad would never throw anything in the trash if it was still usable or if it wasn't used 100%. For example, if we dished our plate, we could not eat half the food and throw the rest in the garbage. Mom and Dad always reminded us of how many hungry children there are in the world who would be thankful to have this food and how privileged we are to have it.

Our community also has a fund for emergencies, such as when a house fire happens or someone breaks a bone and needs surgery. Nobody is forced to contribute to the fund, but most people volunteer to contribute a small amount every week. Five years ago, my uncle's house burned completely down to the ground in the middle of January during the winter. The whole community came together, and they had a newly built house within three weeks.

In my community, there are a few pretty wealthy Amish people who often help young people buy property. However, you can never tell who among the Amish is wealthy, as they all look the same and dress the same.

My Dad owned and operated a sawmill, meaning he bought large amounts of timber that we then cut up into railroad ties and lumber for woodworking. When I turned 14, I graduated from 8th grade and started working at the sawmill along with six other employees who worked for my Dad. I did not get paid by my Dad. This is how every family operates in our community. The kids contribute to the family financially until we are 21 years old. In the meantime, all our clothes, food, and basic necessities are provided by our parents. Most likely, when we turn 21 and go out on our own, we will get help from our parents in some way. Sometimes this means helping the children buy their own place or giving them a new horse and buggy.